The First Time

For Beth

By arrangement with the BBC
The BBC logo is a trademark of the
British Broadcasting Corporation
and is used under licence.
BBC logo © BBC 1996
BBC Radio 6 Music © BBC 2008

Published in 2018 by
Laurence King Publishing Ltd
361–373 City Road
London EC1V 1LR
Tel +44 20 7841 6900
Fax +44 20 7841 6910
enquiries@laurenceking.com
www.laurenceking.com

ISBN 978 1 78627 298 0

Commissioning editor: Camilla Morton
Development editor: Alice Graham
Senior editor: Gaynor Sermon
Design: Nicolas Franck Pauly

Printed in China

MATT EVERITT

The FirstTime

STORIES & SONGS FROM
MUSIC ICONS

Laurence King Publishing

Picture Credits

Playlists

To listen to the artist playlists, open Spotify on your phone, press search, tap the camera icon, then point your camera at the code above the tracklisting at the end of each chapter.

Contents

"Do You Remember the Third Time? The Fourth Cut is the Deepest? The Eighth Time Ever I Saw Your Face?"

Matt Everitt

Just not the same is it? The most unforgettable moments are when we experience something for the very first time. Those memories can shape you and echo throughout your life, like a guitar left leaning against an amplifier feeding back long after the band has walked off stage.

The first time I was aware of music was when I was five years old and heard 'Yesterday' on the radio. I can distinctly remember sitting behind the sofa, listening to the lyrics and feeling overwhelmingly sad for the singer. I stayed hidden there for ages, heartbroken. The first song I was obsessed with was *The Pink Panther* theme. Aged six, I'd play the 7-inch single on an old red Dansette record player again and again and again. The final bars of free-jazz cacophony would collapse and fade out and I'd pick up the needle, put it back to the start and wait for that cool opening solo piano discord to arrive.

There's a part of me that still genuinely worries about Paul McCartney to this very day (I still don't know why she went away, or why she wouldn't say) and I'm convinced there isn't a moment in my daily life which wouldn't be improved by someone walking behind me playing Henri Mancini tunes on the saxophone. Which proves my point. These moments stay with you.

The First Time is a way of asking musicians to recall their memories of hearing *that* album, witnessing *that* gig, singing *those* lyrics – the flashpoints that inspired them – and to talk about the music that's inextricably linked to those moments.

My very first guest was Johnny Marr, back in July 2010, and since then BBC Radio 6 Music has broadcast more than 100 episodes of *The First Time With* …. This book collects together some of my favourites, along with playlists of songs mentioned or inspired by each guest. There's also an introduction to each of the interviews which will hopefully give you an idea of why I chose to include them and what it feels like spending time in a small darkened recording studio with someone whose music you've loved for years.

Generally speaking, musicians are pretty good company. I think people occasionally forget that even the most serious, revered and otherworldly stadium-rock icon probably spent a healthy portion of their early career surviving on crisps, living in transit vans and playing gigs to a few uninterested people. So they're often more self-deprecating and friendly than you'd expect. I hopefully that comes across.

Some people didn't make it in. My terrible interview with Nick Cave will remain undocumented (it was purely my fault and his justifiable frown still looms in my nightmares); Prince smelled fabulous but wouldn't let me record our conversation; and every interview I arranged with Amy Winehouse was cancelled at the last moment. Until she ran out of moments. I've still got a box of '60s Blue Beat ska 7-inch singles I was going to give to her as a present.

Every guest was different, but they've all made music, written lyrics or given performances that altered the lives of millions of people. Mine included. The way we think about love, travel, family, dancing, drugs, food, poetry, partying, politics, money, Macca and jazzy saxophone solos has been directly influenced by these artists. *The First Time* interviews, radio shows, and now this book are a way of discovering more about them. The songs, people and events that gave them *their* first times and made them who they are.

It's also a way of saying thank you.

The First Time Norman Cook Interviewed Matt Everitt

Norman Cook: Ok, Matt, what was your first record?
The Jungle Book Disney soundtrack, which is still a banger. That was a gift. The first record I bought was a cassette of *Complete Madness*. I can say this about very few records I bought at that age, but I still like every single track on that album. I still love Madness.

What was your first bite of the musical cherry?
My first bite would've been terrible. It was performing in a school band in the fifth or sixth form. We did a cover of Jimmy Hendrix's 'Purple Haze', with me singing. And you know me, and you know I can't sing. I would've been awful, but I loved it.

What was your first *First Time*?
The very first *First Time* interview was with Johnny Marr.

Was there an actual concept or did you think 'How do I make this more interesting?'
The first one was a bit like that, then I thought that the format worked and the show came from there: first gig, first single, first time you met your heroes. It just works, doesn't it? It's always a big deal, the first time you do something.

What was the first time you suspected someone was lying during a *First Time* interview?
When you say, 'Oh, what was your first single?' and someone goes, 'Oh, it was Neu', or some incredibly rare Afrobeat single, you're thinking, 'It wasn't. It was Bucks Fizz.' And don't try to claim your first gig was Talking Heads in '78. It wasn't. It was The Wombles. Stop it. So that sometimes happens.

Technically my first gig *was* The Wombles. What was yours?
U2 on The Joshua Tree tour at the Birmingham NEC. 1987, I think. I went with my schoolmate and someone said, 'Get there early as the band might arrive and you'll get autographs.' We turned up at

half eight in the morning and just waited round the back of the NEC for bloody hours. U2 came out and signed fans' stuff about 12 hours later, and I remember I didn't have anything for them to autograph so they signed a scrappy bit of paper I found on the floor, which I've still got somewhere.

When was the first time you thought, 'There's a book in this'?
I guess part of the point of this is that the interviews aren't time specific, so I see it as quite an important archive. I think music is really, really important, so to have this as a record, to see that *this* is what this person was like, *this* is what they loved, *this* is where they came from – to put that in a book just made sense.

The only thing I want to ask you, Norm, is about the experience of being interviewed. Is it one that you ever get used to? It's like a therapy, but then again an intrusion, isn't it?

I've found it very, very difficult to be on the other side, because I'm just used to blithering on about myself. And I'm always quite comfortable with that, whereas pressing someone? I feel a bit nosy. Journalists listen, and I don't think I've ever been a very good listener. That's probably why I've always been on the other side of the microphone.

I must say that *The First Time* is a really warm interview. Going back, and thinking, 'Gosh yeah, that began other things in my career or my life.' A bit of nostalgia's healthy, but I think it's good to have a discipline, so I think the way you do it keeps people on point. I remember, when you interviewed me for the show, just thinking it was a lovely thing to do. Because it's always a bit weird, you interviewing me. And then today it was the other way round. I can relax now. All morning I've been thinking, 'How *do* I do an interview?' Now I can leave that to you, and your book.

"We're going to make The Rolling Stones look like choirboys."

ALICE COOPER

Alice Cooper still looks like a witch: long, raggedy arms, a thatch of crow-feather hair and a large Captain Hook beaked nose. Even without his kohl eye make-up, his grey-blue eyes wink out just like they did on his million-selling '70s album covers. His face is creased and his skin is a little looser, but Alice doesn't look that different from how he did when he was a threat to American decency.

He's tremendously easy company – warm, gracious and happy to retell well-worn stories, and laughing while he does. You can imagine him holding court with The Hollywood Vampires (his 1970s fraternity of terrifyingly hard-drinking musicians that included Keith Moon, Harry Nilsson and John Lennon), and you can see why celebrities like Johnny Depp regard him as a close friend. Smart and slightly self-effacing, he's also surprisingly similar to his cameo in *Wayne's World*, where he played the dignified elder statesman of rock lecturing his stunned fans with expert detail about the pre-settlement history of America.

Vincent Damon Furnier may be a sophisticated and sober sixty-eight-year old, golf obsessed Republican, but he speaks with real fondness about Alice, often referring to him in the third person. Hearing about the height of his fame (and let's not forget he was face-on-a-lunchbox, TV-holiday-special, Marvel-comic-about-your-exploits famous), it's obvious he relishes the controversy he caused, but he never set out to corrupt anyone – only to entertain them. And I think that's why Alice Cooper's image works. He is a character played for a lifetime by a great actor who has grown to genuinely love the role; a theatrical vaudeville villain who still delights in scaring us. And we love to be scared.

Matt Everitt: When were you first aware of music?

I grew up in Detroit and the first time I was really aware of something I really liked was my uncle bringing me a Chuck Berry record, 'School Day'. Immediately I got it. I was nine years old. It had the 4/4 beat, and you could really get into it. My dad liked big band, he liked Sinatra, but the first time my ears perked up? Chuck Berry. I was at the beginning in the mid-'50s when rock and roll started being played on the radio. You could sing along to, 'Venus, if you will, please send a little girl for me to thrill' ['Venus' – Frankie Avalon]. Those songs were so easy to like because they were just happy, three-minute songs.

Can you remember buying your first singles?

First single I ever bought with my own money was 'Jim Dandy' by LaVern Baker and first album I ever bought was *All Summer Long* by The Beach Boys. I was about fourteen, fifteen, I'd cut somebody's lawn, I'd get two dollars, and I'd go buy an album. Then, I'm painting the house in Phoenix one summer morning, and I hear this song called 'She Loves You' by this band called The Beatles. I stopped painting and I went, 'What was that?' Because it was something totally new. I never saw what they looked like, didn't matter, it was the song that got me. Then I saw a picture of The Beatles and I was hooked. A tsunami of British bands came over. Every week there was a new band and we would sit there and go, 'Did you see this band The Kinks? Unbelievable. They have hair down to their collars!' The Yardbirds, the Jeff Beck and the Eric Clapton stuff? All of a sudden you're hearing, 'I'm a Man' and 'Train Kept A-Rollin'.' We were the prime kids that were affected by the British invasion.

What was your very first band like? What were they called?

We did a takeoff of The Beatles and we called ourselves The Earwigs. We bought the Beatle wigs and we hired girls to come up and scream for us during lunchtime in the cafeteria. It started out being a total joke but we were bitten immediately by the bug of being up there on stage. The crazy thing is, in our journalism class we had a guillotine. If you were late for an assignment, you were in the guillotine for five minutes. That was part of the fun of it. And we put the guillotine on stage. The very first time I was ever on stage in a rock band, there was a guillotine on stage. How prophetic is that? And I still use the guillotine in the show.

When did you first become Alice?

Well, the first time 'as Alice' I can remember distinctly was in Santa Barbara fairgrounds. It was a big show and we were the third on the bill. There was Blue Cheer, The Nitty Gritty Dirt Band and Alice Cooper. We were called The Nazz before that. But we found out that Todd Rundgren's band was called The Nazz and so we thought, 'We're a bit theatrical and we're a bit dark, let's not call ourselves something like The Poisonous Dragon or whatever it was going to be, let's go the other way. Let's give ourselves a name that sounds like what we're not.' Alice

Cooper sounded like a little old lady that lived down the street that knitted and made cookies for everybody. I said, 'That's perfect.' Because they're going to get us! With the make-up and the hair! Suddenly it had a ring to it, like Lizzie Borden or Baby Jane. Alice Cooper!

The theatrical image emerged quite early on?

Very early. Honestly, we were all art students also, so our idea was, you'd see The Who or The Kinks on [US TV musical variety shows] *Shindig!* or *Hullabaloo*, and you'd see these great bands, but the only thing that I wondered as an artist was, 'Why is it blank behind them? Why isn't anybody painting this picture?' Our idea was to make the lyrics come to life. Why just sing 'Welcome to my nightmare?' Why not give them the nightmare? That was our niche. That was the thing that made us different. We would take the lyrics and bring them to life. That was the beginnings of Alice being a villain, not a hero – a rock villain.

And you were one of the first people to do that.

It scared the parents, and it scared the establishment so much that that helped us. There was really nothing to ban in our show, there was no bad language, there was no nudity, there was nothing in 1964, but we scared the hell out of them because they thought their kids were going to start looking like us. We saw The Rolling Stones and said, 'We're going to make The Rolling Stones look like choirboys.'

"Alice Cooper sounded like a little old lady that lived down the street that knitted and made cookies for everybody. I said, 'That's perfect.'"

'I'm Eighteen', released in 1970, was your first breakthrough hit.

That was it. That was the one we heard on the radio for the first time. We're in Detroit and we're playing every weekend with Iggy and The Stooges, and The MC5, and all these Detroit bands. We're playing every weekend just to eat, not realizing that each one of those bands was going to go on to have a career. We did this song 'I'm Eighteen' with [record producer] Bob Ezrin and I said, 'It's nice and everything, but look what's on the radio. The Supremes, Simon and Garfunkel.' But we're driving along and it's *Pick Hit of the Week* on a local station, and they play it. I mean, literally, you could hear a pin drop in the car because all the guys in the band were afraid they were hearing things. We thought, 'Well, at least we got one play', but the song went on to be number two on CKLW which was the biggest breakout station in the United States. That's when we knew something was going on; we actually had a hit record.

That song turned out to be a massive influence on punk. John Lydon has often said it's one of the songs that he sung at his audition for the Sex Pistols.

We were trying to be The Yardbirds, we were trying to be a complicated band, but Bob Ezrin kept saying, 'Dumb it down.' We'd go, 'What does that mean?' He says, 'Take three more chords out of that song. It's got to be so basic. This guy's going, "I'm eighteen and I like it." That's the message.' We didn't realize that's exactly what kids wanted to hear. It ended up being one of the biggest hits we ever had.

Can you remember your first tour of the UK in 1972? People talk about those shows being really important. People like Bowie came to see you, and thought, 'Okay, you can do THIS onstage now.'

We came over with all this controversy and [Welsh Labour MP] Leo Abse and [anti-obscenity campaigner] Mary Whitehouse banned us. Which was the best thing ever. We sent them flowers, we sent Leo Abse cigars, and they could not figure out why we were so nice to them. We were going, 'The more you hate us, the more the public loves us.' The record went right to number one and we sold out Wembley Arena. We realized at that point that the British public got what Alice was about. It was scary, it was anti-establishment, but it had a sense of humour to it.

"Honestly, eat one missionary and you get labelled forever."

We were like a force. We wanted to be the next big band, not a novelty. After we played, the next day you'd look out on the street and the kids were wearing top hats and black under their eyes. Marc Bolan came to the show and we were maybe one of the only bands that knew who T. Rex and Bowie were. It blew a door down, the fact that we could have hit records, be theatrical, be showbizzy and be arrogant about it. It let a lot of bands come through, all going, 'I can do that'. Glam rock was born.

'School's Out' is where things went from huge to very, very, very huge indeed. Can you remember listening back to the record for the first time when you'd done it, and going, 'This is the one'?

It's the only time I ever said, 'This is a hit'. I listened to it and I went, 'I can't find anything wrong with this record'. It's got everything. It's got the kids at the end, it captures that last three minutes of the last day of school, when you're watching the clock, going, 'In two more minutes I'm out of school for three months.' That's in the United States, where, when the bell went *Bzzzzzzzz*, the school went crazy. I said, 'We've got to get that on the record.' Even the guitar riff was almost like a bratty little kid.

Financially a good move as well, then?

Well, we say that's the rent payer. It's always our finale song, it's the balloons, it's the top hat, it's the confetti. It relates to every generation.

You were really perceived as being a threat to the moral goodness of society, weren't you?

Well, I'd wear my girlfriend's slip with a pair of black leather pants and motorcycle boots, with blood all over the slip for no apparent reason. The make-up smeared on, and the hair ratted up. People were looking at us, going, 'What the hell are they? I know they're straight because they've got these hot girlfriends, and they play this rough rock and roll, but it's really catchy. And our parents hate them, so there's every reason to love these guys.' Honestly, eat one missionary and you get labelled forever.

How did that level of fame affect you? It got to the point where you were instantly recognizable, and you'd gone solo …

I was drenched in press. There was no such thing as a day when I didn't do 20 interviews. But it was fun because I was this character, I didn't have to answer to anybody. There was sort of a freedom in not trying to please anybody. I was Alice Cooper. I had the total freedom to be anybody I wanted to be. You're indestructible at that point. Whatever you said, if it was controversial, it made you even bigger.

That's terrifying.

Yeah, but it was fun because, honestly, we never, ever thought we were going to get out of Phoenix. The band was so outrageous, so far out on a limb, that we were either going to be considered brilliant or insane. With the hit records, you turn a corner. If you don't have those hit records, you're a puppet show. If you didn't have something to hang your hat on, people would say, 'They're theatrical and that's it.' You go, 'Well, wait a minute, we've just had three number ones in a row, so we're doing something right.' If you don't have that, though, you're gone in a flash. You were fun for a little while and then you're gone.

When did alcohol first become a problem for you?

I think probably the first drink. I had no idea that my first beer was going to be a series of ten thousand beers. I never drank so much that I couldn't do a show, I never drank on stage. I was totally functional, so nobody saw a problem. Nobody around me was going, 'Hey, he missed a show last night, he doesn't know his lines.' I was totally functional; in fact, I was better with a little bit of alcohol in me. I never got a hangover.

That's dangerous.

And who's my best friend? Keith Moon. That's a prescription for insanity right there. It was like I was riding this giant tsunami wave, and it just kept getting better and better. What was happening, though, was I was starting to collapse inside, physically. I finally got to a point where I'd get up in the morning and I'd throw up blood. That's when my wife took me by the ear and said, 'Let's go'. And we went to hospital. I haven't had a drink now for 30 years, so that's why I'm still here. If I had have kept drinking two more weeks, I would have been gone.

Your career dipped a bit in the late '70s, early '80s. Was that almost a relief?

That's when I eventually went into hospital. It was during the disco plague, so all the hard rock bands couldn't get played on the radio. I was at a point where either I was going to die or do something new. The only thing you heard on the radio was disco. It's funny now, as I like those songs that I hated at the time, because it's not a threat to me anymore. As soon as I got sober, I had to play Alice for the first time in my life sober.

How difficult was that?

I must have worn a hole in the carpet during the first show. I said, 'I'm going to go out there, but what if Alice doesn't show up? I'm totally sober now.' So I designed this new Alice. I looked at the old Alice and I said, 'That Alice was a victim. He was drinking, he was a victim, he

"This was not the beat-down Alice, this was the new, improved venomous Alice."

was society's whipping boy.' That's why kids liked him, because he was representing them. I said, 'This new Alice is going to be a villain. Just a stone cold, Alan Rickman–arrogant type of villain.' A different kind of body language, different attitude. This was not the beat-down Alice, this was the new, improved venomous Alice. The audience was taken aback, but they liked it. He was unreal.

I have to ask you about your first round of golf ...

When I stopped drinking I woke up sober, and I had all day to do nothing. I said, 'The first thing I'm going to do is probably just start reaching for something, I'd better get up and go do something.' I went out, went to a golf course, and I picked up the club. The instructor said, 'Hold it like this', and I swung it back and hit a 7 iron dead down the middle. It was semi-sexual. I was addicted. I played 36 holes a day for a year, so by the end of the first year I was a nine handicap. I was playing tournaments in my first year. Every day I'd play with a pro in the morning and a pro in the afternoon. I was there all day, and I did a lot of bad shots, but suddenly I was hitting more good shots than bad shots, and I was starting to understand what the 7 iron did, what the driver was going to do, how to read putts and stuff. I still play every single day. I'm addicted.

Your 1989 hit single 'Poison' marked your big return – that and your cameo in *Wayne's World*.

Mike Myers called me up, and he says, 'We need somebody that has that "We're not worthy!" prestige. A rock icon.' We were just supposed to do the song, but Mike hands me about five pages of dialogue, and goes, 'Could you do these lines?' When the camera rolled I had the basic patter, but I was winging it. Mike at the end just goes, 'That was great!' Because it was really funny. Just delivering the lines straight.

Now you've become this figurehead with so much affection and respect. The outsider has been embraced, while still maintaining a reputation as someone who puts on a good show.

I never let the show down. I still have a competitive streak in me. I'll be on the same stage as Rob Zombie or Marilyn Manson. They sit there and go, 'We sat and we watched you, and we learned from you.' I said, 'That's great, but you're still competing with me, because when I get on stage my object is to blow you off the stage!'

What is the last song you want to play? Anything you want.

Let's play a song that every time I hear it, I go, 'That's what rock and roll's about'. How about 'Train Kept A-Rollin' by The Yardbirds.

What it is about that song that you love so much?

If you don't get up on that song there's something wrong with you, you don't have a heartbeat.

The First Time Alice Cooper Playlist

1	Elected	Alice Cooper
2	School Day (Ring Ring Goes the Bell)	Chuck Berry
3	Venus	Frankie Avalon
4	Jim Dandy	LaVern Baker
5	All Summer Long	The Beach Boys
6	She Loves You	The Beatles
7	I'm a Man	The Yardbirds
8	I'm Eighteen	Alice Cooper
9	All the Young Dudes	David Bowie
10	Alice Cooper	School's Out
11	I'm a Boy	The Who
12	Poison	Alice Cooper
13	Train Kept A-Rollin'	The Yardbirds

"I picked the guitar up, bought a book, *How to Play the Guitar*, and the next thing was we formed Joy Division."

Bernard Sumner

B ernard Sumner is the first and only person who's cried during an interview I've done. He's describing when he first heard that Ian Curtis had committed suicide. His speech slows down to a halt. Then he breaks down.

In early Joy Division press shots, Bernard looks like the misbehaving kid in the back row of a school photo, eyeing up the next stunt. That slight hint of mischief is still there. He's always nearly smiling, and as relaxed and comfortable as his first band's image was austere. A pretty Nordic pin-up with New Order in the '80s, he still has soft, boyish features, and his blond-grey hair is cropped tight at the side with a fringe gently sweeping over his forehead.

His voice, like his singing, is calm and mellow, his Manchester accent punctuated by a slight stutter from time to time, and his memory is incredibly detailed. When he recalls on what side of his mother's bed the phone was when he answered the first ever call from Curtis, he almost seems as shocked as I am that the information is still lodged somewhere in his brain.

Listening back to the whole interview, I am amazed at how open Bernard is. I'm stumbling for words while he details the death of his friend so honestly, and he keeps talking. He could easily (and understandably) have stopped or refused to answer a question about a tragic event that's become such a focus of hallowed fascination for music fans, but he didn't. Maybe it's a lesson he learned from punk - be honest, be real, don't buy into your own mythology.

The moment passes quickly, and we're soon talking about music again, and he's happy to keep chatting as the interview overruns its allotted time – 'I'll speak quicker', he says – and when the interview comes to an end we stare at each other in mild disbelief. 'Bloody hell', he laughs. 'Thirty years condensed into 40 minutes.'

Matt Everitt: When was the first time you were aware of music?
We didn't have a record player in the house. We had a little '60s radio
I got from my grandparents and my mother. I remember it playing The
Beatles. That was my first recollection. I liked it because it had guitars.

**What was the first song you can remember making an
impression on you?**
The first one was 'Ride a White Swan' by T. Rex, which did end up being
the first single I ever bought. I liked 'Big Yellow Taxi' by Joni Mitchell as
well. That was a cute little track. Anything with a good tune and prefera-
bly with a bit of guitar in it, because I liked the sound of guitars.

When did you get your first guitar?
I was sixteen. Yeah, I was a bit of a late developer. I won't tell you what I
was into before guitars, but …

Girls, I presume?
I would have liked to have been, but I was into scooters. I wore a
Crombie and had two-tone trousers and all that business. It was
about 1972. On my scooter I used to go to North Salford Youth Club.
Downstairs they had a disco and they used to play a ton of Motown and
Stax records. Upstairs, they had more serious music like Led Zeppelin
and the Stones and Free. It was a good place to go and get an education,
because you've got the dance vibes down below and then you've got the
guitar music upstairs, so that was a good place to learn about music.

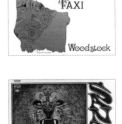

What was the first gig you went to?
I remember hearing Santana on [British TV music show] *The Old Grey
Whistle Test* and thinking, 'I quite like that, a lot of guitar in it.' I went to
see them play live in Manchester. It was the height of their popularity
and I think they'd just done Woodstock, and there were masses of people
there. Then Carlos Santana came on, and the spotlight went on him and
he said, 'Before I start the set,' and he put his hands together, 'please
meditate with me for two minutes.' Of course, this didn't go down very
well in Manchester, and the results were quite hilarious, really. People
chucking stuff, yelling, 'Fucking get on with it!'

**You were at the Sex Pistols' Manchester Free Trade Hall [June
1976] gig as well?**
I was about twenty-one when the punk thing started. We'd read in the
NME about this new, happening music, punk, and we liked the photos
of Johnny Rotten because he obviously didn't give a fuck about what
he looked like, and that appealed to us enormously. There was a local
group that was rumoured to be into that type of music, which was the
Buzzcocks. Then the next thing we heard was the Buzzcocks were going
to support the Pistols at the Free Trade Hall, and we went down to it. It's
a legendary gig, and, as with all legends, when you look at the cold truth,

it wasn't that fantastic. I recorded it on my little cassette recorder, boot-legged it. It sounded really bad but the vibe was fantastic. Local legend is that out of the hundred or so people that were at that gig, 25 groups were formed. It was my road to Damascus.

At that point, you formed a band.
I had those two phases of my early musical development. I had Santana and all those rock bands, and the emphasis in that kind of music was virtuosity. In fact, when I got my first guitar when I was sixteen years old, I just put it in the corner of the room because I thought, 'I'll never be able to play like that.' Then I went to see The Sex Pistols and thought, 'Ah, you don't have to be able to play like that to form a group! And this group looks like it's a lot more fun than the other groups.' At that moment, I picked the guitar up, bought a book, *How to Play the Guitar*, and the next thing was we formed Joy Division.

What was your first impression of Ian Curtis?
We'd met Ian at some punk gigs. They don't look it when you see old film of them, but the punk gigs were really friendly. The whole message of punk for me was 'Don't get too big for your boots. Just have a laugh and enjoy life.' I met Ian at a few gigs, then me and Peter Hook got together and he bought a book on how to play bass and we sat in my grandmoth-er's front room practising every Sunday. Then we're like, 'Right, we're good enough now to be able to write some song.' We decided to advertise for a singer in the Virgin Records in Manchester Piccadilly.

"The whole message of punk for me was 'Don't get too big for your boots. Just have a laugh and enjoy life.'"

Stupidly, I put my mother's phone number on the thing, because I still lived with my mum then. I started getting all these lunatics on my mum's phone at all different times of the day. Then Ian called one night. He said, 'It's Ian, I think you might know me.' And I was so relieved that it wasn't another knobhead that I just gave him the job. I said, 'You got anything to sing through?' He said, 'Yeah, I got a PA system.' I said, 'Alright, come down on Sunday. Let's rehearse', and that's how it started.

What were people's reactions when they first heard 'Love Will Tear Us Apart'?
'Love Will Tear Us Apart'? I can't remember anything about writing it. We just used to jam in the rehearsal room, and we jammed it out and it became one of the songs. We'd recorded a version down at Strawberry Studios in Stockport and we just didn't like it. Part of it was the studio,

but part was [producer] Martin Hannett, who was either brilliant or crap. Actually, that could be said of us as well. We could hear the potential of this song, and knew that there was something about it. We got the mix off Martin and we didn't feel the drums were powerful enough. So he was bugged that we didn't like his original version, and we just spent a day re-recording it.

About two o'clock in the morning, Steve Morris, the drummer, had gone home and I was still working on some guitar melodies and Martin said, 'Get Steve back!' I said, 'What? He's right over the other side of London.' And he went, 'No, no, get Steve! I need Steve now to finish this track.' Steve drives all the way across London, arrives at the studio totally pissed off, and Martin goes, 'Right, back in! I want you to double-track the snare drum.' You never double-track a snare drum because it makes all sorts of weird noises. Steve was so annoyed and he just whacked the hell out of that bloody snare drum. Whether Martin got Steve in at that time to get some attitude out of him on the snare drum, or whether Martin just did it to piss us all off because we had pissed him off? It's hard to tell, and unfortunately Martin's not here to defend himself.

What were you doing when you first heard Ian had committed suicide in 1980?

There was a band on the Factory label called Section 25, a really great band. One of them had a speedboat and it was a dead nice weekend and they'd invited me over. Ian had split up with his wife and had been staying with me for two weeks. I was pretty much an insomniac and I think Ian got a bit sick of that, going to bed at five in the morning. He was not in a great mental state. He was handling it, but he was pretty upset. That weekend, he went to stay with his mum and dad. I was like, 'I've got to see Section 25. I'm going to go hang out with them.'

We got on the river, a perfect day, beautiful sunshine, we're having a right laugh and I was supposed to be going on tour on the Monday. We get back to the house, I'm just drying off with a towel when the phone rings and it's Rob, my manager, and he just says, 'I've got some bad news. Really bad news.' I said, 'What?' He said, 'Ian's committed suicide.' Ian had already tried to commit suicide about three weeks before. I said, 'What? He's tried again?' He said, 'No, no. He has.'

You okay?

Difficult to talk about it.

Then don't, mate. It's okay.

No, no. I'm fine. Then he was like, 'No, he's dead.' That's all I can say, really. I've not spoken about it for a long time and it's pretty difficult. It was just an enormous shock and I remember the room spinning around and it was like I'd been hit with a sledgehammer. Also, from a selfish point of view, I thought, 'All the work we've done has just been thrown away.' I just didn't think he was *actually* going to do it. You think it's a cry for help. He took a pill overdose a few weeks earlier. I just thought, 'Well, he's tried it again', and then the details came out that he was dead and so that was it, the whole world just fell apart. I was very depressed for quite a long time after that. But what can you do? You just have to accept the things that you can't do anything about in life. Eventually, after a period of depression, I just picked myself up. Well, the whole band picked themselves up, and we just started again. There was no other option. There was nothing else that we could do. There was nowhere else we could go. We couldn't go back to our jobs. We couldn't. We just had to get on with it.

I got approached by a couple of people – 'I'll be your new singer' – but it just felt wrong. What we eventually ended up doing – depending on how you look at it, either very rashly or very bravely – was deciding not to use any of the Joy Division songs, to start from year zero, with a new set of songs. For a year, I think, we went in our rehearsal room and wrote a new album. We were locked away writing new stuff and coming up with a new name and deciding who was going to be the singer. That was really difficult because we needed a new direction, otherwise it would have felt like we were just aping Joy Division minus Ian.

"There was nothing else that we could do. There was nowhere else we could go. We just had to get on with it."

I had the difficult learning curve of becoming the singer and having to learn the art in public. We had to write a whole new set of songs and then I had to learn to be the singer as well. It was a little like pushing a ten-ton boulder up Mount Everest. But you can do it. I'm here today, 28 years later, to say, 'Hey, you can do it. You can get over anything if you're desperate enough.' I was going to say, 'if you try hard enough', but I guess the truth is 'desperate enough'.

The first trip New Order took to New York City in the early '80s – the myth is that's one of the things that crystallized New Order's sound.

We all tried singing – me, Peter and Stephen all tried singing – but we wanted to do it somewhere where we weren't so well known, so we went over to New York, and every night we'd go out. That's where I got an idea for a new direction. I was at a club one night and I heard this great dance music. It wasn't like they were playing back here – like, crappy commercial disco; they were playing really good tracks like Sugarhill Gang and Sharon Redd. I'm just hearing this music thinking, 'I'm going to make a track that you can play in a club and people will get off on it.' The music I was hearing was all still being played on real instruments, but they were

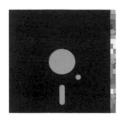

trying to play it tight and rhythmical. I got interested in technology so I thought, 'Well, I could do that if I got a computer and I could link all the synthesizers together, make it super-tight. With the band that was a bit difficult, because they were all grumbling, 'I'm not bloody having a drum machine in this group', and 'You're not replacing my bass with a synthesizer', so I had to battle a bit to get them to do it. I wasn't very popular for a while, until we had a massive hit and then opinions changed.

When was the first time you heard 'Blue Monday' in a club?

It came about by having a new synthesizer – a Moog, but not a very well-known Moog; I won't go into it because it's a bit of a trade secret – a DMX drum machine, and the synthesizer that I built in Joy Division, and linking them all together. I had a mate in New York who used to send me over cassettes of New York dance stations, and I picked a few favourite tracks and I took elements of each. I didn't copy it exactly, I just went, 'I like that track. I'll do something like that for the beat. I'll use an arrangement like they've got. I'll bring some strings in where they bring some strings in. I can do a bassline like this old record.'

What were the songs? Do you remember?

Klein and M.B.O., 'Dirty Talk' was one; 'Our Love', Donna Summer; and 'You Make Me Feel (Mighty Real)', Sylvester, for the bassline. Kraftwerk, 'Radioactivity', the voices at the start. A lot of different influences, and pulling them together. Again, it was just the right record at the right time. It was designed. It's not really a song, 'Blue Monday', it's more like a machine-designed sound system in nightclubs. DJs loved it. I was in a club in Berlin a couple of years ago and we're playing all these fantastic records, modern productions, and then the DJ knew that I was there, so he puts 'Blue Monday' on, and everyone got up and it just wiped the floor with all the modern production.

Why did New Order split up – for the first time – in 1993?

There was a tension in the group between members who wanted to go out and tour and members who wanted to be in the studio and write stuff. I felt like we were touring just to keep the coffers up at Factory [Records, New Order's label] and touring was taking a toll on my health. I actually ended up in hospital in Chicago. I was drinking too much and having too many late nights. The doctor had a word with me, and it just made me think about the lifestyle I was leading. I didn't want to end up like Jimi Hendrix or one of these guys that just burns out from overdoing it. I just didn't want to do it.

I wanted to chill out with the touring, and that met with opposition. I was still getting a bit of opposition for using synthesizers as well. Plus there were two enormous business financial strains on the group. I felt like every record that was a hit and made a lot of money was just liquidated in the Great Factory Records Cash Liquidation Machine. It either went into the Haçienda [nightclub in Manchester, co-owned by Factory

Records and New Order] or it went into the record label. I got pissed off with it. I thought, 'Well, I'm not doing it if we're just wasting our money.'

NEW
ORDER
TEMPTATION
1987

You do have a sense of lyrical style. Do you write prose or poetry or lyrics?

I write stuff, and I'll tell you the truth, I haven't really got a clue what the bloody hell it is about. I do write from a subconscious. I don't mean that in a pretentious way. I find the best stuff that I write is when I can forget myself, and I think that's true of most things. If you take athletes, for example, they just forget themselves. The brain doesn't get in the way of the body, you know? It's the same with writing words, but in a different way. It's not your brain getting in the way of your body; it's your conscious brain getting in the way of your subconscious. If you can just stop thinking about it, and you listen to the backing track and see what that's saying to you, then it just pours out. I don't know if all lyricists write that way, but that's the way I write. It works for me.

What's the final track we should play?

If it was a New Order track, 'Temptation', because that's a track that New Order fans really love, and I love playing it. It's the one track I never get bored of playing, and there's something really special about it. I don't know what it is. If I knew what it was, I'd write another one like it.

The First Time Bernard Sumner Playlist

1	True Faith '94	New Order
2	I Saw Her Standing There	The Beatles
3	Ride a White Swan	T. Rex
4	Big Yellow Taxi	Joni Mitchell
5	Jingo	Santana
6	Mother of Pearl	Roxy Music
7	Boredom	Buzzcocks
8	Love Will Tear Us Apart	Joy Division
9	Beat the Street	Sharon Redd
10	Dirty Talk	Klein and M.B.O.
11	I Feel Love	Donna Summer
12	Radioactivity	Kraftwerk
13	Blue Monday	New Order
14	Get the Message	Electronic
15	Temptation	New Order

STRAWBERRY FIELDS
FOREVER

PENNY LANE

JUSTIFIED

WONDER WHIP

Freshly Made For You

BPM

"The music thing?
That was never planned;
that was an accident."

BILL DRUMMOND

B ill Drummond is made of ideas: from his Soup Line project
(he drew a straight line on a map from Belfast to Nottingham
and announced that anyone whose home lay on that line
could contact Bill and he'd go to their house and make soup), to
The17 (an evolving choir that he created, always comprised of 17
members of the public whose performances are never recorded for
posterity), to his and Jimmy Cauty's musical and conceptual excur-
sions as The KLF, The JAMs and The K Foundation. When you meet
Bill, you're aware that you won't be doing a conventional interview.

Tall and broad, with a face you can imagine on an ancient
Roman coin, he talks quickly, precisely and with absolute assurance.
It's like he's reading from an invisible, memorized script that he
prepared after looking through all of my questions the night before.
It's slightly disconcerting, and adds to the feeling that I'm a bit out
of my depth during the interview – which, in all honesty, I probably
am. He challenges me to explain myself in more detail more than
once, but he's not intimidating. He's charming, polite and generous
with his time, and talks about music in the detail of a pop historian
and with the passion of a lifelong fan.

In 2012, Bill stated that he'd stop doing regular interviews and
only answer two hundred questions before his death: four each from
just 50 people, and only questions he's never been asked. So I'm
glad I got to speak to him before that point, and attempt to find out
where some of those ideas come from.

Matt Everitt: When was the first time you were aware of music?
I remember going to a Christmas party at Penninghame Prison, in South
West Scotland, when I was about three years old. My father was the
chaplain and it was a party for all the children of the officers and anybody connected to the prison. I guess I would have known what church
music was, and pipe band music, but we didn't have a record player.

There was this thing that happened on stage: there was a man who
had a box in front of him and there was a kind of wooden bit that stuck
out of it, and there were some strings on it and he was bashing this thing;
it was the loudest noise I'd ever heard. And there was somebody else who
got this thing that my granny used to wash the clothes, and he was making a load of noise on that. And then there was a tea chest with a broom
handle in the corner and a string that he was plucking. It was just this
wall of noise, but it was the most exciting noise I'd ever heard in my life:
it made me want to jump up and down. It was only afterwards I thought,
'That's maybe music. That's maybe music as well as church music.'

That was the first lasting impression of experiencing music, and
nothing since has ever seemed as loud. And for those that don't know,
it was a skiffle band.

What about the first music that you owned?
You see, you're making a fundamental mistake there. You're saying what
was the first piece of recorded music, as if that's somehow a prime thing.
I owned music from the word go; I was owning that music that I heard.
But you're asking me what is the first record I owned?

What's the first record that you owned?
Okay. The first record I bought was on 17th February 1967, 'Penny Lane'
backed by 'Strawberry Fields Forever' [by The Beatles]. I bought it in
the HMV record shop in Corby, Northamptonshire, at 4:47pm.

What do you remember from listening to it for the first time?
I had this record, but I'd never actually put a record on before. I got it
at the right speed but it took quite a bit to pluck up courage to put the
needle into the groove. I'd seen *Top of the Pops*; I knew that some people
leapt around to pop music, and I also knew some people thought about
pop music. I didn't know if I should be one of the people that leapt
around or one of the people that should think about it. The music started
and all I was thinking was, 'I own this record. This is my record. This is
mine.' I played it three times before I realized it had a B-side as well.

**Can you remember performing – doing something for the
appreciation of someone other than just yourself?**
I've always felt music shouldn't be 'The Performers' and 'The Consumers',
that it should be a thing we're all part of, and I guess that's because it's
only a twentieth-century thing. The evolution of technology so music
could be recorded pushed music into being a thing that you either do

or you sit and listen to. Of course, you had great piano players or great violinists, but it was a thing you did all together. I'm just skirting around the answer. The answer is I sang in a church choir when I was a kid.

Okay, let's say your first communal music experience with like-minded souls?
That would be church when I was a kid, and then in school, but if you're asking me when did I first get up on the stage with an electric guitar and make a lot of noise? That's a different question.

I'm asking that question.
Okay. That would have been when I was about fourteen, yeah. It was in the Girl Guides hall. Some friends of ours had a band and, because I could play a few chords, I went up and met with them.

There were two things we were playing that afternoon: one was Roy Orbison's 'Pretty Woman', and the other was The Isley Brothers. I can't remember the name of the hit just now. If you had a guitar here, you see, I'd play it straight away. It goes E, G-sharp, A.

"I didn't know if I should be one of the people that leapt around or one of the people that should think about it."

The story of your life and career is a parallel of music and art. Can you remember your first piece of art?
Yes, definitely. My dad did watercolour paintings; that was his way of escaping and relaxing. I'd often go with him into the countryside near where we lived, and while he was off doing watercolour paintings I'd be climbing trees. We used to go down and stay with my granny in Norwich. We would go to the museum, and they had all these watercolour paintings and big oil paintings. That had a big impact on me. I was always into drawing; I ended up going to art school because I could draw.

The music thing: that was never planned; that was an accident. I never had dreams of being a rock star or anything. That was purely accidental. When I was twenty-three or twenty-four, that started happening.

Big in Japan was your first recognized band. What do you remember from those times?
It wasn't supposed to be a serious thing. I was sitting in a pub in Mathew Street in Liverpool called The Grapes, and there was myself and this guy called Clive Langer, who went on to become a successful producer. He was the main musician in this band called Deaf School, who were from Liverpool, and he was going to me and these other two guys, 'You've got to form a band.' He says, 'You can have our equipment while

we're away in America [on tour], and when we get back in three weeks' time, I want you to be a band and I'll join you.' That was the beginning of Big in Japan. We only lasted a year and line-ups kept changing, evolving. I guess it was great, in a way.

You formally joined the music industry when you formed Zoo Records and managed Echo and the Bunnymen and The Teardrop Explodes. What was the first mistake you made as a record label boss?

I don't think I formally joined the music industry. Okay, okay, okay, I know what you're asking ... Seymour Stein, who co-owned Sire Records and had Talking Heads and The Ramones [and later signed Madonna], approached us about signing Echo and the Bunnymen. I remember writing out a long letter to Seymour saying, 'Well, this is all very well, but you'll have to understand: if they sign to your label, they will not make albums.' I was totally against albums. As far as I was concerned, albums were the worst thing that had ever happened to music. I compromised on that. He said to me, 'Bill, the music industry right now is defined by album sales.' I allowed Echo and the Bunnymen to record albums.

The other thing was that Tony Wilson, who had Factory Records in Manchester, and I had built a rapport between the two of us over the previous 18 months. He was always telling me, 'You must never sign your bands to major labels in London.' And I used to say to him, 'That's all very well for you to say that, Tony. You've got a comfortable job at Granada TV, you know? We're all on the dole.' He was adamant we shouldn't have anything to do with those people down in London. I wasn't from Liverpool, I didn't have this fierce sense of Liverpudlian pride, but he might have been right. Maybe those are two mistakes.

"I was totally against albums. As far as I was concerned, albums were the worst thing that had ever happened to music."

What was the first thing on the agenda for The KLF – if you had an agenda, mental or otherwise?

The first record that we did together [as the Justified Ancients of Mu Mu] was called 'All You Need Is Love'. It was only going to be a one-off. It was just an idea that I had about what you could do with samplers. I loved the fact that rap and early hip-hop were presenting a completely new way of putting music together.

I liked that we could just get rid of rock music, everything rock music had represented – guitar, bass, drums, lead singer, that whole mythology that goes with it. I love that that could all just be dispensed with. I didn't want us to be making music that was mimicking what American hip-hop or rap acts were doing, but to try and make a British version of it. That's what we aimed to do right at the beginning. I remember, I went through my record collection noting down the key every song was in and the BPM, the beats per minute, making these cross-referencing things. So I could see if you took two seconds of that, something by James Brown, and you put two seconds of that by Abba, you could cut and splice them together. I liked the idea of building things up like that and completely rethinking the whole way music has been put together.

Tell me about your first book, *The Manual (How to Have a Number One the Easy Way)*.

It hasn't been in print for a long time; we often get asked by publishers to reprint it, and Jimmy [Cauty] and I always say no. Obviously, it exists on the net – it's there if people want the information – but its influence carries on and on and on, which in one sense I find surprising. I guess I'm flattered. I don't know how well it stands up now. But I also know one of the influences for me behind wanting to write it: there was a book called *Play Power* by Richard Neville, which came out in about 1970, that said you can do what you want, you don't have to wait to be given permission, and I wanted *The Manual* to be like that. Don't wait for somebody to say, 'Yes, you're allowed to make pop music now', or 'Yes, you've been sanctioned. We've signed you to this record label so you're now official', or 'You've been written about in the *NME* so we'll venerate you'. You know, sod all that. If you want to do it, go and do it.

When did you realize that The KLF were no more?

Everybody knows that bands or singers have a natural life. You might get into a certain artist and enjoy following their career, but usually it is pretty early on that they make their defining record. If you haven't done it by your third album, you're not going to. And pop music, we both thought, should be short term. We had actually got some plans for other things, but we realized, 'No, no. Let's just stop now.'

There were also other things we wanted to do that were nothing to do with music. Music is a very jealous mistress. Music had never been the whole thing for me or for Jimmy, but it sucks up all your time, and everybody around you wants you to do it all the time. I'm not saying that they're leeches, totally, but you get sucked into doing this thing and I just think we both knew it was now time to stop.

What was the first emotion you felt when you were setting fire to the first note of that alleged one million pounds? [In 1994 Drummond and Cauty, under the name K Foundation, burned a million pounds in cash, an amount representing their total earnings as The KLF. The action was filmed.]

About a year or so later, Jimmy said, 'Look, we have this film.' We actually filmed the whole thing. We started showing that at places and we felt we owed it at least to our families to come up with a reason. When we showed the film, all people wanted to know was, 'Did you really do it?' We realized it didn't matter how much we said or attempted to prove that this was for real, the ones that didn't want to believe would not believe, and the ones that wanted to believe would believe.

The other thing everybody wanted to know was, 'Why?' You do something like that, you've got to be able to justify it. We realized that there was no way. There was never a reason that was good enough for people. We decided this is not down to us. This is down to other people. They've got to come up with a reason. They've got to come up with a reason why somebody should want to go – or why two people should want to go – and burn a million pounds.

Somebody we were working with suggested to us, 'Look, you've got to stop talking about it. The more you talk about it, the more it waters it down, dissipates it. Give people enough time to take on board this thing and then they can come up with the reasons why this had to be done or why anybody would want to do this.' I know I haven't answered your questions, but that's the answer I'm giving.

"Nobody should make art bigger than themselves, because big art is bullying art."

That'll do.
It's not a good enough answer for my children, I can tell you that.

Do you think anyone has the potential to make art?
If you're in my position, you think long and hard about it. It doesn't mean you get any closer to an answer, and it doesn't matter. I set up a website called openmanifesto.com, and this website exists for people to say what they think art is and what it should be about. In one sense, it's the complete antithesis of an art manifesto. This is about finding the open manifesto: it evolves; it changes; it takes on things and rubbishes what happened yesterday, but then maybe celebrates what happened ten years ago. And it's there for everybody and anybody to put things on.

The only thing that I could feel strongly about is that nobody should make art bigger than themselves, because big art is bullying art. It makes you think, 'Oh wow. That's fantastic. It's just fantastic because it makes me feel small and insignificant.' That way dictatorship lies. There's part of me that wants to rip down anything that's trying to make me feel small, to overawe me with its volume, its size. In my head, that's a negative thing about us as people. That's why people will follow Hitler. That's why we follow those things instead of actually looking into ourselves.

Let's talk about 'The17' choir project; what was the first one like?

I first did it as a trial in Leicester. I've got a friend [Kev Reverb] there who's got a studio. I said, 'Kev, there's this noise I can hear in my head. It's a choral thing.' As I mentioned earlier, I sang in choirs as a kid. Choral music's always been a natural thing for me to listen to and think about. I put together something there with him, and initially it was to make a very primal-sounding choir that didn't use lyrics, didn't use song structure, didn't use rhythm. It was almost like starting music again. But I wanted to use big, big chords. I could hear these sounds in my head. I tried it once as a performance in front of an audience and realized that was a mistake. I wanted The17 to always be with a different group of people. It's just done for the people that are taking part, so there's never an audience. There's lots of different scores that can be performed by The17, which I've been doing all around the world, and some are hardly music.

You're not tempted to make music for mass public consumption anymore at all? There is a beauty in giving something and making it available forever, not deleting it.

It'd be crap; it'd be rubbish. It's a zeitgeist thing. It's not just one's own talents – if one has talent – it has to be at that right time with whatever else is going around. The mistake most artists make, they think it's them that's the great one. In actual fact, they're just part of something. They're just part of a thing that's happening at a certain time.

What's the last song we should play?

Fairport Convention's 'Who Knows Where the Time Goes'.

Why?

Because it's one of the greatest songs ever written, and that's the one that just came into my head.

The First Time Bill Drummond Playlist

Bill Drummond: I would not describe these as my 'all-time favourite tracks' but what they are, are pieces of music that had an influence on my life at the time, some of which still resonate down the years. I have never been one for mix tapes or playlists. Most of the pieces of music on the list, I will not have heard for years, and would have no problem if I was never to hear them again. But that does not take away from the influence they have had on me in the past. The truth is I rarely listen to music, other than the music in my head, which is there all the time.

"Music to me was this other, almost religious, spiritual thing that seemed to hover around my life. Any time I came in contact with music, I 'felt' more."

BILLY CORGAN

Billy Corgan collapses all 6 feet 4 inches of himself into the studio chair opposite me, wearing a heavy-looking green parka. He's got an equally heavy cold and a long scarf is wrapped repeatedly round his neck. This, combined with a cosy-looking striped hoodie, makes it look like his perfectly round, bald head has been dropped from above onto the rest of his body like a cherry on the top of an ice-cream sundae.

For a long time, Corgan was regarded as a difficult interviewee, prone to needling other musicians and appearing to resent not being given the respect he felt he was due. But here there's no aggression or animosity. He's thoughtful and responds to every question. He's amused when I point out the controversy that occasionally surfaced during his career, and good-naturedly exasperated at how people have tried to categorize his music.

I think Billy finds his own reputation frustrating, inspiring and funny in equal measures. He doesn't care what people think about his personality, but he cares deeply that they listen to his music without the baggage that his celebrity creates. He also clearly enjoys pushing against his fans' expectations, and constantly challenges himself by doing the opposite of what anyone expects him to do.

Which would explain why – before reforming Smashing Pumpkins for a lucrative greatest-hits tour in 2018 – he started a professional wrestling league, opened a tea shop, became a high-profile cat enthusiast and performed a one-man improvised eight-hour synthesizer interpretation of a Hermann Hesse novel. These are not the actions of a man who gives a shit about what's expected of him.

Matt Everitt: When were you first aware of music?

My father was a musician so there were always records around, and my earliest memories of actually playing records on my own? About two years old. I had a little toy record player. My father loved soul music. People like Al Green. There was a lot of soul music in the house.

Were you fascinated by music from an early age?

Music to me was this other, almost religious, spiritual thing that seemed to hover around my life. Any time I came in contact with music I 'felt' more. Which, when you're a kid, doesn't really make sense to you. Because you feel the way you feel. And then when music would be on, I would have more feelings, which was strange to me. Why was I having a different experience when music was on? All I knew was that music provided me with an experience that only seemed to come from music.

What about the first record that was yours?

We had a street sale when I was five years old. I found *Meet the Beatles!* Didn't know who The Beatles were; I was attracted to the album cover, actually. It was 25 cents. That was the first record I ever actually purchased for myself. I remember putting it on and having this, like, electric shock go through my body, because I could not believe what I was hearing. I remember really being struck by the sound of their voices. All I knew was it made me feel very, very excited and I listened to that record incessantly.

What about the first music obsessions you had that were maybe more pertinent to your generation?

Well, honestly, I had an uncle who was a drummer and he had a very progressive record collection: Jethro Tull, Yes, Queen … and that was when I was eight years old. That's when I first came into contact with Black Sabbath.

Which was a big deal for you, obviously.

I love Black Sabbath, personally. I always have, and it's been a joy to get to meet them and stuff like that, but the sound of Black Sabbath is something I've just never been able to get out of my mind. It's about the combination of the darkness, the size and the power. It's something that's influenced pretty much everything I've ever done.

What's a track that would best sum that up for you?

The first track that I heard. I was eight years old and my uncle had Black Sabbath's *Master of Reality*. I put the album on – I wasn't supposed to play his stereo – it was *verboten* – and I heard what I now know is Tony Iommi coughing from a big bong hit or something into 'Sweet Leaf'.

What was the first gig that you can remember going to?

On one hand, my first experience with music was watching my father rehearse with his band in the basement. But my first actual, real concert that I saw? Asia, 'Heat of the Moment' [laughs]. I was fourteen years old. I'll tell you a funny story. A couple of years ago, Smashing Pumpkins played in Chicago and we actually played the opera hall where I'd seen Asia, and I pointed up to the rafters – I'd had the worst possible seat at the very, very top – and I said, 'Hey, you in this T-shirt', and the person waved, and I said, 'That's where I sat when I came to my very first concert, so I'm gonna …' and I brought the person down to the front row.

What about the first band that you were responsible for?
My first proper, professional band was a band called The Marked. One of the worst names ever. So named because I have a big birthmark on my arm and the drummer had a birthmark on his face. And we played, interestingly enough, a kind of Bauhaus meets Black Sabbath. So a progenitor of what became Smashing Pumpkins, this combination of very alternative '80s UK meets kind of '70s classic rock. We did it very crudely and poorly, and the band broke up after a short time, but that sort of sowed the seeds for what I later did with the band.

You mentioned Bauhaus and the UK indie invasion, that's another key thing for you. The Cure is a band that gets named – can you remember hearing The Cure for the first time?
I had this girlfriend when I was seventeen, and she was, like, the cool girl. She listened to The Cure and Joy Division and all this stuff, and so she made me a tape, and I'd never heard The Cure before. I have a disabled brother – I used to have to take care of him a lot, so I'd spend a lot of time at home practising, and I was so bored because I had to play guitar by myself that I kind of invented this weird style where I'd play with a lot of open strings so it would be more interesting for me to play, almost as if I was playing with another person. When I first heard The Cure I was like, 'Oh my god! Somebody plays guitar the way I'm playing guitar.'

When you first started playing with [original Smashing Pumpkins bandmates] James, D'arcy and Jimmy, was it an instantaneous thing? Did it feel different? Did it feel special?
No.

Brilliant! [Laughs] People normally just go, 'Yeah, yeah, there was just something there! It was just magic!'
No, to be honest, I first realized something special was happening was when we were growing up in Chicago. Often, because we were a new band, we would get the terrible slot of Wednesday night or something. So, you know, there'd be people at the bar, you're the band that's on, they're not really there to see you, they're talking, and I noticed, because I'd been in other groups, when the four of us were on stage, people paid a different attention. They just looked at us differently and they would watch us differently. And I don't know what that was, but I noticed that right away. That's the first time I thought, 'Something's happening'.

Legend has it *Gish* wasn't exactly an easy record to make. Would that be a fair comment?

It was slightly difficult, but for the most part I think it was pretty smooth sailing. The only real politics was the fact that Butch [Vig, producer] was not crazy about James and D'arcy playing on the record because they weren't very skilled musicians and so that caused some basic dissension.

It's still a very ambitious record, that first album. You can tell a lot of concentration and love has gone into it.

Well, we felt that the kind of music we were playing at that time, particularly in the Midwest of America, was not really supported by the media. We saw fans responding to it, but we knew, media-wise, we weren't going to get support. So, in a weird kind of way, we thought, 'Well, if we're not going to get supported, we might as well just make the record as weird as we want to make it, because it's probably not going to get good reviews no matter what we do.' We were playing a very aggressive style. In the early '90s, to play solos and to be aggressive on the drums and the guitars was a bit bourgeois to the indie intelligentsia.

Did you resent being put in the same box as Pearl Jam, Jane's Addiction and Nirvana, or didn't that really bother you?

Oh, it drove me insane.

Why? Was it the simplification of art?

Well, we all go through this experience in life – in America we call it high school. You start to realize, 'Oh, the girl that I like likes the quarterback because he's handsome and dumb, so my intelligence means nothing. The weird girl in class who everybody makes fun of thinks I'm cute because I'm weird looking, but I want the cheerleader to like me.'

"If I'm not going to get it handed to me ... I'm going to have to take it. And I'm going to have to have a band that's better, meaner, faster, crazier."

You start to figure out who you are, in the social world. Well, the same thing happens in music: you start off with an idea, and then as you enter into the world, you start to find out, like, oh, your voice is too weird, your band will never be successful; your name's too stupid, your band's never going to be successful; oh, you're from Chicago? Oh, nobody likes Chicago, you'll never be successful.

You start to get all these things put on you that don't have anything to do with whether or not you're good. And this still happens. People

Billy Corgan

make decisions, very snap decisions, on the way somebody looks, you know? The way somebody sounds. Even at this point, the things I say in an interview will overly colour the way people hear my music. So as we went along, we saw ourselves being dumbed down.

So, this drove me insane to the point where I thought, 'Well, if I'm not going to get it handed to me like I see it handed to other people, I'm going to have to take it. And I'm just going to have to have a band that's better, meaner, faster, crazier.

With *Siamese Dream*, 1993 …
Speaking of crazy …

This is the record that really hurled you head-first into the mainstream. How much of it was born out of the frustrations that you were just explaining?
Well, this is a bit psychological. Smashing Pumpkins' reaction as a unit to pressure was to embrace it and then destroy it. So, for example, the first song on *Siamese Dream* is 'Cherub Rock': five-minute song, total prog rock. It opens with a riff lifted right off the Canadian rock band Rush ['By-Tor and The Snow Dog']. It goes into some massive thing, and the first lines are all about how indie rock is completely false.

A statement of intent straight away, isn't it, really?
'Freak out and give in, doesn't matter what you believe in' – that's the first line of the record. So it's basically saying it doesn't matter what we do, you're going to change us into something we're not. And that became part of Smashing Pumpkins' operating ethos: they're not going to let us be who we are, they're not going to embrace who we actually are, so we're going to become almost larger than life. If you think we're dramatic, we're going to be overly dramatic. If you think our concerts are long, wait till we really play a long concert. We overreacted, but we did it on purpose. We would be written about as if we were too stupid to realize why we were being annoying, or how we were being annoying, and we were like, 'No, we actually realize we're being annoying, we're doing it on purpose. Don't you get the joke?'

I suppose it's one way of dealing with being in that world.
Listen, when you're a kid and you don't have any power, what do you do? You say, 'I'm not going to eat my broccoli.' What was our way of not eating our broccoli? You're not going to tell us how long our songs should be. You're not going to tell us how many songs we should play in our concerts. We used to end our concerts with a 45-minute song, and half the audience would leave, you know? Any manager would tell you, 'Look, when people leave before the concert's over, they don't buy T-shirts, they leave frustrated, because obviously they're thinking, "Oh, I've had enough of this."' You're hurting yourself, right? You're consciously saying, 'We don't care if half the audience leaves.' I mean, we were all smart people.

We just didn't care at the level that people wanted us to care, because we cared for something else, which is: we're going to be ourselves no matter what you say. And *Siamese Dream* was very informed by a sense of 'Okay, you think we're this?' Like, people would say about *Gish*, 'Oh, you guys are kind of classic rock.' So we're like, 'Oh, you think we're classic rock? We'll give you classic rock.' And then we made an album of Boston, Electric Light Orchestra, you know – basically, we wanted to shove it up everybody's arse. We were brilliantly dumbing ourselves down to almost play a joke on everybody, and people actually began to believe we were that dumb, which became even more comical, and we fed into it even more, and it started this thing that's just never stopped.

"We were like, 'No, we actually realize we're being annoying, we're doing it on purpose. Don't you get the joke?'"

When did you think your time with Smashing Pumpkins was over?
That's a really good question. It's hard to say, because when I should've left I didn't, and then it's one of those things, like, once you stay, there's no easy exit. If I had my life to do over again, I would've left the band immediately after Jonathan Melvoin died [in July 1996]. He was our touring keyboardist, and he overdosed on heroin, and Jimmy Chamberlin, our drummer, too, right before we were playing two sold-out Madison Square Garden shows. We're on the eve of this crowning achievement in American life – to play Madison Square Garden is a big deal – and here we have two sold-out shows, and the night before we're supposed to play these two sold-out shows, our drummer and our touring keyboardist overdose. Jimmy survives, Jonathan dies. It becomes a huge thing in the media and they're debating it on [US TV news show] *Nightline*, you know, drugs and music, and suddenly we were in the middle of a social argument and our drummer leaves. That's when I should've taken myself out of the picture. It was completely dysfunctional. I was sober, you know, and I'm on TV talking about drugs. I mean, it was a total joke. That should've been my 'You know what? This drama is over and I'm going to go' moment. Instead, I stayed for another four years and allowed the situation to completely drain every ounce of blood out of my body. Out of some sort of warped concept of loyalty.

I have to ask you about Bowie. You've made no secret of your love for Bowie. When did you first meet him?
When did I first meet David Bowie? I think I first met him in a festival situation where we were both playing, or maybe it was a TV show? I honestly don't remember. I know that sounds terrible …

[Laughs] I'd remember when I first met David Bowie.

No, I mean, honestly, it sounds terrible, but the reason I don't remember was because I had been lucky enough to meet David, you know, 10 to 15 times. Enough that you're no longer, like, in awe that you're talking to 'David Bowie', but instead you're talking to David and he's a nice person, and you can have a conversation and not turn into a fanboy. David's a lovely guy. Always very, very gracious and very, very kind to me. Really meant a lot, because, to me, he's such a special artist, such a unique artist, so influential, such a gifted singer. The fact that he chose to be this avant-garde artist really says a lot about him as a person. I have nothing but great things to say about him. I still listen to his music all the time, I'm still inspired by him. His ideas still mean something to me.

If we're going to play a Bowie track, which one should we play?

I'm partial to 'Moonage Daydream'.

And the last question: we ask everyone on this show to pick the last song, so it can be anything you want.

A song by The Cure, because The Cure is one of the greatest UK bands ever. I used to have a Robert Smith haircut. Let's see. 'Primary'.

Why that song?

I just love The Cure. Everything Robert does is imbued with this sort of special Robert-ness, and I just love him as a person. I think The Cure, as a band, their influence and their legacy, is only going to grow.

The First Time Billy Corgan Playlist

1	Today	Smashing Pumpkins
2	L-O-V-E (Love)	Al Green
3	I Saw Her Standing There	The Beatles
4	Sweet Leaf	Black Sabbath
5	Heat of the Moment	Asia
6	I Am One	Smashing Pumpkins
7	By-Tor and The Snow Dog	Rush
8	In Between Days	The Cure
9	When I Was Born, I Was Bored	Shudder to Think feat. Billy Corgan
10	Cherub Rock	Smashing Pumpkins
11	Moonage Daydream	David Bowie
12	Primary	The Cure

"I feel the presence of God with me when I go to write a song."

BRIAN WILSON

Brian Wilson often ends his own interviews. Out of the blue, normally after about 20 minutes, he'll suddenly stand up, unannounced, thrust out his hand to shake yours, and say in a polite, almost whispered voice, 'Thank you for the interview. Goodbye', then make for the door. His team either holds him back by the elbow until formal goodbyes are done or guides him out of the room. And you're left there thinking, 'Did that really just happen?'

Wilson is probably the greatest composer of America popular music ever, and his most beautiful melodies and intricate harmonies were just 'there' in his head, waiting to be realized. But drug issues, mental illness and the weight of just *being* Brian Wilson have left him shaken and hesitant. His speech is slightly slurred and his face is lopsided and still. His skin is pale and his eyes are set deep under brows that arch in a permanently worried shape, as if he's expecting bad news.

At the start of the interview, we get through a lot of questions. Many of his answers are abrupt, or even just 'Yes', 'No' or 'I don't know'. But then – and it's hard to describe – he comes into focus. His replies get longer, he tells stories, does impressions and enthuses about the sounds he created. He's funny, too. I ask him how he regards his back catalogue: 'It's impressive', he chuckles. Then, after a while, I can feel him become distracted, and his character fades.

Every time I've interviewed Brian, he's seemed a little further away. It's like spotting a star in the sky that you're told is gone, but you can still see it how it was millions of years in the past. The genius shone out of Brian Wilson for so long, and so powerfully, that everyone saw it. Eventually he started to burn himself out and collapse, so what we see now is a shadow of what he was, but the light that's reaching us from all those years ago is so brilliant, we'll see him forever.

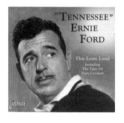

Matt Everitt: When were you first aware of music when you were a child? What was the first music you ever heard?

I was two when I heard George Gershwin's 'Rhapsody in Blue'. That's when I started listening to music. I would say to myself, 'Hey, I love this song', because I wasn't able to talk then, right? But I remember hearing it later, though many years later. When I was twenty-eight years old.

And it had a massive effect on you straight away?

Yeah. I was blown away. When I was twenty-eight I learned how to play the prettiest part, the violin section, on piano. I went from my hi-fi set back to my piano, back and forth, back and forth, until I learned it.

The legend is that you could sing even before you could talk. Is that true?

No, no.

But you did come from a very musical household?

My dad was a good songwriter. My mum could play the organ good, too.

What sort of records did they have about the house?

Well they had Les Paul and Mary Ford records, and Tennessee Ernie Ford. I loved them, yeah.

When was your first performance? Can you remember the first time that you sang as a kid? Was it in a church choir?

No, my first singing was at a high school assembly. I sang, then Michael [Mike Love] came over and we sang a song called 'Bermuda Shorts' [The Delroys, 1957], which just goes, 'Bermuda, Bermuda, Bermuda, Bermuda Shorts', you know? We sang that at a school assembly. It was a thrill.

The Four Freshmen were one of the biggest vocal influences on you. Can you remember hearing their records for the first time?

I learned two things from The Four Freshmen. One, I learned how to sing falsetto from Bob Flanigan, the high voice in the Freshmen. I imitated him at a piano, and I wrote 'Surfer Girl' after I heard the Freshmen. Then, two, their harmonies taught me to make harmonies, too. I never dreamed there could be that kind of harmony until I heard their harmonies.

I want to ask you, as a producer, about your first tape recorder – obviously quite an important thing for you.

I didn't know much about it technically, but it was a little mini four-track recorder, you know? A tape recorder that I used to ping-pong voices back and forth. So I learned to sing all four parts of the Freshmen songs on my tape recorder. I was fifteen. I absolutely loved it.

'Surfin' was the first single by The Beach Boys, recorded in October 1961. What can you remember about making it?

We wrote it in our house, but we recorded it at a studio owned by my dad's publishers. I remember it was raining the night we cut it. I looked out the door and it was pouring down with rain and there was just this mood, you know? We did 'Surfer Girl' that night, too.

When we first heard it on the radio, each day the DJ would go, 'Call in and vote for your favourite song.' So I'd call and say [affects deep voice], 'This is so-and-so and I would like to hear "Surfin", and then [in a high, girlish voice], 'Hi, will you please play "Surfin"?' And so 'Surfin' won the vote and they played 'Surfin', and all my family goes, 'It's on the radio! "Surfin" is on the radio!'

After we did 'Surfin', I wrote 'Surfing Safari' and '409' – Mike Love wrote those lyrics – and we went on a little tour around California; we went to Riverside, San Bernardino and did local gigs and stuff. Quite a memory. It was quite a thrill, of course.

In 1963, the *Surfer Girl* album was the first time you were credited as a producer in your own right. Did you find it easy to write and record at that time? Because it seemed like it.
Yeah, yes, very much so, yeah. From the time we first wrote 'Surfin' up until 'Surfin' USA'. When 'Surfin' USA' came out, the Boys were becoming popular around the country. The songs just poured out of us. We can't go in the studio until we write a song, so we'd write a song, then go to the studio, and then from there I just heard it all in my head. When I heard a song over the speakers, I'd go, 'Let me hear the bass and the drums please.' Or 'Add the guitar, Alan, let's hear your voice.' It would ping-pong back and forth. You get all the different ingredients together.

We'd move very fast. I'll sit at the piano and go [mimes hammering a keyboard] *Blamp! Blamp! Blamp!* like that, and I'll say, 'Wait a minute, I need to put this there', and then all of a sudden there's an arrangement. When we get to a studio there's a lot of love in the booth, and that love goes out into the studio where the musicians are, and they get the feel for it, and then we start recording. We pull up the bass and the drums, guitars, pianos, violins and horns. We get them all balanced and then we do the vocals. The albums are based around harmony. It was like four or five voices all blending together overdubbed three times and you have a choir. Mike Love was on one microphone and the rest was around one microphone, so what would happen is he would sing and we would harmonize behind him. By the time the vocals are done, we have a record.

Usually, me and my collaborators are going, 'Hey, we're into a good song'. But it's very hectic … It's a thrill because I feel the presence of God with me when I go to write a song.

It's something you've said before, about having the music in your head, fully formed, and you just have to play it so it matches what's in your head. Did you hear these songs so complete in your mind?
Yes.

What are the songs that you think you got perfectly right – when you thought, 'The sound in my head was the sound that came out of those speakers'?

The sound in my head? The perfect example was 'Surfin' USA'. Because it starts out, 'If everybody had …' [starts singing] 'Oooooooh ….' Then 'Oooooooh bap! Across the USA, Ooooooh bap!' Like that, you know? It just came out just right.

Phil Spector was someone that you admired greatly. Can you remember hearing some of his records for the first time and thinking, 'Wow, he's going somewhere interesting'?

When I was twenty-one, I was driving down the street and on the radio they said, 'Here we go with "Be My Baby" by The Ronettes'. I listened to it and I had to pull my car over because it blew me out so much. I had to pull over to the side of the road. It just totally devastated me. And then I met Phil Spector at his recording studio, Gold Star, and told him, '"Be My Baby" is the greatest record I ever heard.' He goes, 'Well … I think "Then He Kissed Me" was a pretty good record, too.' He was a character.

Can you tell me about your decision to stop touring with The Beach Boys? Because there was a period when you just stopped going out on the road with them.

Right, in 1965 I told the guys, I said, 'Look, I want to stay here in town and write songs for you. You guys go out and do the tour and I'll stay

"It was an absolute rave. People were absolutely blown away by it. *Pet Sounds* is my favourite album I ever produced."

home and write the music.' Michael had a little tear, and I could see the guys were a little sad to hear that. But when they came back off tour, they were very proud of what I had written for them. As soon as we recorded 'God Only Knows', we'd ventured off into another avenue. I didn't know, really, where I was going until about two or three songs into *Pet Sounds*.

In 1966 *Pet Sounds* comes out and changes everything. When it first came out in the States, people didn't quite know what to make of it. But in the UK we loved it straight away. Can you remember people's reactions when they first heard it?

You know, Americans are slow [laughs]. UK audiences love our music, they love it. People started calling me up, people like John Lennon. He called me up and said, 'Brian, I love your album *Pet Sounds*.' A friend of mine named Lou Adler [record producer] called me and said the same thing. Then all of a sudden, after a couple of months, after it was released, I had all kinds of phone calls about it. It was an absolute rave. People were blown away by it. *Pet Sounds* is my favourite album I ever produced.

The story is that you heard *Rubber Soul* by The Beatles and that inspired you to make *Pet Sounds*.
Oh, well, *Rubber Soul* is the best album ever made. It's my favourite album, period. Oh, I think it was fantastic. *Revolver* was a very good album, too.

What was your state of mind at the time? The songs are very hopeful, they're very positive. Were you in a really good place?
Yeah, we were. My lyricist, Tony Asher, was really, really into it. He was really into the lyrics. He just let the lyrics pour out of him. I would play the melodies and he would do the lyrics, you know? I remember [guitar-ist] Al Jardine came over to my house and he played some of the chords to 'Sloop John B' [a Bahamian folk song originally. Wilson's version is based on the 1958 recording of the song by The Kingston Trio]. I said, 'Let me take it from there', and I wrote and finished off the whole song in about two and a half hours. Not arranged, but written. It took me an-other week to get it arranged, then it took us about two days to record it.

Can you remember the first time that you took drugs?
August of 1964, I was turned on to a drug called marijuana. My friend called it pot. He goes, 'Want to try something that you won't believe? Smoke this and then drink a glass of water, see how the water tastes.' I took some tokes on a marijuana joint and about ten minutes later I went, 'Oh, I never really tasted water before! Oh, I've never really heard music before! I've never heard music ever like this.'

'Good Vibrations' is, in my mind, your best work. Do you think it's one of your greatest achievements?
Well, it was an achievement of recording, but it was a labour of love. It took six weeks to record. It's hard to get that song out of my head.

Still?
Yeah, I just have a tough time getting my head out of 'Good Vibrations'.

How does it make you feel when you hear 'God Only Knows'?
Oh, I feel like a king. I can't describe the feeling. I feel so good I could start crying. 'I may not always love you …' – that was Tony Asher's lyric, I didn't write that. But I liked it. I like the way it sounded, [sings] 'I may not always love you, but as long as there are stars above you …' You know? It was a great lyric. I knew that it was right for my brother Carl to sing, so I turned it over to Carl and he sang it and everybody loved it. Carl loved it, everybody loved it.

Smile has to be the great lost album of pop music, up until quite recently. What happened to *Smile*? Why didn't it get completed as the follow-up album to *Pet Sounds*?

We were taking drugs and we thought, 'Oh, we're too far ahead of our time', and we shelved it. We threw it on the shelf. We were very, very, very, very concerned with how far into it we were getting.

Did you fall out of love with music afterwards? Because you stopped recording for a while and you didn't play live.

Yeah, I did. I went through a dry period, but my wife said, 'You've got to get cracking. You get off your ass and start making music!' [Laughs].

After the first solo album people were so happy to have you back, and that kicked off you re-recording *Smile*, and then that was followed by a tour that got the best reviews I've ever read of any tour. Do you remember that, debuting *Smile* live?

Yeah. I can't explain it; it was just a different world. I couldn't believe it. No one could believe it. I got the feeling of love from the audience and we gave our harmonies to them.

"I do have my paranoia. But I definitely have an ear out for people liking my music because that's the only music I've got."

People often call you a songwriting genius, and you're *the* Brian Wilson. It's an enormous reputation. Are you comfortable with that?

Well, yeah, of course. What if someone said 'You're a genius!' to you?

I would love it!

Yeah, it would make you feel good. I'm a little paranoid about it sometimes, though. I do have my paranoia. But I definitely have an ear out for people liking my music because that's the only music I've got.

It's pretty good music, though.

It is [laughs]. It is impressive.

How is songwriting for you these days? Do you find it easy?

Yeah, it's starting to happen again. I have a song called 'Shelter', which I'm happy about, with good harmonies.

Was there anything you learned from writing your autobiography? From looking back at your whole life?

I learned that I shouldn't have taken drugs, of course. That's about it. I've learned not to take drugs. So I don't take drugs. I also learned don't stay up late, and now I get to bed early.

Is the music still in your head?

Yes.

What should we finish the show with?

I would like you to play 'Daa Do Ron Ron' by The Crystals. Because I love the beat. I like the rhythm on it.

Then we shall finish with that song. Thank you very much for your time.

Thank you very much. What's your first name?

Matt.

Matt, I'm Brian.

The First Time **Brian Wilson** Playlist

1	Wouldn't It Be Nice	The Beach Boys
2	Rhapsody in Blue	George Gershwin
3	Sixteen Tons	Tennessee Ernie Ford
4	Bermuda Shorts	The Delroys
5	I Remember You	The Four Freshmen
6	Rock Around the Clock	Bill Haley and His Comets
7	Surfin'	The Beach Boys
8	Be My Baby	The Ronettes
9	You Stepped Out of a Dream	The Four Freshmen
10	How High the Moon	Les Paul and Mary Ford
11	Sloop John B	The Kingston Trio
12	Good Vibrations	The Beach Boys
13	If I Needed Someone	The Beatles
14	God Only Knows	The Beach Boys
15	Da Doo Ron Ron	The Crystals

"I love making music. That's what I do ... There always seems to be lots of different muscial adventures to get into."

BRYAN FERRY

T here's a joy to meeting someone you know only through rock folklore and finding out they're *exactly* how you'd expect them to be. They're not shorter, or less amusing, or less handsome than their public image would suggest. It's like this when I interview Bryan Ferry. He's the most Bryan Ferry-ish Bryan Ferry imaginable.

His HQ is a short saunter from Kensington. The ceilings are high, and huge photographs of Roxy Music album covers hang near expensive-looking white bookshelves tastefully packed with expensive-looking art books, and there, reclining on a pristine cream sofa, is an expensive looking Bryan Ferry.

It's a cliché to talk about his appearance, but avoiding it would be like flying 13,000 miles to Easter Island and then not talking about the giant stone heads. Elegantly dressed and with salt-and-pepper hair, he looks enviously good for sixty-eight – in truth, he'd look enviously good for forty-eight – and he exudes style. There's a music-industry story that Bryan tore up his new passport on the eve of a French tour because he didn't like his photo. I asked someone who once worked for him if that was true. 'Oh yes', they said. 'And he got David Bailey round the next day to shoot a replacement.'

He's polite, gracious and happy to tell stories of the early days, chuckling when he remembers how otherworldly and brilliant Roxy Music were. Bryan's solo work has been as sophisticated and immaculately delivered as his tailoring, but he seems slightly bemused that we're doing an interview at all. I couldn't shift the feeling that he was waiting for something more interesting to happen. Either he doesn't like the fuss of interviews, or Jerry Hall was waiting to emerge from behind a curtain wearing a tiger-print minidress as soon as I'd gone. I'll never know, but that would be *very* Bryan Ferry.

Matt Everitt: When were you were aware of music?

One of my aunts was a big fan of American music and I think her husband had been in the Air Force or the Navy, so they'd been familiar with AFN [American Forces Network radio]. I must have been five years old, and I remember she used to babysit me and she was always playing The Ink Spots, so I love those records, and I actually inherited them; I still have them somewhere – 78s, of course.

Then I was a little bit older, all of ten years old – that's what I generally put down as my first time consciously listening to something on the radio, which seemed to affect me a lot. And that was Lead Belly. I'm not sure which song he was singing, it might have been 'Rock Island Line', but I became passionate for music from that day on.

What was the first music you owned?

There are a few records that I bought at the same time. One of them was 'Bad Penny Blues' by Humphrey Lyttelton. The first EP I remember quite vividly; I learned every note of it: the Charlie Parker Quintet with Miles Davis. Four songs in a cover with a photograph. I was so passionate about that EP. I treasured it until somebody nicked it very recently [laughs]. About a year or two ago, it just disappeared. It had my little autograph on the back of it because you used to always have to sign your records in case somebody borrowed them or …

… if you took it to a party, you'd know that it was yours.

Exactly. My first LP I won in a Radio Luxembourg competition. You had to write in. Bill Haley and His Comets were about to do the first major rock and roll tour of Europe – I was just about to sit my eleven-plus exam – and I won this LP of Bill Haley and His Comets and two front-row tickets to see them. And that was my first concert.

What was it like?

It was incredible. If you've ever seen the movie *Forrest Gump*, it was like a great moment in history. It was the first rock and roll tour. Teddy Boys rampaging around, jumping up and down on the seats. This was all very new to England – new to anywhere, really – all this 'electric' music, and electric guitars, and a sax player playing upside down. Very interesting.

Did it resonate with you straight away? Rock and roll?

I just thought, 'Wow, this is incredible.' Even though I was a bit stuck-up about rock and roll. I was really passionate about jazz, which I thought was much more meaningful, deeper, more obscure. Nobody else I knew – certainly no one aged ten or eleven – was into it. It was my own thing.

You went to art school. Was there a rivalry between the art and the music as to which was dominating your interest at that age?

Well, it began to happen gradually. I'd been geared to go to university and to study, and I decided to study art. First of all I thought I was going to be an art historian, because I didn't know if I had any real talent as an artist, but the more I studied it, the more I began to think, 'Maybe I can be an artist too.' That's the coolest thing you could ever be.

"I was a bit stuck-up about rock and roll. I was really passionate about jazz."

But then I started doing music for a job. I was quite poor. Very poor, in as much as my parents didn't have any money. I was given a grant to go to university, which I was very grateful for, but I had to always do jobs in holiday times, whether it was in the local factory or a building site. Then the summer before I went to university, I bumped into somebody. He said, 'Oh, I've got a band, and we're doing a lot of gigs, and I need a singer.' He said, 'Can you sing?' I said, 'Oh yeah.' I did my audition, and passed it, and suddenly I had this great summer job.

Then it was time to go to college and I started my own band there. And so music gradually took over. Within my art school, the students were very into music, so I started hearing lots of different music. It's interesting when you meet the people from your own generation who have similar interests, and they turn you on to other things.

That first band, what was it called?
The very first band was called The Banshees [laughs].

Which turns out to be a very good band name.
Yeah, it is. Not bad.

And what were your musical obsessions at the time?
Chuck Berry and stuff like that. But with the second band, which was called The Gas Board, we did much more sophisticated R&B, like Albert King, Freddie King, B.B. King and Otis Redding. All the Stax artists. I was a singer and I played harmonica and a bit of sax. We had a big saxophone section, so we thought we were very cool indeed [chuckles]. The band dropped out of college and became professional musicians, but I stayed on to get my degree as I wasn't sure at that point how much I wanted to go into the world of music and leave the world of painting.

After I graduated, I moved to London and started writing songs, and thought, 'Hmm, maybe I'll try and make my own music. Maybe I can think of something which will express myself creatively as I would've been doing as a painter.' So I started looking for like-minded people. I was already working with [bassist] Graham Simpson, then I met [oboist and saxophonist] Andy Mackay, and then [synthesizer player Brian] Eno, and [drummer] Paul Thompson and [guitarist] Phil Manzanera, and gradually put together our band.

What were your first impressions of those guys? Did it feel like a band very early on?

Oh yeah. What's that film? *The Magnificent Seven*. They all meet each other and go, 'Ah, yes. You're going to join our gang.' It was a bit like that. It was just … strange, really. I wanted to do electronic music, something strange. I couldn't quite figure out what it was, but I knew I hadn't heard it yet, what I was imagining. I didn't have a synthesizer, not many people had them. And a friend of mine knew Andy Mackay, and said, 'I know this guy. He's got a synthesizer, and maybe he can work with you.' And so he came over, and then I discovered he could play oboe – that was his instrument. I said, 'Oh, you must play sax as well', because that's one of my favourite instruments. And he was really good. And for a while it was just the three of us.

"I wanted to do electronic music, something strange. I couldn't quite figure out what it was, but I knew I hadn't heard it yet."

We didn't have a tape recorder, this was before cassettes were even invented. So he said, 'God! We must tape what we're doing.' Because we thought it was really quite interesting. He said, 'I know this guy called Brian Eno. He's got a great tape recorder.' And sure enough, he turned up later with this huge old Ferrograph tape recorder. Beautiful thing, studio quality, but it was enormous. It was bigger than him, and he lugged it into the room, with microphones, and he recorded us. He said, 'Oh, this is really interesting', and he stayed and joined.

I was teaching art a couple of days a week to make ends meet. I was writing the songs, and trying to rehearse whenever we could. And I was taking this demo tape around all sorts of places. I did send a tape to a really good music critic from the [British weekly music newspaper] *Melody Maker* called Richard Williams. And he did a big piece on us, and that helped us to find a manager and a record company. John Peel, who was the famous DJ at the time on BBC [Radio 1], invited us to play on his programme. All this before we had a recording contract.

In terms of the visual aspect of the band, you did cut a wide swathe. Was that an intentional part of the game plan?

It kind of happened once we had the music finished. With the first album [*Roxy Music*, 1972], we didn't really have any idea what to do visually at that point, as I remember. I just thought, 'Oh, great. The music's finished. I better do the cover because I'm an artist, and I should design it, I guess.' To have a glamour girl on the cover seemed the obvious thing to do. I didn't want to have a group picture; I wanted a solitary memorable image, rather than six guys standing looking moody in a street, which was pretty much the norm at that time. I felt something more fabulous was required. So we did this kind of 'ultimate pin-up' picture of this beautiful girl called Kari-Ann [Muller].

And my friend – who I'd only just met – [fashion designer] Antony Price helped me do the cover, the costumes, the outfits that we wore. And we developed this over the next year or so. Then after *For Your Pleasure* [1973], the second album, we started toning it down a bit because the whole glam rock thing had just killed it a bit and made it look less special. So we thought, 'The sequins have got to go!'

You mentioned *For Your Pleasure*, the second record. Is that when you first felt like the band really hit mainstream consciousness? Is that the first time you felt famous?
Yeah. Because I felt that we weren't a flash in the pan. I wasn't really that interested in Roxy having a particular style musically. It was more a case of playing around and experimenting with many different styles, because my influences in music were so varied. From Ethel Merman, Broadway, show business, Fred Astaire, musicals, to Lead Belly, and very primitive field blues singers, Motown, psychedelia, Velvet Underground. Édith Piaf! I'd absorbed so much music since I was ten, I was bursting with ideas: 'Oh, let's do something like this!' And the interesting thing about the first Roxy album is that it had my take on all these influences played in interesting ways by the band and collaged together. So it indicated the many different futures for the band. Which one would we follow?

"My influences in music were so varied. From Ethel Merman, Broadway, Fred Astaire ... to Lead Belly, Motown, psychedelia ..."

And *For Your Pleasure* seemed to be a kind of direction. I'm not sure how to describe it, but it seemed a much more assured album. It was our second time in the studio so we felt we were learning quite fast, I thought. Three albums came out that year, I think. *For Your Pleasure*, and *Stranded*, and [Ferry's first solo album] *These Foolish Things*.

It's very rare for an artist to have this kind of parallel solo career, with a full band career at the same time.
It wasn't intended, either [laughs]. I felt a bit burned out after doing *For Your Pleasure*. I'd had to write it very quickly as a follow-up to the first album. And I remember I had this cranky car, a Renault 4, with that

strange gear-lever thing. Not very glamorous but I thought it was kind of cool. It was very *nouvelle vague* and French cool. And I remember filling this car with keyboards, and a tiny tape recorder – I didn't have a cassette player, they hadn't been invented then – and driving up to Derbyshire. A friend of mine, Nick de Ville, who'd helped me with the first album design, lent me his place in Derbyshire, and I went up to this remote place and wrote these songs, 'In Every Dream Home a Heartache' and so on, which formed *For Your Pleasure*.

From the album *These Foolish Things*, you released 'A Hard Rain's A-Gonna Fall', the start of your public love for Dylan. When did you first hear Bob Dylan?
Well, after doing *For Your Pleasure*, I was a bit burned out. I thought I'd like to do something completely different, just as a cathartic thing. And I thought, 'Well, I'd love to do an album of songs written by other people, so I don't have to do the painful bit, the writing bit', which I had found quite agonizing. I was very anxious to do more and more records but didn't want to go through the agony of writing. And I thought, 'Well, it'd be interesting as a singer, and producer, and arranger to do something.' So I did that first solo album as a one-off. I didn't think it would be particularly successful, or reach such a mainstream audience, which it did. So in some ways it … Well, it did start off a whole new career, but I hope that it helped bring a different kind of audience to Roxy Music. Which was my main love because it was my songs.

The very definable, international playboy image you had – people assumed that this was actually what your life was like.
It's very hard to talk about. People say, 'Well, how do you live?' I say, 'Well, I don't know. Like everyone else.' I like to work, I like to enjoy myself, I like to go out to dinner, have a social life. I've got a great range of friends, I guess, that I've built up over the years, a lot of them from the world of visual arts. I guess you would hope that if you're as old as me you would have a good group of friends. So I don't know, I just live a life.

People always get obsessed about what clothes I wear, and they say, 'God, you're really smartly dressed for being in the music business.' And I say, 'Well, it's not so hard.' You know? [Laughs]. We all have to make choices every day, and decide to wear this jacket or another. Some people like to wear hoodies and stuff. Well, it's not really my thing. All the movies I ever watched, and all the great musicians who are kind of hero figures for me – Charlie Parker, Miles Davis, all those be-bop players – they always dressed up to go to work, to go on stage. They're just cool guys, you know? And I guess I always wanted to be cool like them [laughs].

When did you decide to leave Roxy behind? Because it was off the back of *Avalon*, which was a massively successful record.
Oh yeah, *Avalon* [1982] was the most successful album we ever did.

So off the back of that, why leave the band?

Because I always like to be difficult and do the wrong thing. Life's much more interesting that way. It's like being the baddie, you know?

It was at the end of a very, very long tour, and I just got a bit fed up with it, really. And I thought, 'I don't want to be in a band anymore.' I'd left before; I'd had this parallel career going on as a solo artist anyway. It's important to feel you can work with whomever you want to.

Are you going to keep making music?

Oh, I love making music. That's what I do. There's always something else to do, I think. As you get older, obviously your body of work gets bigger, and you want to add to it, but only if you're doing something slightly different and not repeating yourself. So yeah, there always seems to be lots of different musical adventures to get into.

And the final question – after all these firsts we have the last. The last song. A song you get to choose.

Well, that's very, very kind of you. And after talking myself hoarse, I'd like to play a track from the new album. This is the last song that we finished, 'Reason or Rhyme'. I like the tune, I like the lyrics. There's some very good playing on it – probably my best bit of piano playing for a long time. I don't usually get to play piano on my solo albums; I'd normally have another, much better piano player than me. But for my own songs, I always play. And so it was great for me to be the piano player again.

The First Time Bryan Ferry Playlist

1	Street Life	Roxy Music
2	I Don't Want to Set the World on Fire	The Ink Spots
3	Rock Island Line	Lead Belly
4	Bad Penny Blues	Humphrey Lyttelton
5	Billie's Bounce	Charlie Parker Quintet
6	(We're Gonna) Rock Around the Clock	Bill Haley and His Comets
7	Virginia Plain	Roxy Music
8	These Foolish Things	Bryan Ferry
9	In Every Dream Home a Heartache	Roxy Music
10	Like a Rolling Stone	Bob Dylan
11	The Way You Look Tonight	Bryan Ferry
12	Avalon	Roxy Music
13	Reason or Rhyme	Bryan Ferry

"I hated Elvis when I was at the age when everyone else thought he was the most wonderful thing in the world."

CHARLIE WATTS

To say The Rolling Stones are always late is inaccurate. Like visiting dignitaries passing from one engagement to another, they have their own schedule. You're just one name on it and they'll reach you when they're ready. Pondering all this helps take my mind off the fact that I'm about to interview genuinely legendary people, but doesn't prepare me for actually meeting them.

When I do, they're the full, 3D, surround-sound, high-definition versions of the characters I've seen on stages, posters and album covers my whole life. They're everything I could want and more – hugely charming and unfailingly polite. Mick is smart and inquisitive, and conducts the interview in the direction of his choice; Keith is deliciously gnarled and garrulous; and Ronnie still has the air of an overexcited six-year-old at the best birthday party ever.

Then there's Charlie – bemused at the fuss surrounding him, endlessly enthusiastic about jazz and affectionately dismissive about the music he's been playing with the Stones for the past 50 years.

We meet in a suite at the Dorchester Hotel. He looks, as you would expect, immaculate: double-breasted, wide-collared suit, a blue shirt with a bright white collar and perfectly folded double cuffs, finished off with heavy gold cufflinks. His grey hair is swept back off his broad forehead and he flashes a big toothy smile. He looks not a little like the world's best-dressed undertaker.

'What's this interview for?' he asks, sitting down and gently tugging at the creases of his suit trousers (my granddad used to do the same thing). He looks confused when he's told, exclaiming, 'BBC 6? Never heard of it. Where is it? How do you get it? Digital? I haven't got a digital radio. I only listen to Radio 3', before grinning at me. 'Sorry about that.'

When were you first aware of music?

Parties at my grandparents' house. There's quite a lot of us in our family. Uncles, aunts and everybody got together playing Johnnie Ray and the Four Aces and things like that. We had lots of 78s, and I remember when my uncle first bought a 45 rpm. It was some dreadful record – Gordon MacRae. But it was awful. The songs I remember were by Johnnie Ray and Billy Eckstine. I was brought up on Billy Eckstine's style.

What was the first record that you owned that was yours?

I mean, this has been documented a million times through these types of conversations, but the first record I remember that I fell in love with, apart from Billy Eckstine and Johnnie Ray-type things, was called 'Flamingo' by a saxophone player called Earl Bostic. Soon after I bought 'Walking Shoes' by Gerry Mulligan's quartet. Earl Bostic was a sort of R&B jazz player, and Gerry Mulligan was out and out jazz.

Were you drawn to music straight away?

I don't know why, but I was. Soon after that I heard Charlie Parker, and I loved Charlie Parker and I still do. I listen to the same records now that I played then. They have the same emotions for me. All of them do. I love hearing Gerry Mulligan's band of '54, I think it was.

Do you remember the first concerts you went to?

First concert I ever went to was Billy Eckstine at the London Palladium. He played trumpet and valve trombone. Billy Eckstine was a great crooner, and in the late '40s he had the first kind of wonderful big band – Charlie Parker, Dizzy Gillespie, Miles Davis were in it. The drummer was a guy called Art Blakey. Dexter Gordon was the tenor [saxophone] player. It was an astounding band, and he sang and played valve trombone. It was a very big thing in '48, '49. A very big-name band, but with a very small following, so he couldn't afford to keep it going. He suddenly became just a singer, and he made wonderful records.

Being young, we used to dress like him. He used to wear certain shirt collars that were called Mr Bs [a high-roll collar that formed a 'B' over a Windsor-knotted tie]. That's the impression he had on me. Also he was an amazingly handsome man, in the same way Duke Ellington was. Next person I saw live was Johnnie Ray, who was fantastic but didn't have the same impression on me as Billy Eckstine.

How did this jazz and big-band obsessive set about playing blues and rock and roll for the first time?

I didn't, really. [English jazz bassist] Dave Green, who played in a band I played in – and he's been in most of my bands as a bass player – he's my next-door neighbour, we're the same age virtually. We grew up together from the age of four. We used to play in jazz groups together. We listened to all this music and he went in a jazz direction to [baritone saxophonist] Ronnie Ross's band. I played in a jazz quartet at a place called the

Troubadour, we thought we were The Thelonius Monk Quartet – so it was tenor, piano, bass and drum – and one night [British blues musician and champion] Alexis Korner came in and sat in. About six months or so later, I got a message from Alexis to say would I go and play in this band of his [Blues Incorporated]. I went there, and that's where I met my wife. But rehearsals with Alexis's band were with [blues harmonica player] Cyril Davies; Keith Scott, a piano player who went to Hornsey Art School with my wife; the bass player; and Dick Heckstall-Smith, a tenor player. I'd never heard a harmonica before – certainly not like Cyril played it – and I wondered what the hell they were playing. For some reason, Alexis asked me to join the band, and I did, for years.

Can you remember meeting the gentlemen who would go on to become The Rolling Stones for the first time?
All his life Alexis was a hub for young people, and particularly blues and obscure jazz players. One of these people was Brian Jones. In the early days I played with Brian, and knew him socially through Alexis. And then Mick [Jagger] sang with Alexis a few times, and Keith [Richards] sat in with Alexis a few times, so I knew them as people, and from playing with them. Then I left Alexis and started playing with various blues bands, and then I was asked to join The Rolling Stones.

"I listen to the same records now that I played then. They have the same emotions for me. All of them do."

What were your first impressions?
I didn't really think about them before I was asked to join them. It was another band to join. I was in about three of them, but had no work! But once I joined The Rolling Stones I went to live with them and that's when I formed an impression, because I used to stay in London. I used to hang out and we'd rehearse a lot, and Brian and Keith never went to work, so we'd play records all day, a rather bohemian life. Mick was at LSE [London School of Economics]; he paid the rent.

But you got very famous very quickly.
We were very lucky, in that we never really had a downside as far as audience went. Brian, in the early days, used to work really hard – I mean, the days before we had any work. Really very hard, sending letters and promoting R&B, as he called it, and The Rolling Stones, to all the clubs, and we got a couple of residencies going, one of which was the Ken Colyer Jazz Club in Leicester Square, and the other one was the Crawdaddy Club in Richmond. Very soon, I mean, within a very short time, they

were full up. Ever since I've been with The Rolling Stones – this has nothing to do with me, by the way – but ever since I've been with The Rolling Stones, people have come to look at us. To look at Keith and Brian and Mick, you know? Really. We've always had a following.

Why do you think that is?

I think visually, even in those days, you know, the stage was about four foot by five, and Mick would still do the same thing as he does on a big stage. He used to do incredible things on the tiniest stages of all. Brian had his funny sort of quirky way of doing it, and Mick was obviously on his way to being one of the great onstage people. But he was on a par – I can say this because two of them have gone – he was on a par with James Brown and Michael Jackson for holding an audience. If we do another tour he'll do it again, you know? He's the best.

In 1965, 'Satisfaction' was your first massive number one in both America and in Britain. To go over to the States for the first time, and start seeing some of the artists that you loved over there, must have been a big thrill.

I got to New York and went to Birdland, the famous club. It closed down soon after I got there. Not because of me. But I went to see that and I went to various jazz clubs with Ian Stewart [the Stones' live pianist], and quite honestly then I'd 'seen America'. For me, that was it. Then I went to Chicago and we saw Chess [Studios] and these various places that you longed to see because of records, but for me it was New York.

The Stones' recording sessions always seemed to be very protracted – from the outside, anyway. You took a long time to build the atmosphere for a song before recording.

There's reason for a lot of these things. Andrew [Loog] Oldham [manager] kind of coerced Mick and Keith to write B-sides or songs for artists, and when they were good enough, they were for us. The first albums were done in an afternoon, no mucking about, all finished, done, signed, sealed, delivered. When we earned money, we realized we could work in a studio forever, and subsequently we did. Keith, even now, writes songs in the studio. At that time, when we were young, time wasn't really of importance. A day became a week, so for us to be in the studio for a month was nothing in those days. Mainly because the recording costs were covered. In those days, in the late '60s through the '70s, records made so much, we sold so many records, and made so much money off them, the record company could afford for us to be in there forever. We found out later, of course, it came off our end. But it was still an awful lot of money – you're talking about a lot of record sales.

It was the era of albums and singles selling. You used to have three singles off an album, and the album, all done in a year. Like with The Beatles, it was the norm, that's what they did. We used to have to time singles so that they didn't coincide with theirs, and vice versa. You'd all have an album out and you'd record it and have it out that year. It was that, along with playing every day, which helped make the records sell. It was real work. That's why I never understood why a lot of bands, subsequently – like Amy [Winehouse], for example, bless her, and Oasis is another one – they work all those years, become incredibly popular, then nothing comes out for about three years. No wonder people forget you.

There's this image of it being such a debauched time. But you always seemed quite separate from that …
I've always been separate from rock and roll; it's never been something I've been into. It doesn't mean I wasn't debauched and whatever. But rock and roll? And groupies and all that? I've always found Duke Ellington and his orchestra much more attractive than 90 per cent of what the white groups that were very fashionable at the time were playing. I was in a white group myself … But I was never brought up on rock and roll. Keith taught me, played me Elvis. But I hated Elvis when I was at the age when everyone else thought he was the most wonderful thing in the world. I would never have wanted to look like that. I wanted to be a black man in a club in New York. Don't ask me why.

There was this incredible run of records – *Beggars Banquet* [1968], *Sticky Fingers* [1972], *Exile on Main Street* [1973] – when the band seemed to be producing some astonishing work.
Well, a lot of that is to do with the songs. For me, that period with [guitarist] Mick Taylor is probably the peak of The Rolling Stones band. It was a live thing as well. Mick brought a quality to The Rolling Stones that they never had before, or since. I don't know why, I don't know how. Bands are weird. Seeing the 'Mick' thing work. Ronnie brings another thing. But Mick Taylor brought a thing to Keith. I think Keith prefers

"I've always found Duke Ellington and his orchestra much more attractive than 90 per cent of what the white groups were playing."

playing with Ronnie in that guitar way, when they weave and that, but there was an era, as a band, with certain people, and particularly players that I've met and love, when we played what we call 'rock and roll'.

Can I ask about the possibly mythical, definitely legendary, story about Mick referring to you as his drummer? [Jagger reportedly referred to Charlie as 'my drummer' in a meeting in 1978. Watts is said to have punched him to the floor.]

[Interrupts] That's Keith. When it happened, nobody said anything. I've never ever spoken about it. I never, ever said anything. Mick annoyed me by calling me 'his drummer', and I was drunk, so yes. Yes, but, it's not something I'm proud of, and it's not something I'd ever mention again, but thanks to Keith, it's now in print. It's not something I'm proud of.

Keith mentions that you've always maintained a distance from the narcotic overindulgence of the band. But you did have your own battles with drug addiction in the '8os.
Yeah, and drink. I was lucky that I never got that hooked on it, that bad, but I did have … Yes. I went through a period of taking heroin.

When did you first realize it was a problem? How did you get off?
I used to get off it whenever I went home. I think when my marriage started to go a bit wobbly, and my wife noticed I wasn't the same. I fell asleep on the floor during *Some Girls* [1978] and Keith woke me up and said, 'You should do this when you're older.' Keith! Telling me this! And it stuck. It kind of … I just stopped, along with everything else.

In 2004, you were diagnosed with throat cancer, and underwent a course of radiotherapy.
I had two operations, and radiotherapy, which is the way they do it. I found all this out, having gone through it.

"We're just getting to an age where it's a bit difficult to get it together, and it's such a bloody performance, getting us all together."

How did you react, when you first found out?
I thought I was going to die. I had a lump in my throat, which I'd had for a couple of years, and I went in to see Mick's throat guy, the best man in the world, Peter Rhys-Evans, who's a surgeon. They looked for the thing, and it was benign, this lump, but they took it out, looked on the slide, and it had tiny cancer cells in it. So I'd had that operation – and I hate hospitals; I'd never been in one before – I'd done that, and they said, you have cancer of the whatever. And that night, I thought I was going to die.

I just thought that's what you did, if you got cancer. You'd curl up and you'd waste away and die. I went back for all the other stuff, and then the operation, another operation, to take the lymph nodes and all that out. It was on my tonsil, actually, so that went. Then I went on radiotherapy, which is six weeks long. I felt like shit at the end of that, which you do. Then every week, every month, every year, and now it's five years and it's cleared. I cannot say enough for Peter Rhys-Evans, the doctors and the nurses. They're amazing people.

How come the Stones are still together? Bloody-mindedness? The music? Is it that nobody wants to be the one to quit?
I think it's about two of those, at least. Or three of them. I think no one wants to quit, because the others get to say, 'You quit!'

Like the secret to a good marriage is just not getting divorced? Just sticking with it, regardless of the infighting?
It's been a bit like that, in part. We are getting to an age where it's going to be very difficult. You know, it would be lovely next year to do some shows, because it would be 50 years, you know? As I said, Ronnie plays, I still play. Mick sings, and you know he can do it anyway. I think Keith's doing some records, you know, whatever. We're just getting to an age where it's getting a bit difficult to get it together, and it's such a bloody performance, getting us all together. It's incredibly expensive.

For the final track, at the end of this show, we'll play a song that you choose. What should we finish the show on?
I can't think. 'Just Friends' from *Charlie Parker with Strings*.

The First Time **Charlie Watts** Playlist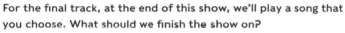

1	Paint It Black	The Rolling Stones
2	Three Coins in the Fountain	The Four Aces
3	Such a Night	Johnnie Ray
4	She's Got the Blues for Sale	Billy Eckstine
5	Flamingo	Earl Bostic
6	Walking Shoes	Gerry Mulligan Quartet
7	Night and Day	Charlie Parker and His Orchestra
8	Watermelon Man	Alexis Korner
9	Come On	Chuck Berry
10	(I Can't Get No) Satisfaction	The Rolling Stones
11	Manhattan	Sonny Rollins Trio
12	All Down the Line (live, 1974 concert film)	The Rolling Stones
13	Elvin Suite	Charlie Watts Meets Danish Radio Big Band
14	Just Friends (*Charlie Parker with Strings*)	Charlie Parker

"I didn't mind success. But that was never really the object."

CHRISSIE HYNDE

C hrissie Hynde is preparing to perform for a small audience in a London bookshop. I'm hosting a Q&A before an acoustic set marking the release of her autobiography, *Reckless*. We've been sorting out timings, seating and her route from the dressing room. Dull, necessary details that Chrissie engages with politely, but with a noticeable mood of 'Is all this really necessary? Just point me at the stage.' But when soundcheck starts, her attitude totally changes. She's happy and completely focused: playing over phrases until they feel right, pitching arrangement and harmony ideas with her guitarist, bitching good-naturedly at the soundman. Then, looking up from under her famous fringe, she grins, says, 'That's it!' and strides off to find some tea.

Which is all you need to know about Chrissie Hynde. Much more than a celebrity, hero or a style icon, she is first and foremost a musician. Everything else simply happened as a result of her love of rock and roll.

For someone with a reputation for being a tough interviewee, she's enormously easy to speak to. She's direct and reflective, with an endless enthusiasm for other musicians. She's witnessed, or been within yelling distance of, an amazing number of historic moments in music history – the British beat explosion in the United States, the birth of garage rock and the moment punk happened – but she's got little interest in the social significance of the events; for her, it's only ever about the impact of songs. Likewise, she seems unaware of (or chooses to ignore) her own importance as a songwriter. Her impressive back catalogue is simply the product of being a working musician: finding like-minded people, getting in a van, playing gigs and getting good.

The Q&A at the bookshop goes well enough. Chrissie is funny, frank and, much to the delight of the audience, shoots down my more pretentious questions. But more than once during the conversation I notice her glance over my shoulder, to the back of the stage, to where the guitars are set up. Waiting.

Matt Everitt: When were you first aware of music as a kid?
I can remember being in the kitchen in Cuyahoga Falls [Ohio], so I must
have been three. A song called 'Love and Marriage' came on the radio.
I think it was a Frank Sinatra song. The reason I remember it is because
the actual lyric goes, 'Love and marriage, go together like a horse and
carriage.' But as a two- or three-year-old, I heard 'horse and carrot', and
I had this image of an enormous carrot whenever I heard that song. Years
later I realized I had the lyric wrong and then I realized that's rock and
roll, you know? You make up your own words.

Was music always an appealing thing?
Yeah. I think there's certain things that you bring into the world from
birth. And you can't deny those things. People have different things they
like. And for me, music really was the life-changing thing. Music and
animals. I also always had that thing … you know? Animal rights people,
they'll always say that. Nurses, too.

What is the first record you owned?
I can remember where I was standing when I saw the first Beatles record
in this big discount house where my parents used to shop. 'I Want to
Hold Your Hand' – that might have been one of the first ones. But before
that, I bought a song by Freddy Cannon called 'Palisades Park', sort of a
fairground-sounding thing, and The Orlons, 'South Street'.

What about the first album?
Oh, that's a big one. I think one of the first songs was Mitch Ryder and
The Detroit Wheels. I think someone gave it to me for my birthday. The
first Beatles album, that was my period. It might sound kind of benign
now. They had blues through America. And it just … it didn't sound like
The Beach Boys! But there were harmonies. It just was different. It was
English! English was magic. It still is. What's left of it.

What about live music? Seeing a performance on stage?
Mitch Ryder and The Detroit Wheels at Chippewa Lake Park amusement park. I saw the afternoon show and there was a punch-up on stage,
which was riveting. I'd never seen anything like it. The main thing was
the guitar player. I was always partial to guitar players, and I was mes-
merized by him. Jimmy McCarty. That was real life-changing for me.

What was he like?
Just a fucking great guitar player. I must have been about fourteen –
and I remember thinking, 'Wow, the guitar is actually plugged into him.'
I mean, the whole band was one of my favourite all-time bands. So I
begged my girlfriends to stay for the show that evening. And they had
the same punch-up, and I realized it was staged. And that was, like, the
coolest thing I'd ever seen. So I think that's when I started subconscious-
ly knowing I had to do something like that.

What was your first guitar like?

Well, I first had a baritone ukulele, which I think my parents gave to me as an Easter present. Then I had one friend and she had a guitar, and we started trying to play together. My first guitar was called a Zim Gar. It was a great big hollow-body, nylon-string, classical-type thing. And I had real little hands; it was real hard for me. But that's good to learn on, because it makes your hands stronger.

Did you have guitar heroes?

I wanted to play like all of them, but I never thought I could. And I couldn't jam with anyone because they were guys, and I was too shy to play with guys. So I just kind of stayed by myself. I wasn't good enough to play along to records, which is how most people learn. Still can't.

I had a Mel Bay book of chords. So that's how I learned – by looking at the chord charts – but I found out early on that if you only knew a couple of chords you could make your own melody up around it. So I got sidetracked doing that. I guess that's how I started songwriting. As for my guitar heroes … I loved at the time Johnny Winter; Mike Bloomfield, who played with The Paul Butterfield Blues Band, was a hero; John Hammond Jr; James Brown is probably my number one. James Brown was my big, big hero.

"They had the same punch-up, and I realized it was staged. And that was, like, the coolest thing I'd ever seen."

What James Brown song we should play?

The great thing about James Brown is that he could write a song around one chord. That's an inspiration for a rhythm guitar player. 'I Can't Stand Myself (When You Touch Me)' – that's a good one on one chord. 'The Payback', one of my favourites, with one of the most sinister background choruses of all time. Or if you go earlier into James Brown, I had an album called *Lost in a Mood of Changes*, and there was no singing on it and it was him predominantly playing the organ. So that's another one. You can get a lot of his great vocals on something like 'Prisoner of Love'. I'd say that would be the one to play. It's just the perfect love song.

What were your first impressions of London when you moved here in 1973?

I've always loved London. And my first impression was that it was just paradise. I've always felt like that. I'm in love with it. I always have been. Everything was in black and white. And it was very primitive but in a way that really appealed to me. I had to put shillings in the meter to get

hot water for a bath. I was living on a pretty basic level: hand-to-mouth kind of thing, from day to day. I remember walking down the street with some guy and he goes, 'I'm going to get one of those'. And I couldn't figure out what he was pointing at. He was pointing at a TV and I realized it was a colour television. I was in love with the place, always have been.

Did you always think, 'I'm going there to find a band'?

Not consciously. Mainly I wanted to leave the States, and I knew I wanted to see the world. It just seemed the obvious first stop, because I spoke no other languages and I was in love with all those English bands and I was in love with horses when I was a kid. I thought everyone over here rode horses. You know, I had no knowledge of England at all. I thought Chelsea was a city. I had no clue about England. But I knew I loved it.

Can you remember the first Pretenders gigs? You'd been in a lot of bands, but this was a more fully formed group with focus.

We went to Paris and played. We didn't have a name yet, but [producer] Nick Lowe had referred to our sound in the studio as 'dinosaurs eating cars', so that's what we called ourselves for a while. The first London gig we did was at The Moonlight Club on West End Lane. I don't remember gigs very well unless something goes really wrong. The same with watching a gig. I can remember when someone freaks out or there's a fight – those are the stand-out moments, the memorable things. When everything goes smoothly, there's not much to remember, really, is there?

Did it feel like a unit with a lot of potential right from the get-go?

Once the unit was in situ, yes, it did. I knew that it could do anything. I just knew I had my band.

The first single was 'Stop Your Sobbing' [1979]. Why that track?

Because Nick [Lowe] liked it. And I was trying to get Jimmy Scott to join the band and leave his girlfriend and his job in Hereford. And I knew he loved Nick. So I thought if Nick produced it, Jimmy would join us. The punk songs like 'The Wait' and other ones that were on our original demos were a little too angry for Nick's taste … a little too angry for Jimmy's taste, too. But when he heard the cover of 'Stop Your Sobbing' [The Kinks, 1964] he said, 'I want to get in on that Sandy Shaw song.'

Did you enjoy success?

I didn't mind success. But that was never really the object. I mean, you wanted success and you wanted your records on the radio. But I never wanted to know chart positions or where we were; I've never read reviews. What I really liked was playing with the band. And then the rest of it is just, you know? You just have to do that to get through it.

Something that happened with me, which was really to my benefit, was that it took me a long time to get my band together. I had a lot of

Chrissie Hynde

false starts. And the whole time I always had jobs. I've always worked, so I had a lot to compare it to. Whatever I go through in the band, I always know that's better than waitressing, or better than modelling in an art college, or better than cleaning houses or hotels, or better than building picture frames. So I always feel grateful for it. I would never complain about aspects of it that aren't as much fun.

The other thing is, when you're starting to get success in the early days – hopefully this is not the way it is anymore – you know there's a lot of drugs and other stuff going on. I had my first number-one single the same week my flatmate died of an overdose. So, you know, there's always the two sides. Right when you're about to get happy about something, there's something else that you have to grieve over. So it kind of keeps you in the middle. And I think in the middle is a good place to stay.

"I'd rather have a number eleven or a number twelve than a number one any day."

Your first number one was 'Brass in Pocket' [1980]. The legend is that you didn't even want to release the track. Is that true?
Yeah, but I don't like to say that because it sounds negative. I just didn't really know what it was. It sounded like it was supposed to be Motown but it didn't quite make it. I don't know. It took me a long time to get over being afraid to get on stage, and maybe about two hundred shows before I got comfortable with it. Hearing my voice was always a real turn-off, so it was a hard adjustment to make, to get used to all that. I try to avoid it when I can, but when it's coming out of shop speakers and stuff, I mean, I didn't really enjoy it so much … I'd rather have a number eleven or a number twelve than a number one any day.

You said that when [guitarist] James Honeyman-Scott and [bassist] Pete Farndon passed away, it propelled you forward with the band. It kept you working under The Pretenders name as a tribute to them. Is that fair to say?
Well, yeah. I didn't see that coming – I mean, even that I *would* continue. Because for two years we said if one of us wasn't in the band – this was me always trying not to be photographed apart from the band – if one of us wasn't there, it could no longer be The Pretenders, that it was really the four of us in it together. And then Pete had so many drug problems the group decided to let him go. And then two days later, when Jimmy died, it was just me and Martin [Chambers – drummer]. Jimmy only lived for the music; that was his only interest. I thought, 'If the whole thing died with him, he would feel that he really fucked up', you know? Dying at the

age of twenty-five, that was a fuck-up. Let's face it. But if the music had died with him, and there was no legacy to it, I just felt that that would have been the real shame of it. So I felt that I had to carry on and keep the music alive. That was all that was left.

'Don't Get Me Wrong' in '86: that's success in America. A whole different level of attention, isn't it?
You might not like being in the States for many reasons, but they love guitar-based rock bands. So you can just tour endlessly there. The great thing is the audience. I've toured with ZZ Top, with Neil Young, with The Who, with the Stones; I've gone with a lot of guitar-based rock bands. And they love it. And that's when all the bikers and the greasers and the waitresses – they're all there. So if you want to tour in a band, that's the place, because you can do it indefinitely in the States.

When did you first become politically active? You work with PETA [People for the Ethical Treatment of Animals]; that's something that people associate with you.
I don't think of it as being politically active. I don't think of it as politics.

"I learned a long time ago that if someone doesn't ask you for advice, don't give it to them, because they'll just hate you for it."

I mean, some musicians stand up to be counted on subjects, some don't. And you're one of the ones who do.
Well, some humans do and some don't. I learned a long time ago that if someone doesn't ask you for advice, don't give it to them, because they'll just hate you for it. You know? So wait to be asked. As far as the meat-eating thing? I can't wait. None of us can wait because slaughter-houses and factory farms and the demise of life on earth – someone has to account for it. And we feel like we're the guardians and we have to step in. It's just the way it's going to be. So if you want to hurt an animal, then you have to go through me. And that's the way it has to be. And if someone doesn't like it, then don't buy my fucking record, you know?

Are you nervous about putting stuff out under your own name without The Pretenders?
I wouldn't say it's nerves. It kind of freaks me out. I don't like it. I always said I would never do it. But now nobody cares, so why should I?

Chrissie Hynde

[Laughs] What do you mean 'nobody cares'?!

I look at most solo artists and a lot of it is collaborative. So that's what I mean – who cares? Doesn't really matter what it's called. It matters what's in the grooves.

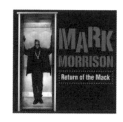

Before this interview, I was telling people I was going to do it and so many said 'She's a hero of mine! She's just such an icon!' Are you comfortable with that kind of hero worship? Because it strikes me that you've never, ever tried to court it.

No one tells you to your face. So I'm very comfortable with it, because I don't have to think about it.

I'm telling you to your face.

Okay, well, no, I'm not very comfortable right now. But it's better than not being an icon or a hero, isn't it? As long as you don't have to do anything. That just happens if you stay in the game long enough.

And the final question: what's the last song that we'll play on the show? It can be anything.

'Return of the Mack'. Because every time I hear him sing it, I really believe him and I really think she lied to him. And whenever I hear that song it makes me want to cry.

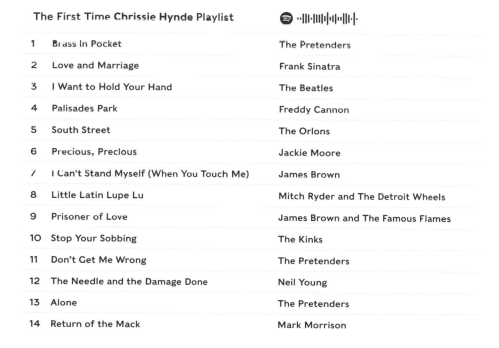

The First Time Chrissie Hynde Playlist

1	Brass In Pocket	The Pretenders
2	Love and Marriage	Frank Sinatra
3	I Want to Hold Your Hand	The Beatles
4	Palisades Park	Freddy Cannon
5	South Street	The Orlons
6	Precious, Precious	Jackie Moore
7	I Can't Stand Myself (When You Touch Me)	James Brown
8	Little Latin Lupe Lu	Mitch Ryder and The Detroit Wheels
9	Prisoner of Love	James Brown and The Famous Flames
10	Stop Your Sobbing	The Kinks
11	Don't Get Me Wrong	The Pretenders
12	The Needle and the Damage Done	Neil Young
13	Alone	The Pretenders
14	Return of the Mack	Mark Morrison

"I decided, okay, I'm going to be the freaky girl that they have to come see after hours."

Courtney Love

We've been waiting in the studio for three hours. 'There was a party', Courtney's minder tells me. 'She's been staying at a friend's apartment. Someone brought the wrong people. Things got broken. She hasn't had a lot of sleep. But she's on her way.' He shrugs and goes back to his Blackberry. We continue waiting for Ms Love.

In an industry full of unpredictables, Courtney Love stands alone. I knew one of her tour managers in the '90s. He spoke of her fondly, and told me a story of Courtney nearly turning herself and the crew of a private jet into a fireball after she unexpectedly opened the plane door, stepped down onto the tarmac and tried to light a cigarette while gallons of aviation fuel washed around her shoes (he claims he threw her over his shoulder and forcibly bundled her back into the aircraft).

Suddenly she's here. Tall, aggressively glamorous, a tangle of thick yellow-blonde hair and a glorious and improbable bust. The first thing she does is apologize: 'the party' is mentioned and, dramatically, 'expensive artworks going missing'. She talks in a raspy, deep-throat drawl – part boredom, part post-party exhaustion and part Valley Girl on Vicodin (brilliantly, she pronounces 'angst' as 'arnkst') – pausing occasionally to yawn from that famously wide, red mouth. She's engaging, aware of her reputation, and genuinely funny, answering every question without hesitation, even when Kurt's name and the subject of her own problems with drugs inevitably arise.

She's also the greatest first-name-dropper of all time – the theory being that anyone who needs their surname mentioned simply isn't that famous. Michael (Stipe), Billy (Corgan), Keith (Richards) and others flit in and out of her stories like guests at a fabulous '90s LA soiree, and I get the feeling she enjoys the naming and dropping as much as I do the hearing.

Matt Everitt: When were you first aware of music?
My parents listened to a lot of Dylan and Beatles. Not so much Stones. My first record was Leonard Cohen's [*Songs of*] *Leonard Cohen*, which I took from my mother's collection. They never listened to it; they never even opened it. I'm glad I started with that record. He was so lyric-conscious and … morbid [laughs]. I was a pretty morbid kid and – you know? – there's real angst on it. My parents were in a record club so they would get all these albums every month. And then the next record, I remember, I think, was *Beggars Banquet* [The Rolling Stones] and then I went out and bought Electric Light Orchestra's 'Evil Woman' [genuinely filthy laugh]. It's a tune! That was my first single.

When were you first struck by the idea of becoming a musician?
I remember staring at the cover of Bob Dylan's *Bringing It All Back Home* and going, 'Oooh, I want to live like that'. And when I was a ward of the state in Oregon, this hippy counsellor came back from the UK with Patti Smith's record *Horses* and also The Pretenders' *Pretenders*, and I was like, 'Wow! Cool!' Patti Smith's 'Rock 'n' Roll Nigger', which is not on *Horses*, to me, that's one of the greatest rock and roll songs of all time. Every time I hear that song I'm just grateful that there is rock. And it's such a hard song to pull off in 1978 – the 'N-word'? I think it's just an insane track; it's a beautiful track of music.

Can you remember meeting Patti Smith for the first time?
Yeah, I do. It was in New York. It was not climactic in that sense, you know? Sometimes it's best if you don't meet your heroes. I mean, Michael [Stipe, of R.E.M.] and Patti are tight as thieves. I'm fine when I see her, but I don't get all 'fan girl'.

Michael Stipe says hearing *Horses* for the first time was a life-changing moment for him.
It's limitless, his passion for her. It outranks his passion for me, which gets me rather jealous sometimes. But he's a great mentor and I'm especially close with him as he's the godfather of my daughter and stuff. But with Patti? It's like, 'Yeah anything Patti does …'

And what appealed about that first Pretenders album? Not that she likes the word, but Chrissie Hynde is an icon isn't she?
Right from the opening track ['Precious']. She's amazing. And she's a great guitar player, and the construction of those songs is great. She even has a Christmas song! Jesus! Christmas songs are where all the money is. If you can write a good Christmas song, you're in for life. You're set, man.

Have you ever tried writing one?
Yeah, I have, actually. It was with Billy [Corgan] and it didn't come out so well.

What was it called?

Oh, I can't remember. Wizzard has one, I mean, and doesn't Slade have one? And every Christmas you play it, you know?

I'm trying to picture a video with you guys all in Christmas gear.

Yeah, me and Billy [laughs]. That's a good idea.

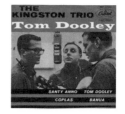

What was the first gig you saw that made a real impact on you?

Probably the Virgin Prunes in Dublin in 1979 or 1980. It was just really scary. Really scary. They looked like they were nine feet tall and they had black hair that was in these giant piles of quiff and they were wearing garbage bags. I liked it! I'd never seen *Top of the Pops* or music like that. I lived in New Zealand and I lived here [in the UK], but I'd never been exposed to musical culture and it was a really interesting time. U2 were first starting and The Smiths hadn't even started yet. New Order hadn't started yet, so that's the period of time I was here. And then I went off to Liverpool. I would go to Echo and the Bunnymen's rehearsals and that was really like school for me. I stole every move from that guy. Between Stipe and Ian McCulloch? I've stolen every move they make. I stole my foot on the monitor from Johnny Cash or Nick Cave, but I still do sing in a British accent though. It's just part of stealing from people. There was also a fellow in between that, Julian Cope [singer with The Teardrop Explodes] – he was the one that got me to Liverpool. By coincidence, we were just listening to a radio station in the car and 'Reward' came on and I said to Rick over there [gestures to the minder], 'Hey, this didn't date well!' [Laughs] It didn't! It's got horns all over the thing!

"I'm a shite guitar player. I have a sound ... I can write a song, I just can't execute it so well."

So what about when you first started playing the guitar? What were the very first songs you learned to play?

The first song was 'Hang Down Your Head' ['Tom Dooley', by The Kingston Trio, 1958], second was 'Danny Boy' – just average stuff. The guitar was very big for my hands. I ended up really fighting with the guitar teacher because he didn't want to teach me stuff I wanted to learn. I learned [Leonard Cohen's] 'Suzanne'. I learned [The Rolling Stones'] 'Paint It Black' on acoustic guitar. Which is really impossible. You can't play 'Paint It Black' on acoustic guitar! You need a riff, and it needs to be plugged in. So much better for me was when I got my first electric and a little amp and then I could learn the songs that I liked.

Who were your first guitar heroes, then?

I'm a shite guitar player. I have a sound, and it's not what it was, but I can write a song, I just can't execute it so well. But in terms of taste? I might shock you right now, but I think Brian May [Queen] is really tasteful. For guitar hero guys, I think Dave [Navarro – Jane's Addiction] can be really shreddy and lame, but other times he can be really tasteful. Peter Buck [of R.E.M.], Keith [Richards] and Noel [Gallagher]. Billy [Corgan] is a hell of a guitar player.

So what was your first actual release?

It would be Hole's 'Retard Girl' [1990]. It took about 20 minutes and cost all my savings, which was, like, five hundred bucks.

Were you pretty focused and driven at that time?

Totally. I had a five-year plan and I was very strategic about things, read every rock critic so I knew their taste, and I absolutely had a strategy: back door through the UK, then you get respected in the US. That's how it used to work, anyway. I mean, it still does work. Lana Del Rey did it.

And what were those first Hole rehearsals like?

[Red Hot Chili Peppers bassist] Flea loaned us his studio, and we would work in the night, because they worked there in the day. I would strip in the day to make the money to buy the backline equipment and the guitars and the drums. I was very good at saving money. The first line-up I knew wasn't going to be permanent, but I worked them six to seven days a week. They complained about it a lot, and were, like, 'The Chili Peppers don't work six to seven days a week!' I said, 'Well, we're not the Chili Peppers. I don't see us selling out [LA venue] The Starwood Club.'

"I had a five-year plan and I was very strategic about things ... I absolutely had a strategy."

And the first Hole gigs?

This was during metal, during that 'poodle metal' time. Poison, Warrant and Cinderella and all that crap. LA Guns and Hollywood Guns, who turned into Hollywood Rose, who turned into Guns N' Roses. During all that crap. So I decided, okay, I'm going to be the freaky girl that they have to come see after hours. Like, 'Let's go see that freaky girl.'

Being an alternative band in LA, the home of glam rock, seems like an odd choice of place to try and get established.

I didn't want to move to Seattle. I knew there was a big music scene up in Seattle, but I'd either die or get chased out of town in a month.

I walked two blocks off the bus when I was thinking of moving there and I just made a snap decision. Sometimes you've got to make a fast decision. It was, 'This is bad. This isn't going to work.' One block from the Greyhound Station I went, 'No, no, no, no. I will be kicked out of this town or die.' I could smell the heroin in the air. You could smell it. It's a very acute smell, Mexican tar heroin. And I could smell it.

So can you remember the first time you actually tried heroin?
Yeah. It was an accident. I was in Hong Kong and I was working at a dime-a-dance club. I was a dancing girl with a number around my chest. They were all little Chinese girls and one German girl; other than that, I was the only white girl. They had these huge petrol cans full of gowns and none of the gowns fit me. One came down to my knees and it had a star on the breast. Anyway, I remember this because there was this Philippines shipping tycoon and he wanted to do cocaine. This girl said, 'Oh, I can get it!' and she went and she got this cocaine. I didn't have any fondness for cocaine, ever. I had a cocaine phase once for about nine months in my entire life, and it was documented and terrible and everyone knows about it and it's just an embarrassment. But I took a very small snort and I woke up on a plane back to San Francisco. So that was that. It wasn't enjoyable. It wasn't something I remember particularly liking. I just woke up on a plane back to San Francisco, in that dress with the star on the boob that came down to my knees.

When Hole first started having hits, did you feel justification after working for so long with so many different people?
I did at the time, though it was right after Kurt died so a lot was going on. I had a baby and responsibilities. And I was also having to go into arbitration, deal with legal stuff about his estate a couple times a week. So I'd have to fly back to Seattle and do that when I was on the road.

I'm assuming that's something of a logistical nightmare?
A fuckshow! [Laughs] Absolutely. A fuckedy-fuck fuckshow. And also I didn't understand the whole thing with death taxes, you know? Wills getting thrown out. It was just a real clusterfuck.

If I can ask you about Kurt, what were your first impressions of him when you first met him in 1990?
I thought he was really cute, but I really didn't like their first single. I didn't like 'Love Buzz' [Nirvana's first release, 1988]. I knew the song, and I knew it was a cover, but I didn't really like 'Love Buzz' so I didn't buy it. But I thought he was cute. I thought he was funny and very enigmatic and dry-witted. And, you know, I had a crush. A lot of girls had a crush on him, but he wasn't aware of it. He didn't know he was a good-looking guy. Took me years to convince him, 'You are a technically handsome man.' Then the minute I told him that, he did all of these things to make himself ugly, like dye his hair red and wear crazy goggle

glasses, you know? It was like, 'Where's the blue-eyed blond boy, what happened? With the nice little sweater? Where'd he go?'

I'm fascinated with just the scale of the attention you got. I can't imagine what that would feel like, when the eyes of the world are constantly on you.
It felt like war. At home was calm, but anything outside was not calm.

So how did you cope?
Just by being isolated. Me, him, our kid, our nanny, boom! No one's allowed in. Except the dealer [laughs]. That's it. Just isolated. Didn't socialize with anybody, ever.

Can you remember when you first heard he'd died?
Yeah, I don't want to talk about that.

"I thought he was really cute, but I really didn't like their first single."

So *Live Through This* [1994] becomes a big commercial mainstream record. Then you've got worldwide recognition. All of a sudden you're a big star. Did you enjoy that attention?
People evolve. At the time I enjoyed it. I don't enjoy it any more. I'm very glad, for instance, that I've been in London for a week, almost, and I haven't been papped once and it's really nice. I used to be papped. It's like there's something that you used to think was just acceptable, and now you can't fucking stand it. It's, like, I see paparazzi and I just put my hand up. I want to make the picture worthless, or put on sunglasses and a dour expression. And that will make the picture worth less money.

When your album *America's Sweetheart* [2004] first came out, it didn't really connect with your audience. There seemed to be this question, 'Is she going to stop making music altogether?' Did you think about that at that point?
I just didn't care about anything at all at that point. Just fuck-off legal stuff and financial stuff. It was taking over my life. It was like the tribbles in *Star Trek*, you know? It was just breeding everywhere. Boxes with 102 credit card receipts in them, and it's, 'Where the fuck did these come from? I don't have 102 credit cards.' So that was what was more concerning to me than the music. I was like, they're stealing my daughter and my fortune, these lawyers that I have, and I don't know what to do about it.

And now you're refocused?
Yeah. Because I know I'll get it back, so it's fine.

So now you're reuniting the surviving members of Hole. When did you first decide to do that? And why now?

I was talking with Dave Navarro and he was talking about touring with Jane's Addiction and how he and Perry [Farrell – Jane's Addiction vocalist] have separate buses and he just kind of talked some sense into me. We're also the last to the dance in terms of those reunion things. I mean, Nine Inch Nails have done, like, three victory laps; Soundgarden do it every year. I said to Tom Morello from Rage Against the Machine, 'You guys, Rage, never did a reunion tour'. He says, 'What are you talking about? 2007 to 2011!' I'm like, 'What?' Okay, well, I'm not doing it without new music. I'm just not doing it without new songs.

And what about dealing with people's preconceived ideas of the kind of person you are? ELO's 'Evil Woman'?

Yeah, that is difficult to live with. So I win them over one person at a time. It's called playing the long game, baby.

And after all the firsts, what's the final song we should play?

The Verve's 'Bitter Sweet Symphony'. Because it's one of my favourite songs ever. I remember hearing it and just feeling this is a beautiful, beautiful, beautiful song for the ages.

The First Time Courtney Love Playlist

1	Malibu	Hole
2	Suzanne	Leonard Cohen
3	Parachute Woman	The Rolling Stones
4	Evil Woman	Electric Light Orchestra
5	It's All Over Now, Baby Blue	Bob Dylan
6	Rock 'n' Roll Nigger	Patti Smith
7	Precious	Pretenders
8	Retard Girl	Hole
9	Tom Dooley	The Kingston Trio
10	Paint It Black	The Rolling Stones
11	Today	Smashing Pumpkins
12	Love Buzz	Nirvana
13	Celebrity Skin	Hole
14	You Know My Name	Courtney Love
15	Bitter Sweet Symphony	The Verve

"I just do 'stuff'. Stuff inspires me here and stuff inspires me there, and I just get on with it."

DAMON ALBARN

I'm in a West London recording studio, preparing for the interview and unpacking my recording equipment. I pause to browse through a book about North Korea that someone's left on the mixing desk as Damon wanders in and explains he's just returned from a visit there. 'Did you find out anything about the people?' I ask. 'Isn't it so secretive that it's impossible to make any real connection with anyone?' 'Oh yes,' he replies, sitting in front of the microphone, smiling, 'but even when people are hiding stuff, they're still showing it to you, aren't they?'

At forty-nine Albarn is still a very handsome man, with the kind of messy hair that either looked that good when he fell out of bed, or someone spent a lot of money making it look like it looked that good when he fell out of bed. He's scruffy and stubbly in old jeans and a denim jacket, and he starts the interview frowning but his face relaxes as his answers get longer. When he does his Artful Dodger grin, a gold tooth winks out.

When he finds a question predictable or stupid, he'll roll his eyes and give a weary sigh, but he'll sometimes circle back on the subject, looking for a new way to approach it. He'll often pause, hang on the first syllable of a sentence, or repeat the same word a few times, like he's casting around for the right follow-up. There's a slow, measured pace to his voice, and when there's an especially long pause in his conversation, if you start to prompt him or ask another question, he'll suddenly cut in and start talking over you (John Lydon does exactly the same thing). You can also hear the soft sibilance on his *s*'s, just like when he sings. He's straightforward, unself-conscious, slightly impatient and clearly very smart, and I often find myself wondering, 'Is he overconfident or insecure?' The answer is probably both.

Matt Everitt: When were you first aware of music?

My mum would say that I was interested in music from a very, very young age – having had a harmonica in my cot that I liked blowing, apparently. But no one played an instrument; I'm the only musician in my family – professionally, you know?

We didn't have that many records, to be honest with you. We had several Indian records: Ravi Shankar and ragas, some Middle Eastern Sufi music, and some more anthropological African records. I had a cassette of *Atom Heart Mother* [Pink Floyd], a cassette of *Catch Bull at Four* by Cat Stevens, *Rubber Soul* [The Beatles], and I think there was some Stockhausen. Then a massive amount of 78s, which ranged from classical to music hall, to early spirituals, to French chansons and Édith Piaf – stuff like that. But certainly eclectic and with quite a bit of a sense of theatre, because my mum [Hazel Albarn] was a stage designer for [theatre director] Joan Littlewood, and my dad [Keith Albarn] was a conceptual artist.

What about the first record that you owned that was yours?

The first record I definitely fell under the spell of was 'Seasons in the Sun' by Terry Jacks – a great record, which actually has a much grander tradition in the sense that it comes from Jacques Brel and that whole era. Then, I'd like to say it was *Combat Rock* [The Clash], but I think the week before that I bought *Kings of the Wild Frontier* [Adam and the Ants].

Is The Clash where the West London thing comes from? You've always gravitated towards West London, and the Westway is where you, geographically, are right now. ·

I came here originally because my girlfriend at the time, Justine Frischmann, lived here. I was living in South East London when I met her, and she had a flat here. At that point, someone who was actually in a position to own a flat was superhuman. That's why I came here, and that was the beginning of my love affair with this part of London. I wasn't that savvy. Even though I'd grown up in Leytonstone, I'd been out in darkest Essex for eight years and I came back as a student and just lived on the peripheries of London.

What was your first gig – do you remember that?

First gig would have been – slightly embarrassing – Nik Kershaw at the Ipswich Gaumont.

What do you remember from the gig? White denim?

He might have been wearing white denim. It was my first gig, but actually it wasn't the first time I'd seen a pop star in the flesh. I'd got the chance through a friend of a friend to go and be in the audience of *Top of the Pops*, the debut appearance of Fun Boy Three with Bananarama [1982]. One of my biggest influences when I was that age was Terry Hall, from Fun Boy Three and The Specials. I absolutely still adore him –

a wonderful guy. I can remember exactly what he was wearing: light-tan moccasins, no socks; rolled-up jeans, quite high; and a burgundy waffle jumper, which I bought immediately when I got home. I was briefly a New Romantic, only for three or four weeks. I had silver two-tone parachute trousers, purple Tucker boots – remember them? – and I had a grey and maroon crossover shirt. There was a lot of maroon going on in the '80s. And I peroxided my hair as much as I could with lemon juice [laughs]. We all wanted to look like David Sylvian [singer with '80s synth pioneers Japan], then I wanted to look like Terry Hall.

What about those first Blur gigs, when you were still called Seymour [Blur's name until 1990]?
It was more about self-harming and being sick than music. It was just full on. It was drink as much as you can before you go on, and play as fast as you humanly can until you collapse in exhaustion. And then that's it. That's the end of the gig. We didn't really do much more than, like, 25 to 30 minutes. But we gave a lot in that brief period.

Even on the first album [*Leisure*, 1991] there's this duality. It's a pop band, but it's also quite avant-garde.
Yeah, it was. When we started we had, if you can call it that, 'a following'. It was years one, two and three from Goldsmiths and also a couple of other art schools where friends of ours were. That was our following, just pissed art students. I think in a way that put me in good stead for everything I've done subsequently. I mean, I do quite weird stuff, like *Dr Dee*, and then I'll do something really mainstream.

"It was more about self-harming and being sick than music."

The first Gorillaz track that was released was 'Tomorrow Comes Today' [2000]. Did you expect them to get as big as it did? Gorillaz arguably became a bigger band than Blur.
They sold a lot more records! But you can't compare them. I thought Gorillaz was me doing a solo record. I didn't put my name on it and I collaborated with a lot of people, but I was essentially generating all the music in a studio on my own. But do you ever do anything on your own? No, you don't. But Gorillaz started off as quite a self-contained, small thing and very tangible and then it became this …

… brand?
That last tour [2010's Escape to Plastic Beach Tour] – I doubt the world will ever see anything quite like it again. Partly because no one would be stupid enough to try to logistically put something like that on the road

again, and you don't make any money. I mean, we made a lot of money in the sense that we played massive gigs round the whole of the world, but, believe you me, when we got the final expenses and outgoings …

Like Lou Reed's rider?
No! Lou was – God rest his soul – a really wonderful person to work with and I enjoyed it. It's a great feeling when he walks on stage, especially at Madison Square Garden, because it sounded like the whole of the crowd were going, 'Boo! Boo! Boo!' But they were saying, 'Lou! Lou!'

Was it fun to just ride that and see how far it could go?
You see, it's weird, because when is it Gorillaz and when is it not Gorillaz? Is it only when it's got the cartoons? Does that make it Gorillaz? I don't know. Because for me it's always the same process: I'm in the studio making music.

The 2002 *Mali Music* album was the first time that lots of people were aware that you'd started to get deeply involved in African music. You talk about the first trip you took there with Oxfam so passionately; it seems almost rehabilitation from a lot of stuff you'd gone through before, like Blur coming to an end.
It was an extraordinary thing, having essentially spent my twenties travelling in a very constrained way and seeing a lot, but seeing very little. Travelling the world in a band starts off by taking the Tube to the airport, getting picked up, hotel, taken to the gig, returned, plane, Tube, home. And then it transforms into being picked up by a taxi, airport, being picked up by another car. So it's quite a strange way to see the world. I had been to other places but that really felt like my first adventure, if you like. I felt like I was back at square one.

What do you mean?
In the sense that I felt like I was just myself going somewhere. I wasn't part of anything, or in any kind of bubble; I was just myself. I felt like that was a very natural place to be and nobody had any idea or any interest in anything about me. I just felt reassuringly invisible. There's not a great deal of pressure on you when you turn up somewhere, in comparison to the previous ten years where travel had been very regimented, and there was a sense that it's all an illusion. Whereas I felt when I turned up in Mali that I was seeing it just as anyone else.

A previous attempt to break out of that bubble had been me getting on a plane and going to Iceland, but within two days of being there, it became very apparent to me that it wasn't really any different from being here. People seemed to have exactly the same sort of perception, and were interested in the image and the whole bubble aspect of it. Whereas there was no bubble [in Mali]. I was bubble-less.

Day one, I turned up at Toumani Diabaté's, who is, I think it's fair to say, the world's greatest kora player, considered, within the griot tradition in West Africa, as someone who can summon the voice of God; he's a revered individual. It's a spiritual responsibility he has when he plays his instrument. So I had this unbelievable opportunity. I suppose you could say that I was still in a bubble, because you don't normally get a chance to meet Toumani Diabaté, but it just felt really terrifying. I turned up with my melodica, and he had this unbelievable 21-string harp, his kora, and immediately he started playing, and I'd been expected to play.

After ten or so years of being put in that sort of situation, I usually feel comfortable, but this was my first ever time improvising with someone like that. You can't tune a melodica, that's the one drawback of it as an instrument, and we weren't in tune, so there were a lot of reasons I was really nervous. I was bit disorientated, I couldn't get my head round the rhythm he was playing, let alone the mode he was playing in. So it was a very good experience, as slowly, bit by bit, I started feeling more comfortable. The distance between that point and now is immense for me because I've had such amazing opportunities to go all over Africa and play with so many different people, and then latterly with Africa Express.

"... I felt like I was just myself going somewhere. I wasn't part of anything, or in any kind of bubble; I was just myself."

Where does this restlessness in you come from, do you think? Because not all musicians have it; you're quite unique ...

I don't think I'm unique at all. I saw an interview with [artist and director] Steve McQueen, who I admire enormously; [film critic] Mark Kermode was being slightly uptight and asking him if he now considered himself more a director than an artist, and he said, 'It's just all stuff. I just do stuff'. And I have exactly the same answer. I just do 'stuff'. Stuff inspires me here and stuff inspires me there, and I just get on with it.

When did you first meet [Afrobeat drumming legend] Tony Allen? He's cropped up in many of your collaborations.

That came out of me really getting into the music of Fela Kuti in the late '90s. In the Blur tune 'Music Is My Radar' I sang a line, 'Tony Allen got me dancing', quite abstractly really, and I think someone pointed that out to him and he invited me to come and do some work on a record, and we just hit it off. I did this tune with him called 'Every Season' on his *Home Cooking* album. I was really nervous about performing it live, but I had this chance to play with him on this TV show in Paris, which also had Ibrahim Ferrer from the Buena Vista Social Club on it. Ibrahim was on the first Gorillaz record, the song 'Latin Simone (Que Pasa Contigo)'

– an absolutely gorgeous man. So there were these two people who I was going to perform with on the same show. Now, I did the first part, which was quite straightforward, and then there was a two-hour turnaround for cameras and everything. MTV presenter Ray Cokes was backstage, and he brought a bottle of Martini white rum, and we started drinking it.

In the two-hour window?

Yeah, and I got really, really drunk. Partly from relief that I got through the first part, and partly because I was really nervous that I was going to screw up the second part because I wasn't sure about this entry point.

Did you get it right? Did you find the intro point?

No! So the moment comes – cameras, lights, action – and … I screw it up, and I'm too drunk to really get my act together. I did eventually learn my lesson and I never drink before I go on stage ever, ever, ever now. I do drink afterward, but not before. I got so embarrassed that I screwed this song up – and this is the behaviour of a man who doesn't really know where he is anymore – that I went round to Tony and got on the back of his chair and put my arms round him while he was playing, and fell asleep on the drum stool, just holding him. He was totally cool with it and continued playing. I don't remember anything else. I woke up in the morning and my tour manager knocked on the door and I asked, 'How did it go?', just hoping for a glimmer of reassurance in his eyes, but he just looked at me and said, 'Deary, deary me. That wasn't good, Damon.'

"I did eventually learn my lesson and I never drink before I go on stage ever, ever, ever now."

You've talked about *Everyday Robots*, your first solo album, being the most personal record that you've written, lyrically.

Yeah, I think that's in part due to [producer] Richard Russell's influence. We were co-producing a Bobby Womack record [*The Bravest Man in the Universe*, 2012], and Bobby has one of those voices that, whatever he's singing, it feels very, very intimate and personal. When we finished that record, we felt like we still wanted to work with each other, and when you want to work with someone it's probably a good idea to continue until that magic disappears. So we played around with the idea of starting a new band, you know, even came up with some stupid names …

Which were?

No, no, I might use them in the future. They were pretty ridiculous. Richard came in one day and said, 'What I would like to do is produce you as Damon Albarn'. And it hadn't really occurred to me. I'd had this sort of vague notion of doing a love-song record, but nothing more concrete than that. Anyway, I thought, 'Well okay, why not?' Having made lots of records on my own that had not been seen as solo records, if this was going to be a solo record, even though I wasn't going to make it on my own, the subject matter had to be something very personal.

Is it a positive album? There seem to be songs about impermanence and it's quite introspective. Was it hard to write?
It's positive in the sense that it was cathartic, and it was a hard record to write. It was really difficult, because you've got that fine balance between becoming too introspective and the references being too oblique …

Just personal to you so no one else can associate with them?
Exactly. But at the same time I didn't want to make it too universal, I wanted it to keep that integrity, which I feel was important for me to sing the songs. They need to have that balance, and it was hard to find that. But I'm proud of the results and I love singing the songs, I really do.

What's the final song we should play? You get to choose it.
Well, it's your radio show. You choose.

Blur's 'Black Book'?
Okay. If you like that song, play that song. Be my guest.

The First Time **Damon Albarn** Playlist

1	Everyday Robots	Damon Albarn
2	Seasons in the Sun	Terry Jacks
3	Rock the Casbah	The Clash
4	The Riddle	Nik Kershaw
5	It Ain't What You Do …	The Fun Boy Three with Bananarama
6	Sing	Blur
7	Colours	Electric Wave Bureau
8	Some Kind of Nature	Gorillaz feat. Lou Reed
9	Niger	Damon Albarn feat. Bocolim & Diabati
10	Every Season	Tony Allen feat. Damon Albarn
11	Lonely Press Play	Damon Albarn
12	Black Book	Blur

FREAK BABY

KISS

FXX

7 P.M
7 $

Naked Raygun

82

CUBBY BEAR
1059 WEST ADDISON • 327.1662

"Everyone should realize that the most important thing is that you be yourself ... Nirvana never tried to be anything but Nirvana."

DAVE GROHL

'Is he really is that cool?' is what everyone asks. It's obviously something of a triumph for Dave Grohl that, despite his former role as drummer with Nirvana, one of the greatest and most influential bands in the history of everything, people's first reaction on hearing that you met him is: 'Dave Grohl! The nicest man in rock!'

It's true. His strategy of dealing with fame is to be really, really, really nice to everyone, to take his music seriously but treat everything else that comes with being a rock star as gloriously, utterly ridiculous and there to be enjoyed. As such, interviewing him is a wonderfully enjoyable experience.

When I picked up the phone to speak to him for the first time, I was greeted by him bellowing, 'DAVE FUCKING GROHL HERE! HOW ARE YOU?', and when we meet to record *The First Time* some years later, he's just landed after a seven-hour overnight flight from Washington – 'Just fucking an hour and a fucking half ago' – but bounds into the studio, gives me a warm handshake and hurls himself into the interview with the same enthusiasm as he plays music. He's sitting up straight, looking directly at me, and his behaviour ranges from thoughtful and measured to wonderfully energetic (he has a habit of smacking the studio desktop with his hands to make a point), and when he talks about favourite bands, it's with the geekiness of an obsessive teenage fan.

Aside from a record company rep frantically trying to bring the interview to a close, it feels very much like a chat you'd have in a bar with a friendly, excitable and slightly drunk random Led Zeppelin fan, which is pretty much who he is – just one who headlines Glastonbury and has his own private Boeing 737.

So in answer to your question? Yes, he really *is* that cool.

Matt Everitt: When were you first aware of music?

My first record was a compilation by K-Tel. My mother was a public-school teacher and so we didn't have a record player in the house, but on the weekends she would bring the crappy public-school turntables home. I bought this record – this K-Tel compilation – and it had 'Fly Robin Fly' [Silver Convention] and 'That's the Way (uh-huh, uh-huh) I Like It' [KC and the Sunshine Band] but it also had Edgar Winter's 'Frankenstein' on it, and it totally changed my life. It was like, 'Oh my god!'

I remember in America AM radio in the '70s was amazing, because it was all super-melodic soft rock like 10cc and Gerry Rafferty and Andrew Gold and Carly Simon and stuff like that, and my mother sang when she was young, so I would sing with her in the car and she taught me how to harmonize. I would sing the lead line and she would sing a harmony and that's when I started to understand, like, 'Oh, so if you put different notes together it makes a chord!' That's what I remember, driving around in our Ford Maverick in the summertime, going to the lake, and my mother singing, like, a Phoebe Snow song or something.

When was the first time you fell in love with The Beatles, because you talk about them, and on the Foo Fighters' *Sonic Highways,* **[2014] the cover photo was done by Ringo Starr!**

Yeah. How great is that? Well, he's a photographer and he took a lot of great pictures of The Beatles and other people as well. He released a book called *Photograph* [2013], which is beautiful. I spoke at his book launch, and when it came time to do pictures for the record, someone called and said, 'Okay, it's time to do band pictures'. I'm like, 'Oh god, I hate doing that,' and, 'Who do you want to use? Do you want to use blah, blah?' 'Nah, we did that.' 'Do you want to use blah, blah?' 'Nah, we've done that.' And then I thought, 'Are there any, like, musicians that take pictures?'

And I just thought, 'I'll call Ringo'. We talked about it and he's so cool, man, and just so humble. He was like, 'Well, I'm a little nervous, you know.' Like he wasn't really sure how to do it, because a lot of those iconic pictures that he took of The Beatles, they were just hanging out in the hotel room – they couldn't go outside because they'd get torn to shreds by the fans. A lot of the best pictures of The Beatles, I think, were taken by Ringo because he caught those really candid moments in the hotel rooms. But he agreed to do it, and he got some really great pictures.

What Beatles track we should play?

My favourite Beatles track might be 'Hey Bulldog'. I loved it when I was young, but then when my daughter started listening to The Beatles, she also said, 'That's the song!' And so we kind of bonded over that.

Let's talk about the first punk rock gig, the one that changed your life – the Cubby Bear [club] in Chicago, 1982.

Oh, totally. Where I grew up in Virginia, unless you were brilliant and had money and were going to some fancy college, you were either going to be a mason or do dry-walling. I used to call them 'Virginia jobs', you know? Just labour. So I worked those jobs and played music in a neighbourhood band and we did Bowie covers and Stones covers, and then I went up to Chicago for a vacation and my cousin took me to a club to see this punk rock band called Naked Raygun. I went to this dingy little club and the band got on stage ... They were so aggressive and loud and simple. It's like, you're used to seeing these monolithic mega rock bands that seem like superheroes, and you have a poster and you listen to the record and you think, 'That's kind of cool', but you could never imagine doing it, just because they're so *good*. And then you go see a punk rock band just, like, spill blood all over the stage, and it makes you realize, 'Well, I could do that'. And that's really fun and exciting.

And so I went home and decided, 'Okay, that's what I'm going to do with my life. I can't imagine that it's ever going to keep the heat on in my building, but that's what I want to do for the rest of my life.' It totally changed my life. It was the most inspiring thing that's probably ever happened to me. And when you're a kid, too, those are formative, impressionable years. I loved music and I had learned to play guitar by listening to Beatles records, and then all of a sudden I see this band bash out three chords and two-minute songs? It totally changed my life. It was great.

Your first gig playing drums with Scream in DC and your experience afterwards sounded like a spiritual baptism as well as a musical baptism, in a way.
Yeah, it's like going to the river. While I was in Chicago my cousin showed me her record collection, and I started finding these albums in

> # "I decided, 'Okay, that's what I'm going to do with my life. I can't imagine that it's ever going to keep the heat on in my building, but that's what I want to do."

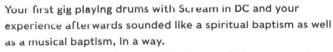

her collection of bands from Washington, DC. I had no idea that there was this huge, influential punk rock scene in Washington. So when I went back to DC, I knew we had bands like Minor Threat and Bad Brains and Scream and all these bands that were amazing, that were right in my backyard. I had no clue. So when I came back to DC, I started going to see shows and stuff. But the DC music scene was *different*.

Washington, DC is the political capital of America and so it's inevitable that that's going to somehow, by osmosis, make its way into what you do. You're just surrounded by it. Somewhere in the mid-'80s, this

guy named Mark Andersen had an organization called Positive Force; he married the music scene with politics and it all came together with a community of people that realized, 'Okay, well, we're a community. We can actually get out and do things to change.' At the time apartheid was still happening, and a hundred of us would grab drums and stand out in front of the South African embassy as traffic went by and just beat the hell out of drums for hours, you know, until the cops chased us away.

Stuff like that was happening all the time. We were doing Amnesty International benefits and animal rights benefits and things like that, because music is such a powerful communicator: not only can it reach out and attract people to something that you're supporting, but you're celebrating life at the same time. So DC was, and is, an amazing city for music because it's more than just music: it's important; there's something else going on. So the first show I played with Scream – I mean, that was a big enough deal because they were my heroes in Washington, DC – we, like, marched up to an embassy and, you know, lit it on fire. I can't remember what we did. Something like that.

What were your first impressions when you first met [producer] Steve Albini? Because – his reputation and character – he seems like a very *singular* individual.

Oh, there's nobody else like that guy at all. Thank god there's only one of him. I first met him when Nirvana recorded *In Utero*. I had never met him before that, but I knew his reputation. He was the smartest, most cynical producer, music critic, band leader, pundit. He was just terrifying. Everyone was scared of him. Then you see pictures of him and he just kind of looks like this skinny little guy – but he's smarter and funnier and better at everything than everyone else in the world. And he had made so many records that we loved. He'd made Pixies records and Breeders records and Jesus Lizard records and Big Black records, and these are bands that Nirvana really loved, so when we went to record with him we were ... I know I was nervous because I knew what kind of dude he was, and I thought he would hate me because I'm such an idiot, you know?

But we got along great. I think he treated me like a pet, actually. Because I was the drummer. I mean, he's one of a kind, and I think he sets a great example, not only for musicians but also for the industry and how to think outside of conventional business, you know? He lives to do things that are real and passionate, and his level of integrity is just unwavering. He just won't bend. And he's stubborn for all the right reasons. So I love him to death; I think he's amazing.

What do you remember about that first Foo Fighters record [*Foo Fighters*, 1995]? The legend is you did 12 songs in six days.

Yeah [laughs]. Yeah, because I didn't think it was a 'record'. I mean, had I taken it seriously, I might have spent a little more time on it. Even before I was in Nirvana, I had this friend who had an 8-track studio in his basement – my friend Barrett Jones. I would go to his house and record his music with him, and then I'd always say, 'Hey, do you have any tape left?' And he'd have maybe three minutes left at the end of a reel. And I would record something by myself where I'd play the drums first, and then I'd overdub guitars, and then I'd overdub a bass, and then I'd overdub a vocal. And I'd take it home and listen to it, and it sounded like a group, you know? It sounded like a band. And I would trick people and play it, like, 'Hey, listen to this new band' [laughs]. And they'd say, 'What? That sucks. Who's that?' I'm like [dejected], 'This is me' [laughs].

But it became this experiment, and then the entire time I was in Nirvana I was doing that in my basement too. I didn't let anybody hear it and I wasn't about to introduce any of my crap to Nirvana. It was like, 'Kurt's writing pretty good songs right now, I'll just sort of do this in my basement.' Then after Nirvana was over I just didn't know what to do and I was in kind of … I was in a dark place and I didn't want to join another band, and finally I just got off the couch and said, 'You know what? I'm going to pick 12 of my favourite songs that I've recorded over the last five years and go to this studio and book five days and just record.'

Because five days to me was an eternity. I usually only had five minutes at my friend Barrett's because I was imposing already, asking for free tape. So I got five days in the studio and I was so prepared, man. I knew what I was going to record each day, and I had this day blocked out for this and then the last day I was going to do vocals, then mix on the sixth day or whatever. And I just banged it out. But there was no band and there was no label – it was just for fun. And then that tape started getting around and people said, 'Hey, do you want to put out this record?' I'm like, 'That's not a record. It's not even a band.' And then it just kind of turned into the Foo Fighters.

"People said, 'Hey, do you want to put out this record?' I'm like, 'That's not a record. It's not even a band.' And then it turned into the Foo Fighters."

Watching the *Sound City* documentary [2013, produced and directed by Grohl], what struck me was how, for *Nevermind*, the studio [Sound City, iconic recording studios] was a bit of a gift, somewhere that had this incredible sound and heritage but was punky and cheap. It gave you the ability to make a record 'sound' like that, and then you helped save the studio by the record being a success.

Well, you know, I think that what that studio represents, or represented, is important. Nirvana made sense at Sound City because we were kind of alike. We didn't need much, we just needed to be ourselves, and it's sort of the same as Sound City. You know, Sound City had that same mixing desk recording console for 40 years, and they never upgraded and they never changed it because they didn't need to. It did what it did, and it had a vibe and it had a sound and it was a one-of-a-kind board. Same with the room: the room was just linoleum tile and perforated sound-board on the wall. It wasn't fancy, but it didn't need to be because it just sounded so good. It was entirely real.

So the artists that recorded there, they all sort of reflected that same vibe or idea. Like, if you put Tom Petty in the middle of the big room at Sound City, it would sound like Tom Petty. But when Nirvana went there to record, we just went there because it was cheap; we didn't know anything about it. We walked in and we thought it was a dump. But it sounded so good, and we weren't used to the state-of-the-art, wonderful new studios anyway. To me, it represents something really important – almost like a lesson for everyone. Everyone should realize that the most important thing is that you be yourself, you know? Sound City never tried to be anything but Sound City. Nirvana never tried to be anything but Nirvana, and the same thing could be said for Tom Petty and Neil Young and a lot of the bands that recorded there.

Fortunately, when *Nevermind* became popular, Sound City became popular again, too. I was very happy about that, like, 'Oh, wow, so now all these people are appreciating it for the same reason that we did.' Rage Against the Machine went there and made their record that same way.

"You can listen to Justin Bieber, that's cool. Just make sure you get a Zeppelin record first."

Can you remember the first time you played Wembley Stadium?
I like that place, I had fun there. I remember the first time we walked into Wembley it was like an optical illusion. It was when we did the Live Earth benefit – this is in 2007 or something – and I remember feeling like, 'There's no way something this big could have an inside'. It just seemed so huge. I jokingly said that night, 'Oh yeah, we'll be back for three nights at Wembley next year!' And then the next year someone said, 'Do you want to really play Wembley?'

England has always been the country where we really cut our teeth, when we first came over and started playing festivals here; it's where we learned to be a live band, you know? Of all the places we've played here – over the years we've gone from the Astoria to being halfway up the bill at Reading [Festival], to Earl's Court to the O2 to Hyde Park to Wembley. It's just kind of ramped up over the years and now, honestly, I don't get nervous to play the stadium. I walk out there like, 'Here we go! We got three hours! Let's do this!' and it's so much fun. I'm totally into it.

When did you first fall in love with Zeppelin? I'm looking at the Zeppelin tats you've got going on.

Led Zeppelin is just … like the clouds and the air and the trees! It's just everywhere all the time, you know? Someone's older brother has a record, it's on the radio, 'The Song Remains the Same' is on TV – it's just everywhere, and it should be, because it's important for people to have that as some sort of musical foundation. Like, you can listen to Justin Bieber, that's cool. Just make sure you get a Zeppelin record first, you know what I'm saying? But, yeah, it was such a huge part of my life. I was really, really into Led Zeppelin for years. I mean, bootlegs and bootleg videos – I never got to see them play live because I was too young.

What's the track we should play?

Right now? It's hard to pick a favourite Zep track. That's like picking your favourite child. 'Trampled Under Foot' has always been one of my favourite songs, because you've got John Paul Jones on that Clav[inet]. It sounds so cool, and there's the one epic drum roll at the end that's so fast it doesn't even sound like it's single hits. It's like [hammers his hands on the tabletop in rhythm]. That's a good one!

And the final song we're going to play?

We should play the song called 'Congregation' which we recorded in Nashville for our *Sonic Highways* TV series [laughs].

	The First Time **Dave Grohl** Playlist	⬤ �·ıⅼ∥ıⅼ∥∥ıⅼ·∥·ⅼ∥ⅼ·
1	Everlong	Foo Fighters
2	Frankenstein	The Edgar Winter Group
3	Every Night	Phoebe Snow
4	Detroit Rock City	Kiss
5	Hey Bulldog	The Beatles
6	On a Plain	Nirvana
7	I Lie	Naked Raygun
8	Gods Look Down	Scream
9	Heart-Shaped Box	Nirvana
10	Let's Dance	David Bowie
11	This Is a Call	Foo Fighters
12	Trampled Under Foot	Led Zeppelin
13	Congregation	Foo Fighters

"It was one of those lucky things where the whole was greater than the sum of the parts, we came together and created something that was wonderful."

DAVID GILMOUR

An atmosphere of patience surrounds David Gilmour. While a crew faff around him with cameras, suggesting talking points and tweaking microphones, he'll find a nearby guitar and start strumming it, nodding and smiling calmly. But generally, he just waits for the conversation to start. David (always David, never Dave) spent most of his life in a world-famous band who all tried very hard not to be famous people, so talking about himself is pretty low down his list of priorities.

He is, however, a lovely interviewee. Enjoyably laid back and unpretentious, and his occasional self-deprecating comments are accompanied by a wide, warm smile. He chooses his answers carefully, and speaks steadily in a low, thoughtful voice. He deftly sidesteps questions about his own moments of excess, and there's a surety about his answers. While it's hard to imagine him losing his temper, there are glimpses of a quiet determination that bring to mind John Dryden's line 'Beware the fury of a patient man'.

Broad-chested, in his unvarying uniform of black T-shirt and jeans, Gilmour has bright blue eyes, full lips and tightly cropped grey hair. He's remarkably handsome, with a face that has something of the Michelangelo sculpture about it, with a profile not that dissimilar to his Renaissance statue namesake.

Pink Floyd created immensely ambitious albums that tackled huge conceptual themes about the human condition set against epic, experimental and breathtakingly beautiful music, so it's interesting that one of the main architects of those records appears to be so low-key. I don't think David necessarily dislikes interviews, but just finds them much less preferable to playing music. It's fair to say his guitar playing is more famous than he is. And I think he likes it that way.

Matt Everitt: When were you first aware of music?

When I was a young child, I suppose. The radio was incredibly varied and we were exposed to all sorts of music on the Light Programme [BBC entertainment and music radio station]. My parents had a collection of strange old 78s of blues records. I was immersed, actually. My parents weren't musicians, but they were very musical.

What was your relationship like with that music? Was it something that you found yourself drawn to?

Yes, I loved it. My parents had lived in the USA and had brought back all these old songs like 'Lazy Bones' [Paul Robeson] and 'Life Gets Teejus, Don't It' [Tex Williams] – fantastic old song, an old American 78, sort of talking blues, but sort of hillbilly music as well. But the first record I bought, and that really turned me around a bit, was 'Rock Around the Clock' by Bill Haley when I was ten. Everyone, I guess, has slightly different memories or different things that will spark them off, but that was the first moment where I thought that this was something new, exciting and original. It was superseded within not very long by 'Heartbreak Hotel' by Elvis Presley, which was a step up again, but that first moment was 'Rock Around the Clock'. It's very hard to describe how new and revolutionary that sounded to me at the time.

When did you first pick up a guitar? And what was that guitar like, and was it awful?

The very first time I picked up a guitar was when my next-door neighbour, Bill, was given a Spanish one by his parents and he had no interest in it whatsoever. It wasn't even mine, but I played it at his house and then I think I asked if I could borrow it, and I think I forgot to give it back.

Whose style were you trying to copy at that time?

It's so broad, so varied. I copied everyone. I had a Pete Seeger guitar tutor record when I was about thirteen. The first track was the six notes that the six strings of guitar played, to tune to. He thought you needed to get your guitar in tune – that was fantastic. Then a chord of D. Then he taught you a song where he just strummed one chord and you could instantly accompany yourself. It was great. It was a great LP, and it had a book inside it which showed you all the chord shapes. That is where I learned guitar.

What about your first live-music experience?

It was probably a package tour in Cambridge when I was a kid where all sorts of people played: The Shadows, Gene Pitney and The Everly Brothers. The people who wandered through every town in those days are like a Who's Who of rock and roll. Hank [Marvin] was one of the big influences, because it's like playing a tune, playing a melody. By nature, I'm a melodic sort of person. It's great to be able to combine that thought of melody and music with a more bluesy approach and try and make something that falls somewhere in between all those things.

What was your first band like?

The first band I actually properly joined was called The Newcomers. We were rubbish, dreadful. I wasn't the singer, I was just the guitar player. Then I formed a band with some other guys which we called Jokers Wild, and that was more ambitious. We did lots of Beach Boys songs. We were into big harmony stuff: Four Seasons and all sorts of R&B records, The Beatles, everything – covers of absolutely everything. That was fun.

The Jokers Wild disc is apparently one of the rarest, most collectible bits of vinyl ever.

Yeah, we recorded five tracks. We went up in the van from Cambridge to London and went to the studio Regent Sound on Denmark Street and recorded five tracks and put two on a double-sided single and five on a single-sided album. We printed 50 of each and sold them to our local fans back in Cambridge. I still have the master tape, though.

What was your first experience with Bob Dylan? Didn't your dad send you a record from the States?

My mum and dad were living in the States in 1961 to '62, and for my sixteenth birthday they sent me three albums. One was Bob Dylan's first album – in March '62. I think that's before it even came out in England. I also had the complete Newport Folk Festival 1959, and a guy called Eric Darling, who did 'Walk Right In' with The Rooftop Singers – he was

"By nature, I'm a melodic sort of person."

great. I was like a sponge. I just loved all different types of music. The blues, and Eric Clapton when he started was a big influence, Hank, and folk music – it all combined to help create what I've tried to do ever since.

Can you remember the first rehearsal with Pink Floyd?

I can't remember the very first one. But I can remember one of the first, which was in a school in North London. We were all together, and it was with Syd [Barrett], as well. He got us trying to learn a new song called 'Have You Got It Yet?' It's kind of legendary now, and we played this song for hours. Every time he played it, he changed it so we never did 'get it yet' because every time we joined in, he was doing it slightly differently. It was some elaborate, strange joke that he was playing on us.

Right from the start, did it feel like there was something special happening – that alchemy when certain people play together?

I couldn't really say that about my early moments with Pink Floyd. I thought that I could make them better, and I was trying to understand

what they were trying to do, which I didn't completely get right at the beginning. It took me some time to get really into the flow of what they were attempting. My background was mostly covers of pop songs, and I was moving into uncharted territory, into this psychedelic thing, which I did like, but it took a while to find my feet and to know what to do.

In 1973 *Dark Side of the Moon* comes out. This is your first experience with massive, mainstream success, the kind of success that there isn't really a map for. Did you enjoy it? Did you deal with it well, do you think?

It's a lifetime in pop music, but I joined the band in January '68 and that was over five years later. We had been building up a stockpile of records and music. Our audiences were growing and growing. We had, before *Dark Side of the Moon*, done shows at big places like the Hollywood Bowl, so it was a gradual trajectory. I'm very pleased, glad that it took a long time of very gradual movement towards success. I think that it helped. We started out with not much in the way of fame or acclaim or money and the process was, by today's standard, fairly lengthy. Maybe the length and the hard work helped us to not lose it completely at that moment.

I can see very easily how some people are thrust into something that they've always longed for – a world of celebrity, success, money – and you can see how tricky it can be for them. It wasn't quite that fast for us. I think that sudden leap is a dangerous one for a lot of people.

Do you think, looking back, 'I managed to navigate that well?'

Not flawlessly, I have to say, Matt, not flawlessly. Well, you know, all the usual trials and tribulations and temptations of the rock and roll life were dabbled with.

In 1978 you released your first solo record [*David Gilmour*]. Four solo records in 37 years? It's not a lot.

It's massive, isn't it? [Laughs] I don't know how I managed to keep that up.

Is it because you work better within a band environment?

Now, I'm finding it great to be working on my own and with some chosen people. The band environment is one that I did really like and thought I was well suited to, more than being solo. It was never really an ambition to be a solo artist; it sort of comes up on you. The band environment that you get into when you're very young means you have an absolute lack of respect for anyone that you're with, and treat them all as badly as you can treat your family. That's something that, as you get older and more successful, is very hard to recreate. Now people around me often tend to defer to me too much. I'm not always right. Strangely.

That first solo record wasn't really planned at all. I just went into the studio with a couple of guys that I had played with in my band in Cambridge – Willie Wilson and Rick Wills – and we just knocked it out in, I think, about ten days.

The genesis of 'Comfortably Numb' [*The Wall*, 1979] comes from that session, doesn't it?

Well, yes. We recorded the album in a studio in the South of France called Super Bear, and I did write and play the very first demo of what became 'Comfortably Numb' – just strumming on a high-strung guitar. It was too near the end of the sessions to progress it, I'm pleased to say.

The chemistry when Pink Floyd played together, that dynamic, that sensitivity, the sense of pace, the knowledge and familiarity – why did it work with you guys? Where did that come from?

It's hard to know these things. Whether it's just something that happens when you're young and you create a symbiosis by starting together and playing together and spending the amount of time that we did spend together, on the road and in the studio. The calendar sheets for our first two or three years are just every day, you're doing something. You never

"It wasn't quite that fast for us. I think that sudden leap is a dangerous one for a lot of people."

quite spend that same amount of time with people in the same sort of way when you get older, so to achieve that relationship is tough. I think it's in there, but whether you know it's there, whether you recognize what it is and what you have, is another matter. Tons of great musical acts have broken up and you think, 'Why have you broken up? You've got the thing, you've got the chemistry, you've got that something, but you've packed it up to go on and do something maybe not quite as good.'

I'd like to ask about the first time you met Kate Bush. Obviously, there's an enormous connection. When did you first meet?

A guy I knew called Ricky Hopper was a friend of Kate's brother. He came to me one day and said, 'I've got this tape of this fifteen-year-old girl singing, and I think she's talented.' He played it to me and I agreed. But I thought that with her unusual vocal style and sound, it was unlikely that the record company's A&R people would get it instantly. After various tryouts, I decided to employ a full studio, AIR Studios in London, with Geoff Emerick engineering, and with a friend of mine, Andrew Powell, producing and arranging, and I chose two or three songs out of about 50 that she had. I didn't spend a long time choosing. I thought we'd do those to a releasable level so that they weren't demos; they were actually properly 'ready to go' tracks. I thought that was the best way to take her to the record companies to convince them. The song 'The Man with the Child in His Eyes' was one of those three.

When was first musical collaboration with Polly [Samson – novelist and journalist, and Gilmour's wife since 1994]?

The first music collaboration was on [Pink Floyd's 1994] *Division Bell* album. I was trying to inveigle her into helping me to write lyrics. She wanted me to do it, but she was willing to help and she did more, much more, than is indicated on the record sleeve. It looked like I had done more of it than I had, in fact, done – she wrote most of several of the songs on that album. The song 'High Hopes' was a high point. It's much more than just lyrics; she has brutally honest comments on almost every aspect of every song that we're doing, and she's always worth listening to.

***Rattle That Lock* [2015 solo album] includes 'A Boat Lies Waiting', about [late Pink Floyd keyboardist] Rick Wright. Was it a hard decision to write in such an open way about his death?**

It didn't start off being about Rick. I had written and recorded almost the entire musical track for it before Polly came up with those fantastic lyrics. I think the rolling flavour of the piano in the second half of the music suggested waves, and sailing was Rick's life. He had a yacht, and he loved living on it. I remember sitting and thinking, 'What could we do with keyboards at this point? Where's Rick?' Then thinking, 'No, damn. Who should I get that I could trust to do the same sort of job?' It's tricky.

Do you think Rick's role in Pink Floyd was underappreciated?

I think so, yes. He has been underestimated by the public, by the media and by us at times. I hate to say it, but I think we didn't necessarily always give him his proper due. It's very hard … people have different attitudes to the way they work, and we can become very judgmental and think someone's not quite pulling his weight without realizing that theirs is a different weight to pull.

Do you regret not playing more with Rick before he died?

We all went through moments in our lives. We all had difficult times – all the usual temptations and failures that you go through in life – and Rick succumbed to some of that stuff. Some of the time, he became very irritating to be around. I'm trying to be fairly blunt about this. Later on, from around 1993 onward, we realized what we had and we got to be much more accepting of each other's failures and loved what we were doing a lot more. After that, I asked Rick to play on my solo album *On an Island* [2006] and come on the tour with me. We spent a lot of time playing together. He always said that was the best tour he'd ever been on.

The final Pink Floyd album, *The Endless River* [2014] – that title could be interpreted in many ways.

This title came out of wanting to show some sort of continuum with the *Division Bell* album, as it came out of recordings made during the same sessions. But one phrase, a lyric on *Division Bell*, in the song 'High Hopes', is, 'The dawn mist glowing, the water flowing, the endless river, forever and ever.' That's what closes that album. It's an endless, continuing flow of something wonderful that we've helped create.

Do you think the complexities of the interrelationships in the band contributed to making the music so emotionally resonant and profound? Did the difficulties benefit you musically?
God, that's a tough question. My personal view is that I doubt it. We all had very, very different characteristics. Roger was very forceful and a great lyricist. I had a gentler, more melodic musical thing. Rick had his keyboard thing, which just oozed emotion in a strange way. It was one of those lucky things where the whole was greater than the sum of the parts, where we came together and created something that was wonderful.

What's the last song we should play?
Let's do 'In Any Tongue' [from *Rattle That Lock*].

Why that song?
It's a really great track, which'll make you think.

Make you think about what?
Oh, you'll see.

The First Time David Gilmour Playlist

1	Shine On You Crazy Diamond	Pink Floyd
2	Lazy Bones	Paul Robeson
3	Life Gets Teejus, Don't It	Tex Williams
4	Rock Around the Clock	Bill Haley and His Comets
5	Heartbreak Hotel	Elvis Presley
6	Apache	The Shadows
7	The Bells Of Rhymney	Pete Seeger
8	You're No Good	Bob Dylan
9	Set the Controls for the Heart of the Sun	Pink Floyd
10	So Far Away	David Gilmour
11	The Man with the Child in His Eyes	Kate Bush
12	Comfortably Numb	Pink Floyd
13	Famous Blue Raincoat	Leonard Cohen
14	High Hopes	Pink Floyd
15	In Any Tongue	David Gilmour

"Why would I want to remember the first time? It's not like fucking."

DEBBIE HARRY

I can tell Debbie Harry doesn't want to be here. She's jet-lagged and crushed into a small, low-ceilinged dressing room, staring at me, bored, from under an air-conditioning pipe. She's just done a press conference and a succession of swift sound-bite interviews with rows of journalists, and embarking on a far-reaching and detailed conversation about her life isn't that appealing. She's trying to sound like she's interested, but she's definitely not.

I always loved Blondie. From the moment I first saw them, it was obvious they were the coolest gang with the coolest songs from the coolest city in the world. I wanted to play drums like Clem Burke and dress like Chris Stein; and, as a nine-year-old, I didn't quite know what I wanted to do to Debbie Harry, but I wanted to do it really, really badly. I'm remembering all of this as the interview starts to unravel.

In the broom cupboard, the answers are getting shorter and shorter, until we're down to bored, single-word responses. Then even those disappear. That said, Debbie does bored brilliantly: it's not a petulant mood, more a 'Warhol standing at the back of Studio 54' bored. It's a very cool bored.

After listening back to the interview the following day, I realize it's unusable. So there are 24 hours of frantic calls to her management trying to find another window before she flies back to New York. Two days later I'm waiting in the corner of a Kensington hotel foyer for a second attempt. I arrive at 7pm, and at 9pm Debbie emerges from the lift, spots me and stalks across the lobby. She looks over the top of her sunglasses, gives a lupine grin and asks, 'Have we met before?'

Matt Everitt: When were you first aware of music?

Oh, gee, I don't know the first time that I heard it, precisely. It must've been as a very tiny infant, because my mother loved opera and used to have it on the radio all the time. I think one of the first people that I liked was Fats Waller. Then I went into more popular radio stuff: Fats Domino, Chuck Berry and all that crowd. My first big singing heroes? I guess the first ones were Peggy Lee, Patti Page, Rosemary Clooney, Dinah Washington, Ella Fitzgerald and women singers like that. Lena Horne, perhaps.

What about the first single that you actually owned?

Maybe an R&B song. It might've been Fats Domino, or 'Afro Blue' by Cal Tjader from the album *Concert by the Sea*. I don't know. Some of the *Jazz at the College of the Pacific* albums [by the Dave Brubeck Quartet] I really liked. Then I got more into the white rock stuff.

When did you start thinking that this music that you were hearing was something that you wanted to pursue?

I guess it was always sort of a dream. I can't say precisely – it sort of grew. I sang in different choirs and I liked that, but it wasn't exactly what I wanted to do. It just evolved. I started hanging around more with musicians and going to see bands, and stuff like that. I guess that's what really inspired me – seeing other musicians playing.

What were the first bands that you used to go and see?

Different bands, local bands. It's such a long time ago. None of them are around now. I was into jazz early on – Ornette Coleman I liked. I guess the obvious ones, basically; I'm not so well schooled in it. Sun Ra and His Myth Science Arkestra – I used to see him a lot in the park in New York. And Richie Havens – I used to see him on the streets. The Young Rascals I really liked, too.

What was your first band like?

That was a folk rock band, but I had a little singing group in grade school that was called The Fifth Grade Girls Club. We did Platters songs and things like that. We were horrendous. Folk music was really happening then, in the '60s. My friend married this guitarist [Paul Klein from US folk act The Wind in the Willows] who wrote songs, and I would visit and harmonize with him, and that's how I became the back-up singer.

There were a few early bands, including the Stillettos, which is where you first met [Blondie co-founder] Chris Stein, who was playing guitar. What were your first impressions?

Oh, I think we were more friends before we became intimate friends. He was a very nice guy, sweet guy. I think we shared a lot of ideas, and I think that when you're looking for a partnership or a relationship you want to share. You want to have a mutual understanding and appreciation of things, and I think that's where we started off. Our taste was very varied, actually, coming from New York, where we had a lot of ethnic influences. There had been a lot of music coming out of New York; Jimi Hendrix wasn't from New York, but he played there a lot. I think Chris was really enamoured of The Rolling Stones and blues. He really liked Bukka White, and I think my taste ran very close to that. I always was fascinated with the girl groups too, the early R&B girl groups.

What about the first Blondie performance? Can you remember it? Because there were a few line-ups, weren't there?
Oh, yeah. I don't know if I remember exactly the first one. I think it was a three-piece band, so it was very simple. We covered a wide variety of things. A lot of times we didn't play to very big audiences. We did all kinds of bar gigs and stuff.

What about the first time you were aware that Blondie was forming into something that worked musically?
Why would I want to remember the first time? It's not like fucking.

Was it really that bad? Did it take that long for Blondie to find their feet, musically?
Yes, of course. We were going through different members, in and out. It took us a while to make it all gel.

"A lot of my friends are no longer with us, really interesting musicians, and it would've been nice to see how they developed."

You played a lot at CBGB, a venue and a scene that's passed into history. Was it as romantic as people say?
Yes, that's what it was like. It was very inspirational that there were so many different styles and distinctions, because you could really go and appreciate somebody and it just built this excitement. The Ramones I liked very much. I liked Johnny Thunders, I liked Television, I liked Suicide – fantastic performers and interesting songwriters. If you want to look at it as being chaotic, I guess you could, but you'd always have a good night out if you go in to see any of these bands. I sometimes miss it very much because a lot of my friends are no longer with us, really interesting musicians, and it would've been nice to see how they developed, and would've been great to have them around. It was a more innocent time, historically. The city was completely bankrupt and it wasn't gentrified the way it is now, and it was kind of wild and free. It was great.

Can you remember seeing the Ramones for the first time?

They used to do these presentations, they weren't really shows. They would invite people to see them, and Chris knew Tommy, the original drummer. He said, 'Oh, you coming down to see my band? We're playing here at this little sound studio.' We went down and fell in love. They were great, yeah. Their whole set was ten minutes long.

The first Blondie single was 'X Offender' [1976]. What can you remember about that?

It was great. It was verification, or ratification, or whatever – it was a good starting point, a good launching point. They made us change the name. It was called 'Sex Offender', and they said, 'You can't call it that', so we had to change it to 'X Offender'. It became the first 'X' song, the first X that was used in punk. There had never been that before.

That first Blondie album [*Blondie*, 1976] is a really strong record, but it didn't do massively well at the time. Do you remember feeling a bit disappointed when it came out?

Well, it went to number one in Australia and it launched our career. We went around the world on that album, and this was long before any punk bands really got out, so it was a bit strange, but it was a great adventure.

But Britain very much took you to its heart. Can you remember your first trip to London?

It was sort of traumatic, but it was great. We were opening for Television actually, and we got a great response. Television got a great response. It wasn't like we were going out as brothers for the cause. It was a little bit too competitive. We had some really terrible reviews first off – I think after the first trip I stayed in bed for a couple of weeks with the covers over my head from some scathing review – but it turned around.

Did you always think that the band was going to be enormously successful? That you would become as big as you did?

I think anybody who joins a band in this day and age thinks that they're going to be mega superstars. They want to fulfil that rock and roll dream for themselves. I think that's part of it, yeah.

In 1978, you released *Plastic Letters* and *Parallel Lines*. Firstly, that's two albums in one year, which is impressive; secondly, *Parallel Lines* turned Blondie into this world-straddling band.

And six tracks off that record were all singles. We had paid our dues, and that's what we were working for. It's a little nerve-wracking. It starts out a little bit confusing, but that's what you aim for.

The level of fame that the band enjoyed – a staggering amount of attention. Did you disconnect from reality a little bit?

I don't know if I disconnected from reality, but the reality *changed*.

The reality became something else, so my life was a little less … It was more public. I just had a more public life.

'Heart of Glass' is such a pioneering recording in the use of synthesizers, in the whole feel of the track. Was it very heavily influenced by discos and going out?

I think that was the big contest between disco and rock. Chris [Stein] brought in this little rhythm machine, and set up that *ticka, ticka, ticka* beginning, that little beat, and it just evolved from there. We had that song for about five years before we actually recorded it. It just worked.

Then you have 'Rapture', which everyone says was the first song that was released that had a recorded rap on it.

Not quite, but the first one to go into the charts, reach number one. We had been to see some great little shows, and meet Grandmaster Flash and The Funky 4 Plus 1, and it just seemed like an obvious thing to do.

You spoke in the past about Blondie's predilection for indulgence. Was there ever a point where you thought that the partying or drug use was putting the band's future in doubt? Did it ever become a serious problem?

I think in general for a band, and for most young people growing up, there's that urge to party and to experiment and try things. It doesn't mix well with business in any way, in any business. It's just a waste of time. A lot of fun, but a waste of time. Most people either die or grow out of it. There's very few people that survive and continue taking drugs their entire lives. That's it.

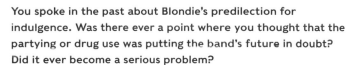

"I don't know if I disconnected with reality, but the reality changed. The reality became something else, so my life was … more public."

When did you decide to split the band up?

Well, the band sort of disbanded. It just sort of fell apart; it wasn't a decision, really. Everything just sort of crumbled, business-wise and personnel-wise. Our record label dropped us, management walked out, and we were dealing with a bunch of problems, and that's just what happened. It was very complicated, period. Very complicated. A lot of issues. It wasn't just Chris's illness [In 1983, Stein was diagnosed with a rare auto-immune skin disease], it was a whole series of things that collapsed. Everything collapsed simultaneously – it just was kind of impossible to carry on. It exploded and imploded simultaneously.

Did you miss it?

No. It was kind of a relief. It was so problematic at the time. What I hear most from young artists is, 'We don't have a manager'. You really need a manager, and that kind of relationship is actually as intimate and as important as another member of the band. It's hard, because business people don't think the way musicians think.

In 1998 you reformed Blondie. What was the decision behind that? It had been quite a while. Was that a tough thing to do?

We had an interest from a management company. Chris also was thinking that if we didn't do it now, we would never get it done. It was timely to do it. They convinced me that we should do it.

Did it take a lot of convincing?

A little bit, yeah. I think that's always the way it is with bands, unless you have terrific management. We always had management problems. Everybody was off balance a little bit – there was no place to settle. That's a very important part of it.

"A lot of the female singers were singing about being in a position of victimization somehow, so to take an aggressive stance seemed like the right thing to do."

Since then, you've had something of a renaissance with your live performances. It seems there's a whole new generation of fans and people that have fallen for the band.

Yeah, it's wonderful. It's kind of a miracle, really. I wouldn't go there, in truth, but it's completely satisfying and wonderful. I think we're doing better now than the original band. I think this band is really terrific.

Do you see yourself as being a ground-breaking figure in music? Because the word 'icon' gets used a lot.

[Growls] That's not good. That word is just completely overused.

But you were definitely an influential figure, and your work still stands up, and people do reference you as being a strong, articulate, single-minded figure.

I guess in a way it was a sign of the times. It was a 'down' period economically, and there wasn't a lot of value placed on what we were doing. I never really thought of myself as a victim, and I really objected to that lyrically. A lot of the female singers were singing about being in a position of victimization somehow, so to take an aggressive stance … I don't know. It just seemed like the right thing to do, and we found other people that were thinking the same way. The pendulum swings back and forth, styles change, and that's what we were part of, fortunately.

I'd like you to pick the final song. What should we play?
Oh, I don't know. God, I'm practically brain-dead. I think something from the new album [*Panic of the Girls*, 2011] I really like – 'Mother'. I like 'Mother' a lot. 'Mother' is about a club that I used to go to [in the Meatpacking District of Manhattan, New York]. It's closed now, but it had gone on for ten years, and it wasn't like a normal club: it was a theme club where you would dress up every week in a different theme. It was great and a lot of fun, and I used to go there. When it closed it was [gasps], 'What do I do now?' By the way, that's one of my favourite all-time lyrics that I've written. I just feel like, 'Wow. I really got succinct and down to the point really quickly, and simply.' I like it.

The First Time Debbie Harry Playlist

1	Rapture	Blondie
2	The Joint Is Jumpin'	Fats Waller
3	This Bitter Earth	Dinah Washington
4	Afro Blue	Cal Tjader
5	Strange Fruit	Nina Simone
6	Somewhere in Space	Sun Ra and His Myth Science Arkestra
7	Good Lovin'	The Young Rascals
8	Pink Stilettos	The Stillettos
9	Sheena Is a Punk Rocker	Ramones
10	X Offender	Blondie
11	See No Evil	Television
12	Picture This	Blondie
13	That's the Joint	Funky 4 Plus 1
14	Well, Did You Evah!	Debbie Harry and Iggy Pop
15	One Way or Another	Jazz Passengers feat. Debbie Harry
16	Mother	Blondie

"Somewhere in the back of my mind is a place that ... I'm better inside of myself."

EDWYN COLLINS

I never had an opportunity to interview Edwyn before he suffered the brain haemorrhages that changed the course of his life in 2005. I never spoke to the strident, chatty, self-deprecating man who fronted Scotland's indie guitar heroes Orange Juice and released the '90s global superhit 'A Girl Like You'; instead, I meet a strident, chatty, self-deprecating, slightly older man who finds it very, very hard to speak the words in his head.

We meet in Edwyn's own recording studios in West London, which is jammed, floor to ceiling, with a career's worth of weird guitars and ancient keyboards. He ambles in slowly, holding a cane, wearing a rather splendid duffle coat and modish check shirt, accompanied by his wife and manager, Grace. He's partially paralyzed on his right side, and his still-boyish features sag a little, but he's smiling, shaking hands, greeting everyone and talking proudly about plans to move the studio to the Collins family seat in Helmsdale, Sutherland. Considering that just eight years previously he almost died and couldn't walk, talk, read or sing, this in itself is nothing short of remarkable.

Edwyn's speech is hesitant. Each sentence is dotted with *um*s and *ah*s, tenses skip around, and he often pauses – patiently, without any apparent frustration – while he tries to find the right name. He is, however, very funny – his laugh is a joyous and cartoonish *hurr, hurr, hurr* – and he'll often start singing to illustrate a lyric. Reading this back, I don't think it really captures the joy in the interview. I remember how welcome I was made to feel, Grace's affectionate piss-taking and Edwyn's laughter. There's was more enthusiasm and fun than the words on the page might suggest.

Teaching himself to sketch animals formed part of Edwyn's rehabilitation, and after the interview he gives me a print of a linocut he'd done of a salmon as a gift. It's so beautifully drawn, and I'm so taken by his and Grace's generosity, that I'm left speechless.

Matt Everitt: Can you remember first being aware of music?
Yes. Donovan. I was eight years old, I think. 'Jennifer Juniper' and 'Poor Cow' on the B-side. Oh, it's a classic. 'Jennifer Juniper' is for kids, basically, but my mum bought it for me. And 'Poor Cow' on the B-side? It's a slow song, an acoustic song, and it's got deep meaning for me. It repeats a melody and it's so emotional for me.

So, even very early on, you had an emotional connection with music?
Yeah. Possibly. When I was fourteen years old, I bought David Bowie – in Boots in Dundee – *The Rise and Fall of Ziggy Stardust* and *Aladdin Sane*. 'Watch That Man' and 'Starman' and everything else. Still good albums.

What was the thing that you think attracted you to Bowie?
The '70s stuff, and the '80s, was not so bad. But by the time the '90s came? [Laughs] *Low*, *The Man Who Sold the World* and *Young Americans* – it's all good stuff. *Hunky Dory* is him experimenting on an acoustic and electric album. To me, *Hunky Dory* is the real thing. 'Quicksand' is a classic.

Let's go back to your first guitar. What was it?
A Hofner – made in Germany – and I bought a Nu-Sonic Burns guitar at the time I moved to Glasgow, in the [indoor weekend market] Barras guitar shop. I got it for 20 quid.

A pretty classic guitar?
Yeah, but it goes out of tune. I've still got them. The original Nu-Sonic is in the studio.

Who did you want to be when you first started practising on your guitar? In your mind, who were you?
David Bowie [laughs]. I loved him. Nowadays, I don't. But I loved him as a small boy. What can I say?

What about your first gig – the first gig that you went to that really made an impression on you? Who was that?
It was Sparks, and supporting was Pilot! – [starts singing Pilot's soft rock classic 'Magic'] 'Whoa, whoa, whoa, it's magic!' – and I went to see them at the Caird Hall, Dundee. *Kimono My House* [1974] and *Propaganda* [1974] were coming out, the albums, and I wore my flared trousers.

What about your first band?
The Nu-Sonics. Oh no, tell a lie. Back in Dundee it was [heavy rock band] Onyx. I played a banjo and they threw me out the band!

What about your first proper band, then?
Yeah, the Nu-Sonics. Steven Daly, the original singer, transferred to drums; Alan Duncan on bass; James Kirk on guitar and that was it.

I remember ['80s pop duo] Strawberry Switchblade – the original Strawberry Switchblade was a song; James Kirk wrote it, but he donated it to Strawberry Switchblade, the band. He coined it. And I wrote 'Ready, Steady, Go'. I admit it was terrible. Its chorus was, 'Ready, steady, go, go, go. Ready, steady, go. Ready, steady, go, go, go. Ready, steady, go.' I wrote that song when I was seventeen years old. Then 'Falling and Laughing'.

What do you remember about recording 'Falling and Laughing', that first single?
In Paisley, on 8-track, I remember. I was twenty at the time. Young and trendy! My original vocalist Steven Daly on the drums, David McClymont on bass, James Kirk on guitar, and also me on guitar. The B-side was called 'Moscow Olympics', a reggae version – James Scott said to me, 'I'm pitching for the Moscow Olympics' [laughs].

The Seeds is a band that you've mentioned. Have you always had a love of garage rock?
I love garage rock. I bought [iconic 1972 US underground rock compilation album] *Nuggets*. What's Patti Smith's original guitarist called? Grace: Lenny Kaye?
Yes. Lenny Kaye. He compiled the songs. [The Seeds'] 'Pushin' Too Hard' – and [Seeds singer] Sky Saxon, he's dead of course – to me, it's full of vigour, the song. It's a good single.

I've got to talk about 'Rip It Up'. It was your first big single, a classic, and it made you a pop star for the first time. Did you enjoy that?
Yes, very much. I admit I did enjoy it. It reached a great height, number eight, I think, in 1983. I did the bass on a Roland 303.

"Nile Rodgers! I ripped off Chic for the rhythm line!"

Which would go on to become the acid house keyboard!
Yeah! But it was quite new at the time. I bought it in Denmark Street, and I wanted to experiment. The Roland bassline, it's kind of like Chic.

I hadn't thought about it that way. It is.
[Laughs] Nile Rodgers! I ripped off Chic for the rhythm line!

Someone that you've said was an influence, which, although a brilliant band, I wouldn't have expected, is Creedence Clearwater Revival.
I bought Creedence Clearwater Revival's album, *Cosmo's Factory,* back

in Orange Juice days. It's still great. At the Mojo Awards, two years ago, I presented to [Creedence singer] John Fogerty! Ahhh! So great! I presented to John Fogerty! Imagine that? I'm a fan, let's say, especially of Creedence Clearwater Revival.

What songs should we play of theirs?
'Born on the Bayou'. The Memphis chords on it. It's so classic.

You've done a lot of producing over the years, as well as being a musician. How do you approach that role?
Seb, my engineer, and I work well together in the control area, and the band is there, and I work it out. For example, take, say, The Cribs – Ross and Gary and Ryan [Jarman] and *The New Fellas* [2005 Cribs album produced by Collins] and the single 'Hey Scenesters!' I'm not pushing them; they're creative and it kind of works out. Plus they're nice lads and Seb and I work well together. I did The Proclaimers too, and they're lovely lads.

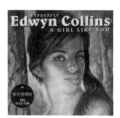

It's about finding people you like?
Yeah, yeah, exactly.

We can't talk about your life without talking about 'A Girl Like You'. When you first finished that, was that a case of 'That's the mortgage sorted! That's going to do all right'?
No. Forty-eight hours later, it's done.

Quick as that?
Yeah. Possibly. It was a good song at the time. I did realize, back in Great Britain, that it's a good song, but around the world? I didn't realize at all. Japan, Korea, Hong Kong. All around Europe – Germany, France, Holland, Sweden. All around America. It wore me out. A year and seven months all around the world.

"I don't remember that time. Grace does, but I don't. I'm haemorrhaging away in the ambulance, and I don't remember."

Did you ever get a bit sick of the attention? Sick of the song?
By the end of it, I was pooped out, let's say, and exhausted and I needed a rest, but I didn't realize towards the end of it, my eyes were puffy. That's high blood pressure, the first sign of it.

Grace: You went to a doctor, didn't you, feeling weird. He said, 'Your blood pressure's up', and he put you on some beta-blockers. And you had some rest after that, came back down, and didn't think anything about it until years later.

Was that the first sign of what was to become ...
Yes, it was. Puffy eyes and a constant headache, and I took eight tablets a day – Solpadeine tablets – to get rid of my headache. But nowadays, I don't take Solpadeine, or paracetamol, nothing. But I take three pills, 24 hours a day, and it seems to work, the tablets. For blood pressure. Grace: Gentlemen, check your blood pressure! [Laughs] The root of all this. We were idiots. It's ignorance about blood pressure.

If I can ask you, what do you remember about having the haemorrhage? How much do you recall?
No. I don't remember that time. Grace does but I don't. I'm haemorrhaging away in the ambulance, and I don't remember the time.

The myth is that you could only say four things afterwards.
Yeah.

"'The possibilities are endless' – it's a good catchphrase."

Is that true? 'Yes', 'No', 'Grace', and 'The possibilities are endless'.
Yes, it was.

There's something really wonderful about that.
But over and over again, 'The possibilities are endless. The possibilities are endless ...' Some people say I'm daft.

I wondered, because you read things on the internet, and you're like, 'Oh, they're not necessarily true,' but ...
No, it was at the time.

There's just something quite lovely about that – Grace's name and 'The possibilities are endless'. Where does that come from? It's rather wonderful, don't you think?
Yeah, yeah, yeah, I suppose . . . 'The possibilities are endless' – it's a good catchphrase. But I'm working, too: for example, my speech is completely away. But somewhere in the back of my mind is a place that ... I'm better inside of myself. And it's a place that's 'Think and think and rethink' and

I'm trying to find … My speech is fucked … No, scrub that. Something in the back of my mind is going on, and on … See what I mean, Matt?

It's a weird feeling. I know I'm striving to capture my songs, and Grace and William, my son – it's sometimes striving and striving and striving to capture this mood. Sometimes, of course, I'm unwell, and it seems to be a kind of vision I strive for.

It must have been a relief when you realized you could still write great songs.
Yeah, yeah, it was. My singing is coming on. My speech is not coming on. It is a bit, my speech, but it takes time.

'Losing Sleep' [2010] was the first thing that you released and recorded, after the haemorrhage. It's a great song. There must have been a certain sense of 'Yes! It's there, I can do this!'
Yeah. Part of what it is, is I'm losing sleep, I'm losing dignity – I'm struggling to find the words to say what I'm meaning. So, it's a challenge [laughs]. I'm fine with the chorus, but the verse takes a lot of time to think of the meaning.

I want to talk about The Isley Brothers – other artists that you love. When did you first let them into your life?
I don't remember. Oh, now I do. What's that? [Hums tune] 'Summer Breeze'. And I like 'My Love Is Your Love (Forever)' – northern soul. But 'Summer Breeze', it's a cover version.
Grace: So somebody covered it, or they covered it?
No. Isleys covered it.

Somebody covered 'Summer Breeze'?
Yes. Right.
[Frantic phone Googling.]
Grace: Seals and Crofts! You're right, Edwyn. Seals and Crofts.
[Triumphantly] Seals and Crofts!

I can hear a lot of soul in the new record [*Understated*, 2013].
Yeah.

Did you used to go to those northern soul clubs?
No. But I was seventeen years old at the time and I used to go to Shuffles, it was called, the club, down in the basement, in Glasgow on Argyles Street. Apparently, Grace is saying to me, back in the day, I wasn't a very good dancer [laughs].

There's this whole generation of fans that have discovered you – when Franz Ferdinand broke through, they namechecked you a lot – a whole other generation of people getting into your stuff. That must be nice.

It is. Basically, it flatters me, Matt. It's good to be flattered [laughs]. But some people still don't get it, my songs. 'Not for me!' the guys and the girls say. But so what?

The final thing we ask everybody on the show is to pick the last song that we'll play. What should we go out on?
What I do every morning, I dig out my album of the day. It's a 7-inch single, and I find it on YouTube, and put it on my Facebook and Twitter.

What was a recent one that you liked?
Oh! 'Groovin'' – The Young Rascals.

Okay, why that song?
It's a good '60s single. Soul and pop combined. A medium tempo. [Starts singing] 'Groovin', on a Sunday afternoon …' It's a summer's day, out on the beach, and it's atmospheric and emotional [laughs].

Then that's the song we should play. It's been a pleasure to speak to you.
Thank you, Matt.

The First Time Edwyn Collins Playlist

1	A Girl Like You	Edwyn Collins
2	Poor Cow	Donovan
3	Quicksand	David Bowie
4	Amateur Hour	Sparks
5	Magic	Pilot
6	Falling and Laughing	Orange Juice
7	Pushin' Too Hard	The Seeds
8	Rip It Up	Orange Juice
9	Born on the Bayou	Creedence Clearwater Revival
10	Hey Scenesters!	The Cribs
11	Born Innocent	The Proclaimers
12	Rock & Roll	The Velvet Underground
13	Summer Breeze	Seals and Crofts
14	Losing Sleep	Edwyn Collins
15	My Love Is Your Love (Forever)	The Isley Brothers
16	Groovin'	The Young Rascals

"Music's been my companion since I was three years old. I'm an anorak. I'm a fan."

ELTON JOHN

We all have an idea of Elton John – as we do for all celebrities – a powerful image in our minds about who he is: flamboyant glasses, a furious temper, outrageous outfits and reawakened hair, acclaimed charity work and his position as a trusted godmother to wayward celebrities. Everyone acknowledges Elton's musicianship and incredible back catalogue, but from the very first moment I meet him, I realize his defining characteristic is that he's a music fan – an endlessly enthusiastic, vinyl-loving, lifelong obsessive.

He's wearing a sharp blue suit, Tequila Sunrise–tinted glasses and a bejewelled brooch that definitely cost more than my house. Right from the off, he's friendly and charming, talking fast and answering my questions quickly and candidly – addressing even his own debauched past head-on, without a flinch of self-pity. But when we discuss other musicians, especially new ones, it's obvious how passionate he is.

There's a myth that in the peak of his drug-fuelled egomania Elton called the front desk of a hotel he was staying in, fuming about the overcast view from his window and demanding the hotel staff 'make it stop raining'. But there's no ranting or diva-ish behaviour on display. I'm just sitting here discussing Kraftwerk and Florence and The Machine with a fellow fan – albeit one who sits just behind Elvis Presley and The Beatles in the list of the most successful artists in the history of the American charts.

Matt Everitt: When were you first aware of music?

It must have been a record or the radio. We had a very musical family, and the radiogram was a big central piece in the living room and all the people in my family bought records. So it was probably Mario Lanza, or maybe [Alberto] Semprini? I was fascinated by records from an early age – just watching them go around on a 78, thinking, 'How did this sound come out of this round thing?' I had a piano, I had a record player, and everything revolved around music. My family loved it.

What about the first record that was yours?

The first 45 I owned was 'At The Hop' by Danny and the Juniors and 'Reet Petite' by Jackie Wilson. Music has been my companion since I was three years old. In times of joy and in times of solace, I've always listened to new stuff; I've always bought records. I'm an anorak. I'm a fan. In 1970 and '71 there was Musicland, on Berwick Street in London, and every Saturday I worked behind the counter. I was fascinated with what people bought. I just loved being around 78s, 45s, EPs, LPs, cassettes, 8-tracks.

We've got a question from someone, a friend of yours ...

John Grant: Elton, it's John Grant. I was wondering – not that I want to bore you to death – who was the first pianist that first made you want to become one yourself?

John Grant? Is he here?

He's in the UK at the moment.

Wow. Got to phone him, then. My first pianist hero was Winifred Atwell, a Trinidadian black lady who was very popular in the '50s. She would play a grand piano when she was doing something classical, and then she'd say, 'And now I'm going over to my other piano!' which was a honky-tonk upright, and she would play pub songs. I loved her. I wanted to be like her. When I first went to Australia she'd moved there to be with her husband, and I met her.

What was she like?

It was one of the best things in my life. She was my hero. She was the person that I really loved because she played the piano so joyously. She was incredibly successful, but it was her vitality. Like Liberace. It was a performance rather than just playing the piano, and that was what Winifred Atwell was about. And then, of course, it translated into Jerry Lee Lewis and Little Richard, which took it to another level completely.

You're a big fan of John Grant's work?

I think he's one of the most important artists of our time. I've been a friend of his through the bad times and now the great times, and I'm very proud of him because he came from a very dark place. When he said in *The Guardian* that he was HIV-positive, it seemed like a whole weight was lifted and he started to fly again. His music just flew. He's an artist that will be around forever, and he will always be taken seriously because he has a lot to say, and he says it brilliantly and with a lot of wit. Kind of like a gay Randy Newman [laughs]. He sang on the *Goodbye Yellow Brick Road* album that we re-did. There's nothing about him that I don't love.

There's a YouTube montage of you singing 'Your Song', from 1970 through to now. Fashions change, the voice changes, but you never phone it in, you never go through the motions.
It's very strange. The more I sing Bernie's lyrics – especially the ones I sing *a lot*, you know? – the more I love them. Every time I sing 'Tiny Dancer', 'Levon', 'Your Song', 'Daniel', something else happens … I don't know. They're just lyrics that you never get tired of singing. I'm lucky to have had a lyric writer that the more I sing their lyrics, the better they get, and that's astonishing. 'Indian Sunset' from *Madman Across the Water* [1971]: when I sing that song [in Las Vegas] I sing it with Ray Cooper, my percussion player, and it goes down better than anything else in the show. The lyrics are so beautiful and so relevant now. Because he's a storyteller, he doesn't date himself.

"The more I sing Bernie's lyrics ... the more I love them."

I listened to *17-11-70*, your first live record. There's a real parallel with that and *Wonderful Crazy Night* [2016]. That band! You are all kicking seven bells out of the performance.
17-11-70 was not supposed to be a live record. It was the first FM radio broadcast done in Phil Ramone's recording studio in New York for ABC Radio. It wasn't meant to be a record, but because bootlegs were so popular at the time, and we were bootlegged up the wazoo, we put it out. It's one of the few records of mine that I listen to. It's the power of the three-piece, the freedom. Bands like The Who; The Jimi Hendrix Experience; Emerson, Lake and Palmer: there's something about a three piece band, you have the space. My musicians are [drummer] Nigel Olsson, and Dee Murray, who was an incredible bass player and singer. I went off on tangents and they would follow me, instinctively.

There's a documentary about Nina Simone called *What Happened, Miss Simone?*, and the guitar player said, 'She would suddenly change key in the middle of the song and I would just follow her.' And it's extraordinary when you get that nuance between a performer and a musician; my band at that time did it, and the band that I have now do it. When we wrote the song 'In the Morning' [1969], they'd come in, learn the chords and play it through with me, and go out and do one take. I didn't tell them what to play, they just *knew* because they're fabulous musicians.

Nigel and Davey [Johnstone – guitarist], of course, have been with me a long time and they play exceptionally brilliantly, and I haven't made an album with them for quite a while, but this [*Wonderful Crazy Night*] is the climax of something that we've been playing on stage.

What Nina track should we play?

'Here Comes the Sun'. We did a Beatles programme. Trudie Styler, who organized it, said, 'Should we have Nina Simone? She's a bit of trouble?' I said, 'You've got to have her! Assign her to me! I'll look after her.' And she couldn't have been any sweeter. I was so intimidated by her and she was so lovely. She'd had a stroke, but she sang 'Here Comes the Sun' and she melted my heart. For me she was the greatest artist of the twentieth century, bar none. Forget The Beatles, forget the Stones, forget Dylan, Presley, any of them, Sinatra, Louis Armstrong … Nina Simone walks over all of them. She covered every territory from classical music to writing songs about the Freedom March, to covering new songs by The Beatles. Anyway, at the end of the evening she sat in a chair and she cried because she got a standing ovation, and I'll never forget it. And she never played again. I was running over, giving her a Kleenex and stuff like that. I was just her maid in waiting, I was so honoured to be on the same billing as she was.

John Lennon joined you on stage at the gig at Madison Square Garden [1974]: it was last time he performed in front of an audience. When did you first meet him?

He was doing a video and Tony King, who works for me now [as a creative director] and used to work for John back then, was dressed as the Queen in one of his music videos at Capital, and I went to meet him. We got on like a house on fire, we hung out together for a couple of years.

"Forget The Beatles, forget the Stones, Dylan, Presley, any of them … Nina Simone walks over all of them."

Why do you think you clicked?

Sense of humour. I found him very kind, very funny. I don't know why we clicked, but we did; we had so much fun. I was quite intimidated by him, because I knew he was razor-sharp and could be very abrasive. But only the kind side and the funny side ever came out with me.

Those recordings from Madison Square Garden are amazing.

Yeah. I've always had good bands and that is why I think I've survived. Playing live is such an important thing, and having a good band is so essential to keeping your enthusiasm up. I've seen so many bands go through the motions. It's why I got out of my old band, Bluesology, because we were going through the motions. So the Lennon thing was quite remarkable. I played *his* last gig … I played in Nina Simone's last gig at the Rainforest Foundation [11th Annual Carnegie Hall Benefit Concert, 2002] and Elizabeth Taylor did her last work with me in 'Original Sin' [2002] in the video. So three incredible legends, I've done their last things with them.

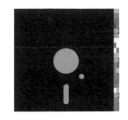

When you started your Rocket Hour radio show, the first song you played was New Order's 'Blue Monday', I believe?
First track I played was Florence and The Machine and 'Ship to Wreck', but the last track was New Order's 'Blue Monday'. It's a fucking amazing record. I've always loved electronic music – always. There are lots of musicians who hate it, hate synthesizers. I absolutely love it. Kraftwerk? I remember getting stoned and listening to *Trans-Europe Express* at my house at Windsor at full volume and thinking I'd seen God. It's amazing. I get up in the morning and I'll put on dance music; I love it. I wouldn't know how to make it, but I accept it and I enjoy it so much.

You've always been very honest about your drug addictions. Can you remember the first point when you were like, 'If I keep on doing this, it's not going to end well'?
Well, I was still working, and I was still listening, and I was still making records, which kept me alive. I didn't take three years off and sit in my room every day doing coke, otherwise I wouldn't be talking to you now. One of the nights I remember … I was in a hotel somewhere and I played 'Don't Give Up' by Peter Gabriel and Kate Bush, and 'Lost Soul' by Bruce Hornsby and Shawn Colvin, and then I played the Enigma Variations [by Edward Elgar], and I just cried and cried, because I thought, 'You're so sick, but you want to live.' I knew I had a big problem, and even though I was crying, music was helping me get through that.

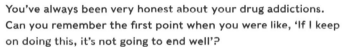

The problem with me is I'm so stubborn; I just couldn't ask for help. When I did ask for help everything changed immediately. It was really Ryan White dying, when I went to his funeral and spent the week in Indianapolis, that I realized my life had reached rock bottom. I looked dreadful, I was so overweight. Six months later I was in rehab, because I thought, 'This boy's got AIDS, he's had it since he was eleven or twelve, he's never complained to anybody. He's been so incredible. His family are incredible.' And I go back to the hotel suite and think, 'Fucking wallpaper. I hate it!' So, that's probably the nadir. And then six months later I was clean. I always say to him and his family a huge thank you, because he showed me, through life and through death, that there was more to life than what I was doing. I was so ashamed and disgusted with myself.

You're still playing live loads. I've got this theory that for some artists, you've been doing it for so long it's your normal state. Do you feel more like yourself on stage than anywhere else?

I'm comfortable with myself on stage now; I'm enjoying playing more than I've ever done. I'm singing better, I'm playing as well as I've ever done, I have the best band since the three-piece. I'm in the prime of my life as a performer, and I wanted to translate that into the record. I'm so happy with it because it's captured what we do on stage – and we really are kick-ass on stage.

You've done so many amazing things, performed with so many incredible musicians. What advice are you going to give your kids? Because it is an unusual life that you've led.

They have no idea what I do; they're not interested. They like coming on stage, but they like shining the torches out in the audience. They like music, but they like 'Uptown Funk' [Mark Ronson] and they like 'Happy' [Pharrell Williams]. They sing 'Bennie and the Jets', they sing 'Rocket Man', but they're young boys – they're interested in Lego.

"I didn't take three years off and sit in my room every day doing coke, otherwise I wouldn't be talking to you now."

When they get older, and they get to a point where they're starting to mature, what advice can dad give?

They'll probably look at me very scarily! 'Oh my God. You did that? You did this? You dressed up like that?!' What advice would I give them? Just be yourselves. I'm not going to force them to do anything. They live a very, very lucky life, but I want them to work for their money. I came from a working-class background, and I earned my money with very hard work. And I loved it. I think a silver spoon is no good to anybody.

They're in a very difficult position because they're sons of someone very famous. Let them be whoever they are and just guide them, and love them and tell them what's right from wrong, and don't spoil them. If they want a new car, they're going to have to pay for it. And they're going to have a second-hand car to start with. That's what I had. They have to have a sense of value. It's a difficult balance when you live my kind of life. But at the moment they're great, just like normal kids.

What's the best thing about being Elton John?

There are certain things that can be a pain – paparazzi, camera phones – but they're all outweighed by the fact that I've had such a long career. The best thing about being Elton John is that I'm still in love with music, as much as I was when I was three years old. It's so important to me and I love making it, I love recording. I like being able to use my voice, and, being gay, to try and help things for other people in less fortunate positions than myself. I'm a good schmoozer. I can meet people and I have a certain respect because of the way the [Elton John] AIDS Foundation has been run. I can hold my own in the Senate, I can hold my own in Congress, you know? I know how to behave in certain situations. The older I get, the more I want to try and change life for those people whose lives are absolutely awful compared to how we live over here.

Using my notoriety, or fame, to make the world a better place goes hand-in-hand with music. I'm aware of the power I have to do that, but I don't want to boast about it; I just want to get on with it.

What's the song we should play last? Anything you want.
For my funeral? 'Ding Dong the Witch Is Dead' [laughs]. I'd like to play something from the new album: 'Guilty Pleasure'. It's the most up-tempo song I've ever done apart from 'Your Sister Can't Twist'. If I was a punk, that would have been the punk song I'd have done.

The First Time **Elton John** Playlist

1	Levon	Elton John
2	La Mer (The Sea)	Alberto Semprini
3	At the Hop	Danny and The Juniors
4	Reet Petite	Jackie Wilson
5	The Poor People of Paris	Winifred Atwell
6	Sweet Painted Lady	John Grant
7	Your Song	Elton John
8	Someone to Watch Over Me	George Gershwin
9	Honky Tonk Woman	Elton John
10	Here Comes the Sun	Nina Simone
11	Whatever Gets You Thru the Night	John Lennon/Elton John
12	Blue Monday	New Order
13	Trans-Europe Express	Kraftwerk
14	Don't Give Up	Peter Gabriel and Kate Bush
15	Lost Soul	Bruce Hornsby
16	My Terracotta Heart	Blur
17	Guilty Pleasure	Elton John

"I've just always been quite attracted to morbid, kind of gothic fantasy."

FLORENCE WELCH

The first time I interviewed Florence was after a gig that culminated in her leaping into the venue's ornamental fountain, then crawling under the tiny stage and not coming out. It was a showcase in a small bar at the annual South by Southwest music-industry festival in Austin, Texas, in March 2008. We'd only heard one song by then, and she was accompanied on stage by one guitarist – the only other instrumentation came from Florence herself walloping a drum. Apart from a splash of gold glitter across her face and a sequined cropped jacket, there are no theatrics when she walks onstage; she's tall, with bare feet at the end of long legs, and a big mess of dark copper hair. When she speaks on stage, she's chatty, garbled, funny and totally unaffected by the audience talking amongst themselves. But then she starts singing. And they all stop.

I interviewed her again just before she took to the stage at the Glastonbury Festival in 2010. By then she was high up the bill, her debut album *Lungs* had sold over two million copies and won the British Album of the Year award at the Brits, and her costumes were being designed by Gucci. She'd also been on tour essentially non-stop since the Austin show: I'm reckoning 206 gigs in just over two years. She's shaved off her eyebrows, her face is pale, her hair is dyed bright scarlet and she's wearing a feathery white bodysuit with a gauzy cape. She's exhausted, limp, totally dazed and completely disconnected from her surroundings; I remember thinking about Bowie's lost space traveller in *The Man Who Fell to Earth*. Our interview is disjoined and brief before she's ushered up on stage to join her 11-piece band, and I actually start worrying whether she's going to be capable of performing, whether the success, attention and motion has broken her. Then she starts singing. And I stop.

Matt Everitt: When were you first aware of music as kid?
I think it was probably Disney movies, and learning the songs from them. Ariel [*The Little Mermaid*, 1989] had a really big impact on me [laughs]. You know, it's the first film I ever went to see. And it's interesting because that's all about her voice; she loses her voice. But I think, also, singing hymns in school assemblies and at church in school.

What about the first single that you had?
The first single I remember buying myself on CD was Eminem, 'My Name Is'. I must have been maybe eleven? Before that I had The Corrs on tape. I loved them. And I had the Spice Girls on tape. I had a Coca-Cola CD player – I was really little. I stuck the album sleeve on the wall – The Corrs! I did listen to No Doubt. And then I got into American skate punk and Green Day's *Dookie* was the first record that I bought. Before that there was, you know, a bit of The Corrs in there [laughs].

And the first album was *Dookie*?
Yeah, and I think that's the first time I thought of music not only as just music, but as an identity that you could have. I started going to ska gigs and going to Download Festival. It was not only that you listened to the music, but it meant you fancied a certain kind of boy, you wore a certain kind of clothes, you hung out with a certain kind of people. And you could congregate together in school, the same people, and my three best friends then became the other three girls at school who dressed like teenage skaters.

What was the first gig that you went to?
The Voodoo Glow Skulls at the London Astoria! They were a ska punk band. But my actual first gig – I think my parents took me to it – was Nick Cave, which was really good. But I didn't … I'm such an enormous fan now, but when I went, I didn't even recognize what an amazing opportunity that was. I think it just washed over me. But the first gig that I went to was the Voodoo Glow Skulls at the Astoria. And our friend's dad had to sneak us in by wearing a suit and pretending he was an A&R man, but who had brought all these kids. It was weird [laughs].

You mentioned Nick Cave. When was the first time that you fell in love with Nick Cave's music? What was the record that made a big impact on you?
Do you know what, I've always been a fan, but this latest record has just completely blown me away – I think it was 'Jubilee Street'. He took music to a place that I longed to go. That's where I want to get to. You know, when I'm listening to something or I'm making something, that feeling is what I'm looking for. I mean, there are songs that sometimes make me have to lie down on the floor, and I can't move, I'm so overcome by them. I've always had that feeling from certain songs, and I think that song is so magical.

What was the first band you were in? There seem to be lots of different bands and different names. Where did it start?

Well, I started a band at school called Flo and the Roses, which my friend Rosie was in. I wrote lots of dramatic love songs about break-ups that hadn't happened because I hadn't had a boyfriend! It was ridiculous, all this pseudo-romantic stuff. I used to get into trouble for writing lyrics in library books. But yeah, loads of really, really heartfelt heartbreak songs. I mean, I didn't even have a boyfriend until I was eighteen!

When was the first Florence and The Machine gig, then? What do you remember from the first incarnation?

It was at a Christmas party. But, actually, my name then was Florence Robot Is a Machine. My friend Isa Machine [Isabella Summers], who's still in the band, wrote 'Dog Days Are Over' with me, and that's where it all started. I was Florence Robot, she was Isa Machine. There was like a big folk scene going on in London at the time, and I was at art college and I wanted to do music, but this band didn't exist. Florence Robot Is a Machine – it was just me. There was no band.

"I think, in my head, because the songs were so violent, I wanted to look even more vulnerable."

I met Mairead [Nash], who went on to become my manager, in this club – I was really drunk. She ran club nights, and I was talking about this band. She was like, 'Yeah, we'll book you.' I was like, 'Great!' Then I got the phone call from her asking if I'd play her Christmas party. I said, 'Yeah, sure.' But, I mean, the band didn't exist. I had to get my friend Matt [Allchin] to come and learn these songs. And then I actually had to get a band. Mairead asked me to sing covers! We were supporting Kitty, Daisy and Lewis – it was a folk night. My dad came. There was eggnog.

I only had four songs, though. I bought some pop socks. I had special loafers – I was going for a kind of 'lost schoolgirl' look. And so I would walk on stage holding books and my bag. I think, in my head, because the songs were so violent, I wanted to look even more vulnerable.

Why were the songs violent?

Well, there was 'Girl with One Eye', 'Kiss with a Fist', 'My Boy Builds Coffins' – all of my first songs dealt with really dark stuff. Because I've just always been quite attracted to morbid, kind of gothic fantasy. Especially around that time, when I was in my teens and early twenties, it was really what I was into. I was hanging out with a lot of Camberwell art college punk bands – that whole swashbuckling drunk-pirate gothic scene. I think these gothic folk tales came out of it.

'Kiss with a Fist', when it first came out, got a lot of attention pretty quickly. How did that feel?

I guess it was funny, because 'Kiss with a Fist' was *of* a particular time in my life. I grew up in Camberwell [South London], and there was a big punk scene, and I was feeding off those bands. But when I started trying to make a record, I realized I didn't want to make songs that all sounded like that. It was all of a particular time, for me – very much reminds me of being seventeen, eighteen, that kind of that feeling. I think I knew quite quickly that I wanted to move beyond it, or evolve from that genre.

"I was hanging out with a lot of Camberwell art college punk bands – that whole swashbuckling drunk-pirate gothic scene."

Another very important first, as it's a place that means a lot to you, would be Glastonbury. Remember your first?

Yes. Oh my god! I'd never been, and we got booked to play *The Guardian* tea tent on Sunday morning. It was just me and Matt, who was my first guitarist; 2008? I don't know. So we were playing on Sunday; we arrive Friday night, and I've got no tent, no wellies – I'm wearing boat shoes! And whatever happens at Glastonbury for those two days happened. And on the Sunday morning I had to play. I woke up in somebody else's tent [laughs], pretty much in someone else's clothes. And this was the mud apocalypse Glastonbury; I had to be frog-marched through the mud to this tent on Sunday morning.

Matt was lost on the other side of the festival, and we were going to completely miss our slot. He hadn't shown up. Weirdly, I don't know why, but Suggs from Madness was there, and he did an impromptu impression of Mick Jagger for 15 minutes to stall for time because I was crying back-stage. I had to do the first half of the gig a cappella. Then Matt turned up. He'd trudged through all the mud to get there, and as soon as he got on stage, his whole guitar fell apart. It was a muddy and chaotic first experience of Glastonbury. But have there been any other ones, really?

When *Lungs* came out in 2009 – the first album – were you prepared for the level of attention that it got? It's so expansive, and connected with a lot more people than might have been expected from your first incarnation. Were you ready for that?

Do you know what, it's so hard to remember how I felt about it because it was such a blur. I can remember winning the [Brits] Critic's Choice award [2009], and I didn't really think that much of it, because I didn't know what it was, really. I was like, 'Oh, that's so nice!' [laughs]. 'Oh, thank you!' And then my boyfriend at the time – who was much more internet savvy than I was – went, 'I think this is a really big deal'.

The thing about that time is that we were just touring so much, and it was the first time we'd ever had riders! We had whole huge bottles of vodka every day, and we were allowed to just drink and play music, you know? People were letting us do it. There was no idea that there would be a bigger thing in sight. Every day it was about that gig and we were … we were just *in it*. And it was all so exciting. And doing festivals for the first time – I mean, I don't quite know how we survived [laughing]. Still, I don't. But you're just so excited that you get to play, I think.

When *Ceremonials* came out in 2011, that was your first American Top 10 album. That's where things get a bit unhinged, I guess, when you get that level of attention. I remember seeing you backstage at Glastonbury in 2010, and you looked dazed.
Oh my god. That was more people than I'd ever seen in my life. I couldn't … Like, I remember having a little weird … It was really … It's hard to speak about it even now. It was almost like I couldn't quite process it as it was happening. To go from the tea tent then to, I think, the largest crowd the Other Stage has ever seen – I couldn't quite process it. I can imagine I might have been dazed. I couldn't remember it, when I came offstage. It was almost like my brain went, like, blank.

"To go from the tea tent to, I think, the largest crowd the Other Stage has ever seen – I couldn't quite process it."

Was there a point, when you were doing that tour, when you were in the States, when this record was rolling behind you, the second album, did you feel your grip on normal life loosening a little bit?
It's fine if you keep doing it. It's when you stop. You've got to build yourself completely back up again from scratch. And then you make a new record about it [laughs].

You mentioned Neil Young as being somebody that you love. When did you first feel the love of Neil?
You know, I am quite a late discoverer of Neil Young. But I'm one of those bores who then like goes around telling everyone, 'Oh my god, have you heard of Neil Young?' They're like, 'Yeah, we've heard of Neil Young' [laughing]. I remember I got into a conversation with Win Butler [of Arcade Fire] about pop music, and we were talking about it, but I was

like, 'But I love Neil Young!' I was spending a lot of time in LA, thinking about making a new record, and I just started listening to him. His genius just dawned on me in this massive way. I was instantly a mega fan. Recently we got to play the [annual charity] Bridge School Benefit, the concert he puts on in San Francisco, which is really incredible.

Did you meet him? Was he as cool as you wanted him to be?

He's so cool! I went into his dressing room because we sang a song together, 'Southern Man' – maybe my favourite song – which was such a huge honour. I went in, and I sat down, and I was really nervous. I was like, 'It's so nice to meet you, Mr Young.' And he's like, 'Yeah, it's really nice to meet you, too. When I first heard your record, you know, I thought that you were a man with a high voice. Because I live in the mountains and I was just like, "Hey, a man called Florence with a high voice. That's pretty punk."' I was like, 'Thanks, Uncle Neil!' He can think whatever he likes [laughs]. I was just happy to be there.

'Spectrum (Say My Name)' was your first number one single in 2012. Was it important to you?

Yeah, it was. I mean, it was wonderful. I think it was around Pride, as well; it was on the same day that it got to number one. And 'Spectrum', that song, is a big anthem about just being free and illumination and empowerment. So for it to come around that time was like a really amazing, amazing thing. Yeah, it felt really good.

"Big female emotions? I've got some of them! They need some safe hands."

How Big, How Blue, How Beautiful [2015] – is this record half going back to the stripped-down sound of before and half a reaction to living in a tour bus for three years?

Again, I always approach all the records like, 'We're going to do a much more minimal album!', and then I'm like, 'But I want to add trumpets!' So I inherently can't help being myself. If you like Florence and The Machine, it's still a Florence and The Machine record. But I think what [producer] Markus Dravs managed to find in me is almost like a different gear. You know, I love the big, grand stuff. I love big drum sounds, and the loud bits and the quiet bits, I can do that well. But what Markus encouraged in me is to write from a simpler place. You know, like songs like 'Ship to Wreck', at first, I didn't [like it]; I'd written it, but he really championed it and really wanted it on the record. And I was like, 'But it's just a song! Where's the trick?' He's like, 'No tricks!' That kind of simplicity and purity of songwriting, I think, is what he encouraged.

Are you happy with it?

I am really happy with it. I think, as an artist, the idea that something's finished means it has to be perfect. Nothing can ever be perfect, so inherently you're always dissatisfied. But I'm as happy as I can be, I think [laughing].

Björk is somebody else you love a lot. When did you first fall in love with Björk?

Homogenic [1997] has been a huge record for me, and that's what brought me to Markus Dravs – also, of course, because I love Arcade Fire, and he did a lot of their stuff, but really it was while I was writing. I had a year off, and I was writing a lot of the record, and I was listening to *Homogenic* a lot. And it was just his understanding of emotion on that record. It's produced in a very emotional way. And so I thought, you know, big female emotions? I've got some of them! They need some safe hands.

And finally, what's the last song we should play?

Oh, well, Father John Misty's got a new record out, and I love him so much. There's a song on his latest record called 'The Ideal Husband', which I just think is fucking amazing.

The First Time Florence Welch Playlist

1	Dog Days Are Over	Florence and The Machine
2	Part of Your World (*The Little Mermaid* OST)	Jodi Benson
3	My Name Is	Eminem
4	Runaway	The Corrs
5	Longview	Green Day
6	Charlie Brown	Voodoo Glow Skulls
7	Jubilee Street	Nick Cave & The Bad Seeds
8	Kiss with a Fist	Florence and The Machine
9	Southern Man	Neil Young
10	Spectrum (Say My Name)	Florence and The Machine
11	You Got the Love	The Source feat. Candi Staton
12	Jóga	Björk
13	The Ideal Husband	Father John Misty

"You're not born a pop star. You invent yourself or you, by fluke, turn yourself into a pop star."

JARVIS COCKER

The public figures that we clasp to our collective bosom say a lot about who we want to be as a nation. The UK holds a special affection for people like Fry, Hawking, Lumley, Windsor (both Liz and Babs), Banksy and Mirren. They have (or we attribute to them) qualities that define Britishness: backbone, talent, humour and eccentricity. It's not a role you can apply for; the nation just decides that you're on the list. And in 1994, after 16 long years fronting Pulp, Jarvis Cocker's name was added to it. He became a national treasure.

This is because, if I may put it this way, there's a little bit of Jarvis in everyone: we've all felt like the quiet one in the kitchen while the party kicks off in the bedroom; we've all trailed after that girl or boy who just doesn't realize that underneath our awkwardness lies a brilliant but misunderstood poet and sexual dynamo; we've all wanted to drop the perfect quip at the perfect moment, or wave our arses in the direction of those who take themselves too seriously. Jarvis's songs document those feelings, often with himself in the starring role. He's become a hero for misfits, 6 feet 4 inches of proof that the most seemingly unlikely people can triumph with enough wit, smarts and flair.

He's as funny as he is tall, with long, thin limbs and thick glasses, a greying beard and a rather lovely smile. He's a relaxed, natural storyteller, and his recollections stretch out and meander across our conversation. His large hands float around while he talks, and his long fingers wiggle and point like floating punctuation.

Jarvis is obviously still a musician but no longer a pop star, and the tabloids and paparazzi of the '90s have moved on. Now he's also a writer, critic, producer, director and filmmaker, but he's still a hero. I've seen it. Cabbies, bobbies, hipsters, parents and kids will call out when he walks past. Everyone still wants a bit of Jarvis in their lives.

Matt Everitt: When was the first time you were aware of music?
The first song that I can really remember hearing is Gordon Lightfoot, 'If You Could Read My Mind'. It spooked me because there are these lines in it about somebody being chained up in a dungeon: 'In a castle dark or a fortress strong, with chains upon my feet.' And also the thought of somebody being able to look inside somebody's head. But that song stayed with me over the years. Obviously, at the age of five, you don't really understand what it's on about, but it's almost like they give you a message that you might want later in your life.

Did you equate that with something that you could do?
Oh, that didn't happen for a long time. I always assumed that you would have to do something really *official* to be able to be allowed to make music. I would watch *Top of the Pops* and I liked the *idea* of pop stars, that they got girls screaming at them. Being a shy child, I thought that could be a good way to get girls. But I never thought I could actually do it.

What was the first record you owned?
The first album that I actually bought with my own money was *Changesonebowie*. The first single I bought was '5 Minutes' by The Stranglers. But before that I'd listened to my mum's record collection, which was mainly The Beatles, and I'd listen to *Sergeant Pepper* a lot. The song that sticks in my mind from that one is 'A Day in the Life'.

What was the first song that you actually wrote?
I wish that I could say it was a really meaningful, deep song, but I formed a group in about 1978 when I was still at school. We were so rubbish that we couldn't really play other people's songs. So we started writing our own, and the first we actually finished was called 'Shakespeare Rock': [sings] 'Got a baby, only one thing wrong, quotes Shakespeare all day long. Said baby why you ignoring me? She said, "To be or not to be?"'

Was that the first incarnation of Pulp, or was that later?
Pulp was called Arabicus Pulp at that point, because that was a commodity that we'd seen in the *Financial Times*, but we got rid of the Arabicus quite quick. It amazes me that we came up with that name at that age, because it was very appropriate for that group; it was about what Pulp tried to do, which was to take something quite trashy, the three-minute pop song, and put some meaning in it. 'Pulp' was the word applied to very cheap comics and things that were just supposed to be bought and then chucked away, which is how pop music was thought of – chewing gum for the ears. From the very start of Pulp, I wanted it to be a pop thing.

Legend says that it was your first demos that led to your first Peel Session [BBC Radio 1 music show]. Is that right?
That's true, yes. We started playing concerts in 1980; I was still at school at the time. There was a group in Sheffield called the Scarborough

Antelopes – very catchy name. Their bass player said, 'If you want to record something, you should go and see the Colonel – Ken Patten. He's got a studio in his house.' It was an amazing place, a semi-detached house that he'd wired so you recorded in his bedroom and he mixed it in his kitchen. So we recorded our first demo, three songs on a tape.

Maybe a couple of weeks later, John Peel was doing one of his roadshows at the Polytechnic in Sheffield. I made a very elaborate hand-drawn sleeve and took a cassette down to him. He said he'd listen to it on the way home, and a week later we got a call to go and do a Peel Session.

What was that like?
It was like being told you were going to heaven. I'd been listening to the Peel show for years, pretty much every night because it was the only way of hearing new music. It totally opened the door to a lot of things for me, and I always think that that's where I got my musical education from, really. And so to be invited down – I thought it was never going to get any better that that. We had to borrow loads of equipment, because at that point we were just rehearsing in my mum's living room.

"We got a call to go and do a Peel Session. It was like being told you were going to heaven."

You moved to London in 1988 to go to Central Saint Martins art school, which seems a pivotal moment. Was it intimidating?
I just had to get out of Sheffield, otherwise I'd get bogged down. I was fantastically lucky to get into Saint Martins. I'd just got these two crappy films I'd made on a Super 8 I'd bought at a jumble sale. Really, the main reason I applied there was that the college was in the middle of town, and I thought, 'I want to be at the centre of things'. And the first day, you're scared, aren't you? I was a bit older as well; I was twenty five. I was considered to be a mature student, which was a joke. I was very immature.

When do you think the band started to reach its intended audience, and you could feel some kind of swell of popularity?
Ironically enough, it was when I moved to London and wasn't really doing it so intensely anymore. I think people can smell desperation on you [laughs]. When I was in Sheffield, I used to get really worked up when we were playing a show. I'd, like, stop songs halfway through if somebody made a mistake. And when I moved to London, because I was relaxed and I was doing something else, I enjoyed being in the band more, and I think people who came to see us found it a more pleasant experience, rather than this neurotic idiot having a nervous breakdown on stage.

What was the first hit? I suppose 'Babies'? 'Razzmatazz'?
Well, 'Babies' never charted, really, but it certainly got a lot more attention. The first song in the Top 40 was 'Do You Remember the First Time?', which smashed into the charts at number 36, I believe …

Different Class [1995] took you to the stratosphere, and 'Common People' helped make the band successful. Can you remember hearing that in a nightclub for the first time?
There's a semi-funny story to do with that record. When it came out, the BBC were doing this gimmick where occasionally they would do the Top 40 rundown live. They were doing it from Birmingham that week, so we got invited. They didn't tell us where we were in the charts. We're waiting and got excited, because it got to the Top 10 and we still hadn't been called up. So I started getting ready; I was wearing contact lenses at the time, and one won't go in properly. Then it got to the Top 5, and we still hadn't been called in. And then, eventually, 'Number two!' We were amazed. We got ushered out onto this stage, and it'd been raining, so there were all these puddles, but my vision was impaired because I only had one contact lens in. We launched into 'Common People', and halfway through I did one of my trademark jumps, slipped and crashed to the ground. I remember laying there in this puddle, looking at these disinterested teenagers, thinking, 'Well, this is supposed to be the crowning moment of my pop career and I'm just lying in a puddle in Birmingham.'

"This is supposed to be the crowning moment of my pop career and I'm just lying in a puddle in Birmingham."

Glastonbury in '95 is seen as Pulp's crowning glory. I remember seeing you that morning, looking very, very nervous outside your tent. You weren't initially going to headline – it was going to be The Stone Roses – and you just looked shell-shocked.
I was. That whole week. I can't even remember what the first song was. I remember very vividly the hour leading up to going onstage. I've never been as nervous in my life. I was in this kind of blind panic, thinking, 'There's just no way I can do this.' And then, when it came to zero hour, it goes vague. I can't really remember walking up onto the stage. I can't even remember what I first said when I went up onto the stage. I think I went into another zone. My memory of it only really clears when we played 'Common People', and that was quite weird because I could just hear the audience singing the words of the song so loud.

All I can really remember talking about is that if a bunch of idiots like us can end up on this stage, then that means anybody can do it. And

I still believe that. To me, the beauty of pop music is the fact that not everybody will be a star, but everybody has the potential to do it. It's just normal people who, through whatever circumstances, manage to get to that place. You're not born a pop star. You make yourself a pop star. You invent yourself or you, by fluke, turn yourself into a pop star.

That performance sealed your fame in one way; the incident at the Brit Awards sealed your fame in another [in 1996, Cocker interrupted Michael Jackson's performance in protest]. It was your first entanglement with the tabloids on a grand scale.
You wake up after doing something daft at a party and think, 'Ah, did I really do that?', and in normal life, just your circle of friends will make fun of you. But unfortunately I did it at a very large media event and so the whole country knew about it, and that transformed me into one of the most recognizable people in the country. I realized that I'd not over-stepped the mark, but I'd crossed a line that I was never going to be able to uncross. It freaked me for quite a while.

At least in those days there was still film in cameras, so it did stop occasionally, because they had to put another roll of film in. Now it's dig-ital; it's like they just keep going and going and going. I think it must be ten times worse now. And I'm glad that I'm not in that world anymore.

This Is Hardcore followed in 1998. At the time everybody was quite surprised at how dark it was. When was the point when you first thought, 'Oh, I'm in trouble here'?
Well, it's a hangover record. It was a very conflicted record. Here I was doing the thing that I'd been wanting to do for over 20 years, it was very dear to me, but then I felt that it had been taken away and turned into something that I no longer had any control over. You've had a big hit record! You've got to follow it up! But what it had done to my social life, it just wasn't making me very happy. The thing that I was supposed to do, that I'd grown up loving doing, somehow had got me into a pickle.

I'd spent all this time dreaming about what being a pop star would be, and because of that, I really had not valued the things that were around me to start with. And when they got taken away, I wanted them back, but it was a bit too late. So there was a lot of stuff to sift through. Some people might say, 'Why didn't you just go to a therapist and not burden us with it and make a record about it?' Okay, fair point. I hope that I've eventually managed to work through that, but it took a while.

It's always the drink and the drugs and the going out …
Well, we know that. We've read all those rock-star biographies. We know that it's not a healthy diet – cocaine, alcohol and all those things. But people always think, 'Oh yeah, but that's somebody else. I can handle all that.' And then you find out that you can't, you know? So, yeah, it's kind of depressing. I don't know, you have to do these things. You can't just sit at home all the time. You've got to go out and have a go, ain't ya?

Then we get the beautiful, pastoral, natural-sounding *We Love Life* [2001], produced by Scott Walker. When did you first meet?
I'd been a massive fan of Scott Walker's for years and years, and I think it was when he did Meltdown [Walker directed the London festival in 2000] and we got invited to play. He poked his head in to say hello, with his baseball cap pulled right down, so he was in no danger of making eye contact. I was just overawed. I was a little bit scared about working with him, because you can have too much respect for people, and making a record is a messy business – you can't be too polite. I didn't want to be sat in the corner saying, 'Oh yes, Scott. Do whatever you want' [laughs].

But once you've got over that initial thing of working with one of your greatest heroes, I think it was quite productive. He's an enigmatic guy. I think that really comes down to the fact that he's pathologically shy, but once you get through that barrier, he's quite easy to get on with and he tells jokes, but he's just very focused on what he wants to do.

That record – maybe it tried too hard to be a rehabilitation record after the mess of *This Is Hardcore*, and maybe that was a bit too conscious an effort to tie things up in a happy way. I think there are elements of that record that are okay, but I don't know whether it's totally successful.

"The beauty of pop music is the fact that not everybody will be a star, but everybody has the potential to do it."

It always seemed to me that Pulp had a quiet finish: it didn't implode, it just seemed to fade gently. What happened?
I was moving to France, and it seemed to me that public interest wasn't at a peak, shall we say? And I just thought, 'Why make a big deal about it?' So we didn't split up, it's just that we decided not to bother doing it so much anymore. We just drifted, I suppose. I'm still drifting.

Can you imagine a time when you'll get back together?
I'm flattered that people even remember the group, and I'm flattered there's still a place in their hearts for it. Like I say, when I started the group, the reason it was called Pulp was because I was in love with that throwaway element of pop music, so the fact that we're still getting played 15 years on is quite weird.

It's also nice to leave people with a nice memory. Like wedding-video syndrome – a wedding video can never really capture what that day's like, and in a way it undermines it, because then you *see*. When you're in a situation you see what you want to see, or you project what you want onto it, then when you're faced with the cold, hard evidence, you say, 'Oh, well, god, yeah, I look a bit hungover,' or 'I was looking a bit pudgy that day.' So I'm grateful that people think of Pulp with affection, but then if they were faced with the actual, real thing on the stage in front of them, I don't know whether that would be so good.

Now we find you happily ensconced in a solo career. What was that first solo record [*Jarvis*, 2006] like?

It'd been quite a long gap, so it was okay. I'd thought I was going to retire, and then I started writing songs and thought, 'Oh, maybe I've still got something to contribute' [laughs]. It was weird making that record. Even though I wrote the words in Pulp, everybody had a vested interest in it and it really was a band. Whereas with that first solo record, I had written the songs on my own and I only got people in to help me when we were recording it. I had more of a feel of responsibility, and I felt a bit more grown-up.

I had a big sense towards the end of Pulp that I was holding the rest of the band back, and that was one of the reasons why we drifted apart. I always felt that the band would love to be out playing concerts and would love to be making a record, and it was just Mr Fartypants here who was having 'a moment' and couldn't come up with lyrics or felt too fragile to go and play. I felt guilty about keeping the rest of the band hanging around all that time. I think that's another reason why I thought, 'Well, I'll go off and do something else and then people can get on with their lives, rather than hanging around for me to get me act together.'

We've had all these firsts; what's the last track we'll play?

Maybe we could just play 'Get Down On It', by Kool and the Gang. I really like songs that just put you in a good mood.

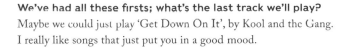

	The First Time Jarvis Cocker Playlist	
1	Babies	Pulp
2	If You Could Read My Mind	Gordon Lightfoot
3	Space Oddity	David Bowie
4	5 Minutes	The Stranglers
5	A Day in the Life	The Beatles
6	Turkey Mambo Momma	Pulp
7	Plastic Palace People	Scott Walker
8	Do You Remember the First Time?	Pulp
9	This Is Hardcore	Pulp
10	Don't Let Him Waste Your Time	Jarvis Cocker
11	Get Down On It	Kool and the Gang
12	Running The World	Jarvis Cocker

"I realized a movement was about to happen, and I kind of realized, too, that I'm a part of this movement."

JIMMY CLIFF

For a man who helped introduce a large part of the planet to a whole new genre of music, and wrote some of the most universally loved reggae songs ever, Jimmy Cliff is very low-key. Some musicians' egos arrive ahead of them in the form of entourages or lists of requirements, but Jimmy just brings a gentle charisma and quiet pride in his remarkable artistic achievements.

His meeting with Island Records founder Chris Blackwell in 1965 and a move from Kingston, Jamaica, to London propelled him onto the international stage, but he'd been writing songs since he was fourteen, honing his craft with iconic reggae producer Leslie Kong. For music fans outside Jamaica, some of the very first reggae they heard would have been Cliff's incredible tracks, such as 'Wonderful World, Beautiful People', 'Many Rivers to Cross' and 'Vietnam' – a song whose political content might have damaged his US success, but which Bob Dylan called the best protest song he had ever heard.

Cliff also starred as outlaw Ivanhoe Martin in 1972's *The Harder They Come*, Jamaica's first major film production and its most influential movie of the era. It helped define the country's culture for the rest of the world as hip, charismatic and dangerous, and was accompanied by one of the greatest soundtracks of all time, which turned Jimmy into reggae's first international star.

Jimmy himself is courteous and unassuming, and I can hear the smile in his soft, musical voice. There's a certain assurance in his answers, and hints of the confidence that helped him become a star – he's definitely aware that many of his songs are all-time classics – but there's no ego here.

The Rolling Stones, Bruce Springsteen, Elvis Costello, Paul Simon and Joe Strummer have all invited him on stage over the years, reinforcing his status as someone who genuinely changed the musical world, and remains probably reggae's greatest living singer. In fact, it was Jimmy's friend Keith Richards who perhaps described him best: 'Unbeatable songs, and the voice of an angel.'

Matt Everitt: When was the first time you were aware of music?
I guess it must have been going to church with my family. I liked that part of church – just the music part of it [laughs]. I went to one of those churches where there's *a lot* of music. I saw the people moving, and it moved me as well.

Was it quite a musical family that you grew up in?
Everyone sang. We didn't have instruments in those times, but everyone sang. We would sit around and make music together. I had quite a big family and everyone was quite musical.

When did you make that jump from thinking 'I like music' to thinking 'I'm going to be a musician'?
It was also in school. Maybe eight, nine. It was break time and I was in the classroom singing, and some girls walked out and said, 'Where's the radio?' So I thought to myself, 'Oh wow, I have something here!' And those were some girls who really wouldn't normally look at me!

Who were your first musical heroes, when you were young?
Well, there was lots of indigenous music in Jamaica, you know? There was music for almost everything: working, weddings, digging, all those kind of things. So, those were indigenous music. But besides that, there were people from New Orleans – jazz people from New Orleans, and R&B people like Professor Longhair, Fats Domino and people like that – because those were the ones we could pick up on the radio. Fats Domino, 'Be My Guest'. He was one of my greatest people who inspired me a lot – that beat, you know? His unique sound of a voice and the piano playing. Fats Domino, great.

And then you moved to Kingston, didn't you? To be a musician?
Yeah. Then after listening to all that music on the radio, I heard one local artist, Derrick Morgan, and one of my teachers said, 'That's a local artist. He writes his own songs.' So I said, 'Oh, how does he write his own songs?', and he said, 'You just write it!' So I did just that. I sang them to a few people, and they said, 'Wow, you did write that?' I said, 'Yeah.' So it was time for me to go to Kingston to change school. I had four songs in my pocket [laughs], ready to sell when I got to Kingston. I must get them recorded, like this singer that I heard on the radio.

You make it sound really easy!
I was very excited about it. I went to Kingston and I started looking around to get my songs recorded. I entered a talent parade, and I lost one and I won a few, and then after testing many different producers, I finally found one who would record me. His name was Sir Cavaliers Combo. And then after Sir Cavaliers I found Leslie Kong, who was on [record label] Beverley's, and we really had a great relationship. I stuck with him for a number of years.

Tell me a bit about 'Hurricane Hattie' [1962]. That was one of the first breakthrough tracks, wasn't it?

That was my first hit. Hattie was a hurricane that had blown in Belize, in Central America, and I decided to make a song about it. It was an eventful thing, so I made a song about it, and it became a hit, my first number one hit in Jamaica.

That was the start of a run of tracks that you did with Leslie Kong. Could you feel part of a movement that was getting more popular?

I realized that it was a movement happening, because the music now had a name – they called it ska. And when I first went to Kingston, it didn't really have a name. So, yeah, I realized a movement was about to happen, and I kind of realized, too, that I'm a part of this movement.

How did you first start working with Chris Blackwell at Island?

Chris used to come into Leslie Kong's record shop, and somebody told me, 'He's Chris Blackwell. Oh yeah, that's Island Records, he's a producer.' Then in 1965 I went to the New York World's Fair representing Jamaica. Because then I had a few hits under my belt, and I've always been a good performer, so they asked me to fill that slot. That's when I met Chris Blackwell, and he invited me to come to England. I said, 'Well … America here is pretty good for me' [laughs]. But he said, 'Look, you know Millie Small? Look how well I've done with Millie Small [her 1964 cover of 'My Boy Lollipop' sold more than seven million copies and helped establish Island Records]. You have a really good voice and you're a good performer. You could achieve just the same or more.'

What was London like in the mid-'60s?

Well, London was exciting to me because there were lots of clubs around. In Jamaica there were clubs, but here it was different, and there were various kinds of music from Africa and the Caribbean Islands. I was open to more rock music, and music that I was not so exposed to in Jamaica.

Did you face much discrimination?

Oh yeah, I faced some kind of discrimination. I remember one incident, at the first flat I was staying in. Somebody got the flat for me, and I was there for maybe two, three weeks, when the caretaker came in and said, 'What are you doing here?' I said, 'I live here!' [laughs]. He said, 'Don't you know that we don't have black people here?' I said, 'Wow. Well, if you want me out, you'll have to get me out on my head.' So I slammed the door. However, the following day I was on *Top of the Pops*, not performing but as a part of the audience. And then the next day he said, 'Oh, I saw you on the telly last night!' So now everything was all right for me to stay. Prior to that, of course, there was the discrimination thing and all of that, but then when you become a celebrity, it's okay [laughs].

In '69 you released the *Jimmy Cliff* album, which included 'Wonderful World, Beautiful People' – a big international hit. You talked about a movement earlier: this is where reggae starts to spread around the world. You must have been proud.
Absolutely. This was, like, my dream coming true. That's what I came to England for, and the dream was happening now. I wrote all of the songs – like 'Wonderful World', 'Many Rivers to Cross' – while on a trip to South America, Brazil. And then I went back to Jamaica and recorded them. So yeah, my songwriting skills were coming to fruition now.

I enjoyed it. At the same time, it had an odd side, too, where I started having to be careful of what I said, because I noticed the two sides. But yeah, I enjoyed the fame. If I walked into a store or something and they recognized me, service would be nice! Doors opened a little easier.

We've got to talk about 'Vietnam', one of your many famous tracks. And we can't mention it without the Bob Dylan quote, can we? Which is pretty impressive.
Pretty, pretty impressive! I found it something natural that I did – and it's something that I still do naturally. I am touched and become sensitive to things like that on the planet – what I consider to be unjust, or not right, and all those kind of things – so it's something I just do naturally.

***The Harder They Come* [1972]: How did you first get involved in that film and the soundtrack? It's quite a piece of work.**
One day I was at Dynamic Sounds, the famous studio where a lot of the hits were made at that time [the first state-of-the-art recording studio in Kingston, Jamaica], and I was recording 'You Can Get It If You Really Want'. I came out and I met this gentleman [director Perry Henzell], who said to me, 'I'm making a movie. Do you think you could write some songs for it?' I said, 'What do you mean, "*Do I think I can write?*" I can write! I can do anything!' He was taken aback with my response. The next thing I knew, he sent a script to me via Island Records. I read the script and I could identify with the character. I *knew* the character as a child growing up. And I'd always wanted to act – as a matter of fact, that was the first thing I wanted to do, even before I wanted to sing. So he came over and ran a scene with me and he was satisfied: 'This is the guy I've been looking for all these years to do my movie!'

It's a seminal film. It's responsible in many ways for helping introduce reggae music and culture to the rest of the world.
Absolutely. During the filming, we all went into the film with vigour and hope and energy. When I lived here in London, I used to go to the West End a lot. I watched, like, four movies a day, and I always thought, 'Wow, what if my movie could be showing here one day?' So we went into it with big expectations, but never knowing if it would do anything or not. I was very surprised, but pleasantly so. Even though I had my big expectations, I was still surprised it had that big of an impact on the world.

The film is regarded as a classic, and the soundtrack is one of the biggest-selling reggae albums of all time. What is it about the soundtrack and the film that make them so timeless?

I think we captured a time and the energy of a time. It was not just Jamaica, that kind of energy, but it was an energy that was going all over the planet, and we captured it in that film. The character that I played, he could've been any character in England or in the US or wherever in the world. That's what gives it its timelessness. In my opinion.

So many people have covered your songs. Desmond Dekker, New Order, Willie Nelson, Keith Richards – an incredible list of people. Who's done your favourite versions?

Well, you know, I appreciated all of them, because it was encouraging for me to have my work covered. I've covered other people's work as well. When I cover someone else's work, I try to make it my own, and that's the thing that catches me when I hear somebody cover my work and it's completely different from mine. When I heard 'Trapped' by Bruce Springsteen, it's completely different from mine, and I said, 'Wow. Now, that's great'. So that's one of them, you know, because it's so different.

Have you ever managed to meet Bruce and talk to him about it?

Yes, as a matter of fact, we performed together. I was doing an event in the US, and he was performing there, and he asked me if I would perform with him. So I went up and we did three songs with his band. We have a good artistic relationship, yeah.

"Back in the days when I recorded with six or seven musicians sitting in the room ... there's a vibe, there's an energy, you know? And I kind of miss that."

You've always liked collaborating with people.

I love that because it brings out something else out of me. I think it's an artistic thing, when you see another artist do something. It's inspiring. That's one of the things that I miss in today's world, with the technology that we have. It has changed that a bit, because somebody comes in with one keyboard, and that one little keyboard can record everything. But back in the days when I recorded with six or seven musicians sitting in the room, and *you* sat in the room, and everybody starts playing, there's a vibe, there's an energy, you know? And I kind of miss that.

With this new record [*Rebirth*, 2012], it's 50 years since you first stepped into a studio. Does it feel like 50 years?

It feels like yesterday! I called the album *Rebirth* because it's a rebirth in many aspects. I am in a rebirth of my career at this time, and with this album I went back to point zero, which is the origin of the music. This album has the original sound that we had, recorded live. I feel my career is on another rise again. There were moments in my career where there was a rise: 'Wonderful World'; *The Harder They Come*; when I got in the Rock and Roll Hall of Fame in 2010. And now I am on another rise, because this album is really a great one. It's positive energy, absolutely.

How did you meet Tim Armstrong from Rancid? A great guy to work with, but I wouldn't necessarily put you two together.

Well, the connection between reggae and punk is quite well known from the sociopolitical point of view, and Joe Strummer was really the one who introduced me to Tim's music. My management suggested Tim Armstrong because I wanted to make a new album, and they said, 'Well, how about Tim Armstrong?' So we talked on the phone and the vibes felt really good, and we went into the studio. It just flowed. He was excited, I was excited, and when I started hearing how he went back to the original sounds that we had at Dynamic Sounds and all of that, I said, 'Wow, I'd forgotten all about that. Oh! That's great!' And the vibe just flowed.

"Music can be used positively or negatively, but I think music is kind of beyond politics. It's on a higher level."

You've been the only living musician to have been given the Order of Merit, the highest honour that can be granted by the Jamaican government to an artist. That's a pretty big deal.

It's a great honour, you know? I mean, to get honour outside of your country is really nice and wonderful, but when you get an honour in your *own* country and one like that? It's a good feeling.

It always seems to the outside world that Jamaican music is closely linked to the heart of Jamaica as a country.

There's great pride in it. The people and the politicians are very much aware of that situation, and sometimes they play with it. From back in the '70s they see what the people are gravitating to, and they sometimes use it for good, or for bad. But the thing with the Jamaican people is that the music is part of our oxygen.

You should have been a politician.
I think the music is beyond politics, really and truly. Like they say, it's the universal language. Music can be used positively or negatively, but I think music is kind of beyond politics, really. It's on a higher level, so I like to stick with that [laughs].

I'd like you to pick the last song that we'll play. It could be anything you want. It can be one of yours, it can be a new song, an old song, something by somebody else …
Well, I really would like to introduce one new song from my album. It's called 'One More'.

Why that one?
Because this song kind of represents what this album is all about. The song is called 'One More': I say I have one more song to sing; I have one more story to tell; I have one more arrow in my bow; I have one more shot at the prize. It's where I am at this point in time in my career.

The First Time **Jimmy Cliff** Playlist

1	You Can Get It If You Really Want	Jimmy Cliff
2	Mardi Gras in New Orleans (from *Mardi Gras in New Orleans 1949–1957*)	Professor Longhair
3	Be My Guest	Fats Domino
4	Moon Hop	Derrick Morgan
5	I'm Sorry	Sir Cavaliers Combo and Jimmy Cliff
6	Hurricane Hattie	Jimmy Cliff
7	My Boy Lollipop	Millie Small
8	Wonderful World, Beautiful People	Jimmy Cliff
9	Mother and Child Reunion	Paul Simon
10	Vietnam	Jimmy Cliff
11	Wild World	Cat Stevens
12	Many Rivers to Cross	Jimmy Cliff
13	I Can See Clearly Now	Johnny Nash
14	The Harder They Come	Jimmy Cliff
15	Trapped	Bruce Springsteen
16	One More	Jimmy Cliff

"I've been out of this country for a few years, and you seriously do need me back here to tell you what's what, all right?"

JOHN LYDON

John Lydon is singing at me in a high pantomime-dame voice: 'Oh, I was moved by your screen dreeeeam, Celluloid pictures of liviiiing. Your death could not kill our love for yoooooo', he warbles. 'I always do sound tests using Roxy Music, chunks of songs.' He explains cheerily, 'Bryan Ferry? I mean, he's not the most talented singer, but I love everything he's ever done.' I haven't officially started the interview, but John's started it for me. I'd followed the advice of his manager, Rambo – 'He can't get good beer or biscuits in LA' – and brought provisions, so John is nibbling on Hobnobs and drinking Kronenbourg, while talking nonstop about life, cracking jokes, asking rhetorical questions and taking the piss.

Interviewing John, after you've set aside his intimidating appearance and history, is a hugely exhilarating experience. You don't ask him questions so much as point the interview in a direction you hope it might go and try to follow him. He delights in confounding expectations and naming influences you wouldn't expect – daring you to disagree – and his face jumps from a beaming grin to a low-browed scowl, often within the same sentence.

More than anything, John really cares about his music. He's intensely proud of his world, and he wants you to follow what he's talking about. He peppers his answers with questions: 'All right?' 'Get it?' 'You see?' Even when it seems like he's finished, and I start to ask a follow-up question, he's suddenly talking again, right over me. Making sure I get it. Making. Sure. I. Understand … All right?

F. Scott Fitzgerald said, 'The test of a first-rate intelligence is the ability to hold two opposed ideas in the mind at the same time, and still retain the ability to function.' By that measure, John's a genius. In the space of one interview, he comes over as a romantic and a realist, sentimental but antagonistic, genteel and bolshie, funny and menacing. I wish every interview were more like this.

Matt Everitt: When was the first time you were aware of music?
From just walking past record stores and seeing the pretty little colours on the discs, and my mum and dad playing their endless mix – between cèilidh and The Beatles. So, I suppose as an act of rebellion, I went out and I bought that hideous 'Ruby, Don't Take Your Love to Town'. Now who did that? That old sod with a beard that became a gambler.

I liked it because it was a strange song. It was dark and it was about being left at home by an unfaithful wife. And, you know, that's the culture of most good music, it's all about grief and pain, and so that's more or less what Public Image really is – dealing with those emotions. This is why I've always told the world, I'm a *folk* singer by nature. Not a *pop* singer, *folk*. Folk music from the heart. I'm dealing with all of the worst emotions you could possibly ever try to run away from, but they are the real elements of what makes you a human being, ultimately. And when you face up to them, you will truly understand what I am doing, and indeed what all good folk music does. It's a painful delivery, but an accurate depiction of the foibles of being a human being.

Who were your first musical heroes?
My mum and dad used to play all kinds of crazy stuff. I grew up with an absolute dislike of The Beatles, and I think it was an accurate dislike, too. I did not find The Beatles to be accurate about human emotion; I found them to be pop craftsmiths, but not genuine. They didn't make me cry, they didn't make me happy. Years later you would get bands like 10cc: wonderful wall of sound, really well orchestrated, but utterly meaningless. And here we are, years and years later, and I give you another example of what I mean: the Japanese. They love jazz music. They put out note-perfect jazz records. But is there one note of feeling or emotion? No. It's just note perfect. And this is the difficulty; this is the career I've chosen. I'm in opposition to what I see as phony and fake and pony, all right?

My songs are all about crying out from the deepest, darkest nether regions of your soul – and sometimes reaching joyous accolades. Because of that, because of facing that problem head on, the Sex Pistols was a really good introduction for me into the wonderful, magnificent world of pop music, all right? And I told it like it is. Beyond belief. I don't think anyone could take that away from me. But there's a little bit further, isn't there? There's that inner pain that you have to resolve between you and the rest of the universe, and you have to be accurate. Now, I'll give an example. It's like, my eyesight's going really, really poor lately, but that's because I'm an avid reader, I love books. Why do I love books? Because the best books are written by people who reveal their soul and their inner nature to you, warts and all. That you can learn from.

I find modern music resents any kind of education at all about anything – anything at all. It's an unlearning process and a flimsy, striptease chorus of overexaggerated breasts and underdeveloped talent. You know? And I'm absolutely not complaining here about the girlies; I'm talking about the men in pop. All right? I'm fed up. Man bras? Stop it.

Taking it back – we're going to go through the whole of your career – what was the first Pistols gig like?

I don't suppose it was very brilliant for very many people, because, indeed, very many people weren't there. But it was good for me. I'd always viewed myself as vaguely talentless, and I sort of proved the point to myself that, yes, I just might be. But I do have a voice and I do have something to say, and I've never looked back from it, from there on in. I don't know if the band understood that, or the management, but I really hung on for dear life from that point on, because up until then, yes, I've read loads of books and I'm a bit of a book worm, and a bit of a football hooligan, too, I must admit, but I really do love to understand what makes the human psyche tick. And I've got the opportunity to do that.

Now the Sex Pistols were really good and I loved writing the songs there, but I wanted a little bit more – you know, that would get into the deeper, darker elements of the human soul. While in the Pistols, just before it broke up, for instance, I was writing songs like 'Religion', which later came to play in the Public Image [Limited] genre. And it was bizarre for me, because as a Sex Pistol, I thought we'd pushed so many boundaries, but at the same time, the band couldn't take the boundaries that a song like that was pushing against. And, matter of fact, they outright rejected 'Religion'. I desperately tried to get Sid [Vicious] to learn the bassline, but he could never grasp it, because Sid had his own emotional problems at the time. And, well, then the Pistols fell apart, and I started Public Image with no money and bugger all help from the universe. But hello, what's changed?

> # "I'd always viewed myself as vaguely talentless, and I sort of proved the point to myself that, yes, I just might be. But I do have a voice and I do have something to say."

But there you go. I always was looking forward to Public Image. Public Image *should* have been the advancement of the Sex Pistols. It wasn't. In lots of glorious ways, because of happenstance and the eventuality of history, they're two entirely separate events. And this now implies that I run a duality with my personality, and I would like you to understand – no: one is part and parcel, leading into the other.

What were you listening to when you first formed PiL?

Everything. The quicker list would be what didn't I listen to. And here it goes: New Orleans trad jazz, all right? I've always been very open and honest about that, which is probably why I cannot get on the Jools

Holland show [UK TV contemporary music show]. It's one kind of music I can't grasp the heart and soul of, and Jools is very wrapped around that, you know? And he does it very well, but it's not my style, it's not my love. I don't feel the heartache in it.

You've always been very eclectic with your taste ...

Not eclectic, expansive. Before the Sex Pistols, I used to be a reggae DJ. Well big deal! I didn't think that was so peculiar or odd. I'd be quite happy down the Hackney Four Aces to spin a Hawkwind track right smack in the middle of it. Nobody was complaining way back then.

Who were the first reggae artists you got into?

Didn't see it as such; just seen it as that's the kind of music I like and love. Tamla Motown I wasn't so hot on, because the orchestrated bits, to me, used to slow the rhythm down. And at the time I was very shy, and the idea of dancing up close with a girl was appalling to me. Because of my illnesses, my willy wasn't functioning perfect [Lydon was hospitalized for a year with spinal meningitis as a child]. So that's what Tamla Motown was: it was more *romantically* led, and I wasn't healthy in that area. But that's the explanation of music to me. Everything and anything, and never really seen a problem with Hawkwind – and this is way previous to 'Silver Machine'; we're talking the really good, dark, 'Hell's Angels on tour' kind of stuff that they used to kick out live – and some serious, good pre-early dub. Everything.

What was the intent behind 'Public Image', PiL's first single from 1978?

We weren't looking to create any new, different, original sound – it was to just tell it like it is. And Keith Levene, the guitarist at the time, loved Wishbone Ash, and I loved that rhythm guitar of Wishbone Ash. And so

"What is Public Image? It's a massive wall of contradictions. I could be wrong. I could be right."

there it is, it kind of creeps in. Could it be that we were just pony magicians getting it wrong and that's what we ended up with? Or is it because we just love music and truly, completely understand that the best music in the world is made once you've learned all the rules, and you throw the rules out the window? But it's very hard to operate in that way until you understand the rules first. So yeah, there is a learning curve, but then there's an unlearning curve. That's what makes life brilliant and genius.

And then Public Image, for me ... What can I tell you? It's the most interesting aspect of my life. It's what I leave out of the record, not what

I leave in. I'll chuck everything in, the barn door, the fridge, right? And when it comes to mixing, out they go. It's what created the initial anger aspect, love, hate, joy, mob, war, kill, hate – all of those things that make your brain freeze or unfold all at the same time. What is Public Image? It's a massive wall of contradictions. I could be wrong, I could be right.

When *Metal Box* [PiL, 1979] came out, it was a really ground-breaking record. Can you remember what the public's reaction was like when it first was released?

Well, hate is … No, not the public. No, the public had never hated me. That's never been a problem. The only people that have ever gotten in between me and the public have been the press, who have consistently tried to send me off to the knacker's yard, all right?

Why do you think that is, then?

Well, if I wrote a blues song, the lyrics would be, 'I woke up tomorrow morning, I guess I'm ahead of my time.' The reality is, it just sounds different; it's not that it's advanced, it's just different. It's how I view things. Now, a lot of people have looked on that over the years and they've imitated it and then it becomes a format. But fair play to me now, I don't think there'd be Oasis without my squealing vocal. Right?

How did you first meet Afrika Bambaataa and come to collaborate with him [on 'World Destruction', 1984]?

Because of hanging around in New York again and talking to people and being open-minded. Afrika was a great DJ; he understood it's not all soul music, disco music, black music. He'd mix Kraftwerk in there with Parliament and style it up a notch. It's why I love the rave culture, too, because of its mix-and-match attitude. You got to keep breaking away from the norm. And I love the bloke, we're mates, what can I tell you? It's like the same with doing 'Open Up' with Leftfield. They're friends of mine. That's a record that was, oh, let's say two, three years in the making. We tried ideas until suddenly or somehow a tune came up and I went, 'Oh yeah, right, I can work with that.' And I went down to the studio, and I laid the vocals down in one night. Then we just started layering on top, because the attitude was right. All right? It wasn't 'Oh, hi, pop groovy diggers, let's go have a hit single here, shall we?' There's a lot of serious work that goes into everything that I do. There's nothing flippant.

Do you feel like the legacy of Public Image Ltd has been overlooked a little bit? Because I hear it in bands like Radiohead, LCD Soundsystem …

Radiohead and Coldplay bug the hell out of me, because it's so soulless. It just seems pointless. It's nice, but it's tosh. It's tosh, mate, and you know it. Look at the condition of the universe you live in, right? I've been out of this country for a few years, and you seriously do need me back here to tell you what's what, all right? That's not me being awfully

grandiose about it, but you need to get some sensibility. That grandiose idiocy – I used to have to suffer that years ago, bands like James, which had the same pompous presentation. It's too much with no content. They care about lining their coffers. There's nothing there you can learn, there's nothing about heart and soul. They don't know about people dying, living, aspiring. They don't sing those songs out of a sense of community; they sing them to you out of contempt, with fiddly studio gadgetry. Is this acceptable? Is this what you want? Well, you got it in spades.

What are my musical influences? Everything, everything, everything. There's a movement saying, 'Can's *Tago Mago*? Wonderful album!' but don't you dare miss Abba out of that agenda, because you are completely misunderstanding me if you do, all right? I don't make music from a jazz-snobbery point of view. I make music because I'm a folk musician for the folk, right? All folk. All of us.

People like Miles Davis, I got on with him because he was a folk musician, not strictly jazz – folk. He understood that basic principle; this was him trying to communicate a human emotion to other people. That is folk music, right? Jazz is a nice term to put on top of that, but it's really a category, isn't it? Like progressive rock or heavy metal or pop music.

What's been inspiring your recent lyrics then?
Life, love, death. Well, there are a few other things in between, I suppose [laughs]. All of the emotions, faults in myself, faults in others – I have to come to terms with being a human being, and realizing that life doesn't end at 21. In fact, it just gets better.

"Don't you dare miss Abba out of that agenda, because you are completely misunderstanding me if you do."

What was the very first PiL reunion gig like? Tell me about that. It must've felt fantastic.
I don't know about the word *reunion*. I've always hated that term. How about 'first PiL gig in a long while'?

Okay, tell me about the first PiL gig in a long while. What did it feel like being back on stage again?
Don't remember that [laughs]. Love it, love it. I loved being with the Pistols and all of that stuff, because that's a celebration of my youth, in a weird way. And that's where I learned to really be a songwriter. But PiL, to me, is something far outreaching that. So being on stage in a PiL format? That's a most excellent period of time, on stage. You really let it rip, and I really tell it like it is – unchastized, untrained, raw, sexy, sensual, erotic … Full of ticks, because I don't wash much.

There's one more question that I want to ask you, which concerns [former Sex Pistols manager] Malcolm McLaren. What were your reactions when you found out that he passed away?
Can't think that anything concerns him anymore, may he rest in pieces [laughs]. Kind of nothing, really. I mean, I'm still grieving about the death of my father, so that's still, to my mind, much more important, and always will be. Malcolm was someone I never really got to grips with – never meant much to me, never did much, really. Seemed to spend an awful lot of his life grabbing credit for things that weren't really due to him. It was a bit sad to hear that his funeral was a bit of a fiasco. Apparently, there was all kinds of squabbling going on, but that's, you know, because he led such a silly life.

I miss his space on earth, as I do at the death of any human being. I don't think I'll ever come to grips with death properly. I know it's a vital part of life, but it's one I think all of us should stave off for as long as we can. I hope he died respectfully. I hope for the first time in his life he stood up and faced it like a man.

What's the last song we should finish the show with?
Well, Mr DJ, play that song for me – 'Rise' [by Public Image Ltd].

Why that one?
It was an important record to make at the time.

	The First Time **John Lydon** Playlist	
1	Public Image	Public Image Ltd
2	Ruby, Don't Take Your Love to Town	Kenny Rogers
3	2HB	Roxy Music
4	Master of the Universe	Hawkwind
5	Anarchy in the UK	Sex Pistols
6	Religion II	Public Image Ltd
7	Mushroom	Can
8	Spanish Key	Miles Davis
9	Open Up	Leftfield feat. John Lydon
10	World Destruction	Time Zone ft. John Lydon/Afrika Bambaataa
11	Death Disco	Public Image Ltd
12	Fernando	Abba
13	Rise	Public Image Ltd

"I had some weird obsession with the guitar. I just had this thing about the shape of it, and I *needed* it."

Johnny Marr

Johnny Marr featured in the very first episode of *The First Time*, and in lots of ways he's the perfect subject. The Smiths were the first great British band of the '80s – the first indie act of the era to have an impact on the pop charts – and the blueprint and potential for all their brilliance is evident in their very first single.

Marr was also, without doubt, the first modern guitar hero, obsessed with sound and arrangement rather than speed and technique (although, it must be said, his technique is pretty impressive). Johnny is one of those unique guitarists who inspired countless other players, none of whom actually sound anything like him. As Noel Gallagher opined, 'No one can play guitar like Johnny Marr, so you might as well not bother.' But nearly every alternative band – and a fair few mainstream ones – owes him a debt, be that Radiohead, Oasis, Arcade Fire, Blur, Coldplay or the Arctic Monkeys.

He's also the first famous musician I ever saw who was perfectly happy to abandon the traditional concept of band membership and leap from genre to genre, and group to group (sometimes just for one record), his tenure based only on how the music felt at that moment. He makes artistic allegiances based on songs, not habit.

When I meet him, he's whip thin and whip smart. A habitual long-distance runner, he's tanned and healthy, with bright hazel eyes and a Great Rock Haircut that goes back to George Harrison's *Rubber Soul*–era mop and can be traced through to the mod cut of Steve Marriot and the bar-room bouffants of Rod Stewart and Ronnie Wood. He's frank, funny and approachable, but clearly has a bullshit detector ticking away in the back of his brain, probably finely tuned over years of negotiating the choppy waters of the music industry. It's easy to imagine him quietly slipping out of his own record-company launch party to dive into a gig – or, more likely, a guitar shop.

Matt Everitt: When were you first aware of music?

I was always aware of it in a big way, because my parents, to this day, still are absolute music obsessives. My parents are both Irish, and they were very young when I was born – when I was a little kid, they were in their early twenties. They came over with their extended family from the south of Ireland and brought with them a load of music – a mixture of American rock and roll music and early country music. Being young, they were very, very into the pop music of the day, so that was pretty much the most important thing in the house.

My dad played harmonica and accordion, and all my uncles and aunties sang and played. There were lots of weddings and christenings – not necessarily in that order. Bands playing, Irish show bands and rock and roll bands from Manchester. I saw an obsessive approach to records. One of my earliest ever memories is seeing two young women standing at one of those little Dansette record players, playing a record like 14 or 15 times, just playing this 45 over and over again and kind of dissecting it. It was The Everly Brothers, 'Cathy's Clown' or 'Wake Up Little Susie'.

One song that really took over the atmosphere of my early childhood was 'I Only Want to Be with You' by Dusty Springfield. It's really stuck with me, and with the way I approach music now. There's a lot of information packed in a lot of those records, those 45s. But my love of Dusty Springfield, it goes way beyond just liking retro music; it's always been there, all my life – this rich, soulful and very British sound.

What was the first record that opened your eyes to soul music?

I got into Motown because my friend's sister had a Supremes compilation record that came out in the mid '70s, stuff like 'Stoned Love' and 'Love Child' and 'Stop! In the Name of Love'. They sounded amazing. All the instrumentation was just so vibrant; it had real energy in it and the songs were so good. I decided that I'd track down these old Motown records that I'd seen in bargain bins. And I never lost my love of that music.

"It's always been there, all my life – this rich, soulful and very British sound."

What was your first guitar? What was the first song that you played on it, and how much did you love that instrument?

The first guitar I ever had was this little toy guitar, a little wooden thing, that I was obsessed with owning. It was in a shop that sold buckets and brooms and washcloths – a utility shop, really; it wasn't like a proper music store. I ended up painting it and putting bottle tops on it to make it look like an electric guitar I'd seen on television. That was probably when I was about four or five. I still remember it.

As young as that?

Yeah, I had some weird obsession with the guitar. I have no idea where it came from. I just had this thing about the shape of it, and I *needed* it. So I had this guitar and couldn't really get anything out of it, and from then on, every year under the Christmas tree would be this triangular cardboard box, and each year that box just got bigger and bigger.

What was the first thing you learned to play?

Eventually, I got a guitar I could get a chord out of, and it coincided with me buying my first record, which was 'Jeepster' by T. Rex, but the B-side of it was called 'Life's a Gas', and it happened to be made up of the chords that I was learning. I saw Marc Bolan do it on the *Cilla* show [British TV variety show] and I kind of copied the chords. 'Jeepster' was my introduction into learning how to write songs, really.

What was your first band like?

Well, my first band was just me and my mate. This was when we were about eleven or twelve maybe – he was my best mate and he was a year older than me. He was a complete Rod Stewart and the Faces nut, so he was Rod Stewart and I defaulted immediately to Ronnie Wood, of course, and that was a good start. I was able to play 'Stay with Me', and 'You Wear It Well' was one that I really liked.

Were you any good?

The band was awful. The guitar playing wasn't too bad for a twelve-year-old, I suppose, but people used to comment that I was pretty good, and that's how I knew I was on the right road. I remember we did a gig on Silver Jubilee Day [1977]; I would've been about fourteen. By that time, I really liked to play 'Suffragette City' by David Bowie, so when I think of my first performances in my first band, I always think of 'Suffragette City'.

You met Morrissey in '82. Did you sit down and start playing records together? Was that part of the early bonding?

Yeah, yeah. The first time we met I went around to his house and introduced myself, and we started immediately talking about records and the Marvelettes. He asked me to put a record on and I picked out 'Paper Boy' by The Marvelettes, and I flipped it over to play 'You're the One' – the B-side – because I liked 'Paper Boy', but I figured that if you were a real aficionado it was pretty well known. And then there was Patti Smith stuff that I used to really like. It was amazing to find someone who I had those things in common with, because in '80, '81, '82? Those things that had become very, very close to me were really quite unusual.

Like what?

Like the Phil Spector records, like '(Remember) Walking in the Sand' by The Shangri-Las. I really liked 'Give Him a Great Big Kiss' by The Shangri-Las too; they were kind of the bands I really liked.

Was that the kind of stuff you were listening to when you were making the first Smiths records?

No, when we did the first Smiths record, that stuff I mentioned was all part of my musical education, what made up my personal identity. You like having stuff of your own, and what Morrissey and I had in common was that our heroes were into that. We got into the girl groups, through the New York Dolls and them covering those songs, but I think at the time I was listening to a lot of Brill Building stuff. I used to like 'Young Boy Blues' by Ben E. King. You've got to remember this was at a time when everybody was listening to synthesizer duos, and in the clubs there was a lot of early electro, which I really liked, but 'Young Boy Blues' is a long, long way away from that. And I used to like 'I Count the Tears' by The Drifters – that was a big song.

But you want to be of your time, you want to represent your age group, so as much as we were unusual when we started The Smiths – and we were personally not very typical of our age group – musically we came out of post-punk, and we wanted to be a modern group. I remember I liked 'Homosapien' by Pete Shelley, off his first solo record, because we were really big fans of the Buzzcocks and that spoke to our generation.

Another very important record was *The Correct Use of Soap* by Magazine [1980]. I really respected John McGeoch, the guitar player, and Morrissey respected Howard Devoto for his lyrics and singing. 'Because You're Frightened' was particularly a favourite of mine off that album.

At the end of The Smiths, much was made of the personal wrangling. Did you start pulling in different ways musically?

That probably would've happened, but we didn't all the time we were together, and the last record [*Strangeways, Here We Come*, 1987], I think it still is my favourite. So we never pulled in different directions when the band was together, but I'm glad that I got to do very different things after that. Sitting here now, 25 years from when The Smiths split, having done so many different types of music, I feel not only fortunate but completely without doubt that it was absolutely necessary. I'm just not one of those people who can stick with the same format year in, year out. I can't stand to play the same music for three, four, five years. I don't want to be playing what I'm playing now in 18 months.

Electronic was the band you formed with Bernard Sumner. That surprised a lot of people. Were you always into dance music? When was the first time you went to the Haçienda?

The Haçienda wasn't really a dance club as people remember it when it first opened. My first experience with the Haçienda was Peter Saville [Factory Records designer] and Mike Pickering – he went on to be M People – who was a DJ there, who brought into the clothes shop that I was working in the blueprints for the Haçienda before it was even built. I was there on the opening night, and I was there four to five nights a week with 12 other people – who were the entire patrons of the place.

The Haçienda didn't have anybody in it, really, until 1986 or 87, apart from the odd rock band, but it was like my front room. Ian Brown will tell you the same. This little group of people: you couldn't help but know each other, because we were stood in a place that was supposed to hold 1,800 people and there were, like, 14 of us there.

The first time I ever worked with Bernard was in 1983: he was producing a record for Mike Pickering's band, Quando Quango, and I played guitar on that. I always played with other people. People have this idea that The Smiths split and then I went band-hopping, but when we did our first album I worked with Bernard, and then when we did our second album I played on Billy Bragg's records, and when we did our third album I played on Kirsty MacColl's record, and when we did our last album I played with Talking Heads.

Bernard was someone I really respected, and I heard from a mutual friend that he was interested in writing some songs away from New Order and wanted to work with me. At the end of The Smiths, I was very keen to do something that sounded different, and I regarded Bernard Sumner as the best electronic musician in the UK – as well as being the killer guitar player in Joy Division. We bumped into each other over the years and then we started writing, and then this very, very tight friendship started. Electronic were together for nine years. I wouldn't change that time for anyone — it was just a really, really good time. We could've been a bit more prolific, but hindsight's a very good thing, you know?

"I can't stand to play the same music for three, four, five years. I don't want to be playing what I'm playing now in 18 months."

There are a couple of musical urban legends: one says that the first time you met Noel Gallagher was in the Haçienda and he passed you an Oasis demo. Is this true?

No, it's half true. He passed my brother a demo – my brother was always being given tapes by people to pass on to me – and he, in his wisdom, didn't bother with a lot of them. He knows his stuff and he gave me this tape, and I just put it on a shelf somewhere. So several weeks had gone by and I was just driving down the road and it was pouring down – we had rain in Manchester, for a change – and I was with my brother, and this huddled figure in this duffle coat was walking down the street and my brother says to me, 'Oh, there's Noel.' I was like, 'Who's that?' He goes, 'You know, that guy whose demo I gave you to listen to, like, two months ago.' So I was like, 'Oh right, okay', and just because it was so pouring with rain, I pulled over and gave him a ride in my BMW.

We went off and he asked me what I thought of the demo, and I just lied through my teeth and I told him I thought it was great, because we got along and I thought he really had a spark to him. When I went back home I went through all of these shelves looking for that demo, and then there it was, this tape, and I played it and thought, 'Yeah, pretty good'. I gave him a call and I went to see him a few days later.

By 2005, you're playing with Modest Mouse, a US alt rock institution. Can you remember seeing them for the first time?
First time I saw Modest Mouse, I was on the stage – played with them! I thought the guitar music coming out of the UK was all getting very obvious – Beatles rewrites, you know? It actually put me off classic rock. So midway through making the second Healers album, Isaac Brock called me from Modest Mouse and wanted to know if I would help them write whatever the record was they were about to write.

It sounded like an interesting experiment. I had no idea how the band operated and how they wrote songs. Having written over an album now of stuff with Modern Mouse, I still don't know how we write together and I like it that way. So I went over there, and me and Isaac met up. We wrote a song called 'We've Got Everything' that same night. I woke up about four in the morning in Portland completely jet-lagged, didn't know where I was, and thought, 'Did we just write a new modern alternative indie A-side tonight?' Turned out we'd turned the key and off we went, because over the next ten days all of these ideas that I had musically just came out. It was a really inspired time.

All the way down the line with the band, it was like, 'Are you going to join? Are you going to join?' It's like, 'No, I don't know about joining another band.' I thought I was done with bands. I'm not someone who needs to be in a band. But if I'm in the right band, it's the most important thing in my life. It just felt like the right band, you know?

When did you become Johnny Jarman? When did you fall in love with The Cribs?
I officially joined actually just as we walked on stage … We played Leeds and Reading [Festivals] in 2008, and we really slammed it at Leeds. It was an amazing night, 18,000 people singing not only the lyrics but the riffs. It was so good and then Ryan said to me, 'So you're in then or what?', just as we were walking on at Reading. It was pretty great. I'm still a fan, you know? I think it's very important to think like a fan; it's one of the things that really made The Smiths tick. I never lost that, and so when a band comes along that you can be a fan of, it's something that I recognize as being pretty special.

When The Cribs' second album came out, I knew that there was an intelligence at work there. First off, I just really liked the music, but there seemed to be a lot going on – a very deliberate kind of sound, deliberate in their approach. I thought, 'This can't be all by accident; I hope it's deliberate.' Of course it is.

There's no great master plan. I really like working without a map. I've always just followed the music, whether it's been other people's records or just joining bands and meeting musicians. I was like that when I was fourteen, fifteen, and I'm still like that now, and luckily for me there's a bunch of these interesting songs with guitar parts and people seem to like them.

Do you feel comfortable about the label 'guitar god'?

Obviously, I'd rather it be said than not said; I don't want to be insincere about it. It's the most incredible thing. It's the highest accolade, and I know that the greatest accolade is for people you respect to respect you. But I can't think about it too much, because you would have to have some gargantuan ego to analyze it. I'm just very, very grateful and trying not to screw up, and I try and live up to it. But the best thing about it is that it validates the path I've taken, which is on my own now, 25 years on.

What's the last song we should play?

I'll pick 'We Share the Same Skies' by The Cribs, purely because it's the most recent single that I've had out and it starts off with a pretty good riff – that's good reason enough.

The First Time **Johnny Marr** Playlist

1	How Soon Is Now?	The Smiths
2	Cathy's Clown	The Everly Brothers
3	I Only Want to Be With You	Dusty Springfield
4	Metal Guru	T. Rex
5	Stoned Love	The Supremes
6	You Wear It Well	Rod Stewart
7	Suffragette City	David Bowie
8	You're the One	The Marvelettes
9	Young Boy Blues	Ben E. King
10	I Count the Tears	The Drifters
11	Because You're Frightened	Magazine
12	Run Through the Jungle	The Gun Club
13	Atom Rock (Fac 102R Remix)	Quando Quango
14	Get the Message	Electronic
15	Dashboard	Modest Mouse
16	We Share the Same Skies	The Cribs

"You just have to assume it doesn't mean anything more important than how it sounds as you're playing it."

JONNY GREENWOOD

There are no lengthy negotiations, no time constraints and no entourage when you visit a member of Radiohead; just a friendly welcome at Oxford station from one of the band's management team and trip to their headquarters in a happily battered Prius. The relaxed atmosphere is more suited to a quick trip to drop off scones at a school bake sale than a journey to conduct a rare interview with the guitarist in possibly the most important British band of the past 20 years.

It's hard to tell, as it's nestled deep inside luxuriant hedging, but Radiohead's headquarters is a large, sprawling cottage containing a recording studio – 'I'd rather not have a photo taken in here', Jonny Greenwood says. 'I promised myself never to be one of those musicians who's pictured in front of their own mixing desk' – a kitchen area I'm delighted to find littered with empty champagne bottles, and lounges full of pianos, amplifiers, guitar cases and comfy sofas.

Radiohead never stopped doing interviews, they just did fewer and fewer. As a band whose every utterance is seized upon like a sermon from the mount, when they do speak, people get a bit overexcited. So I understand Jonny's habit of picking his words carefully: he'll reply with a hesitant 'Right …' if a question sounds like it might have a hidden agenda. But despite his body language – hunched forward, wide eyes often covered by a long, dark fringe – he's actually lovely to chat to. Softly spoken and unerringly polite, he's talkative, thoughtful and intelligent, with a dryly self-deprecating sense of humour and genuine enthusiasm for his band's music.

Months after this interview, I had a chance to interview each member of Radiohead. Similarly, the experience was a joy – to get the opportunity to speak to them all will remain a highlight of my career. I guess if Jonny hadn't liked this first interview, I never would have had that chance. It's nice to able to have this opportunity to say thank you. So thank you.

Matt Everitt: When were you first aware of music?

My first memory is probably being given a plastic recorder when I was about four or five and thinking it was amazing and playing it all the time. I stuck with it, to be fair; I kept playing until I was an adult. I was in recorder groups when I was a teenager, when I should have been taking bong hits in a stolen car or something. Instead, I was playing baroque recorder music. I know, it's a wasted youth – what can I do? Misspent.

What about the first time you were aware of recorded music?

Yeah, I suppose it was cassettes in the car. We had a *very* small collection of the same cassettes being played over and over again. For some reason, my mum always got the fake versions of famous records. So instead of having Simon and Garfunkel we had the Woolworths £1.99 cassettes where someone would just cover the same song as closely as possible, and sell them for half the price.

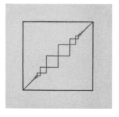

Which other ones, apart from *almost* Simon and Garfunkel?

Musicals, actually. There was the *Flower Drum Song* – bizarre, obscure musicals, always on cassettes. And Burl Ives, we had that on record.

And the fascination with music was immediate with you?

Yeah, I suppose so. Because it was quite a limited collection of music, you'd listen to the same thing over and over again. I remember doing that with records when I was really little. I was very lucky because having a sister ten years older than me, and of course Colin [Jonny's brother] in Radiohead, he's two and a half years older than me, meant I got to listen to their records, and older siblings always have better taste.

What sort of things did they pass down?

I remember for one whole year, every morning, Colin would play, very loudly, 12-inches of The Beat, things like 'Psychedelic Rockers'. He used to play 'Everything's Gone Green' by New Order, and we had that every morning, over and over again. The stuff we heard, I think, stands up.

What was the first record that was yours?

I remember getting hold of a copy of *Cool for Cats* [Squeeze]. I don't think I would have bought it new; it must have been a few years old, even then. My mother threw it away, because it was seen as a bad influence … Which is strange, isn't it? I'm quite nostalgic for those days. Nowadays it feels like parents are keen for their children to form bands and play rock music, but this was the last gasp of it being vaguely 'not the thing to do'. I mean, you see teenagers now whose grandparents were probably in punk bands, so all rebellion is gone. Maybe that's a good thing.

What about the first gig you went to?

The first gig I saw was distressingly cool to admit to, I'm afraid, because it was The Fall in Oxford. And I just couldn't deal with it. I actually left after four songs and waited outside, because I just found it overwhelming – and then went back in again. The volume and the chaos was exciting, but overwhelming. Brix Smith playing guitar – the *Frenz Experiment* tour, I think. I remember standing outside and hearing it by the emergency doors, and still listening to it and just trying to make sense of it.

What do you remember about *your* first gigs?

First gigs as Radiohead? Like a professional jobbing band? We didn't play concerts until just before we signed. We used to play a venue called the Jericho Tavern in Oxford. It feels like we only played that place three or four times, and then, suddenly, we were going on tour with The Frank and Walters, or Sultans of Ping FC in our early days.

What do you remember from that first tour?

Yeah, just so exciting. I remember we all lived in the same house in Oxford, and we'd have a minibus, and just putting the gear in the back, taking it out of the sitting room where we'd been practising and loading up the van and going off. It was the most exciting thing, to be going to Coventry Polytechnic or wherever. I don't mean that to sound sarcastic, because it really was the best thing to do. Nothing like it. It's still the same, the same fun of arriving at a venue and walking into an empty room, and wondering how it's going to go. It's great.

When did you first fall in love with the singular wonderfulness that is the Pixies?

I remember being at school and Thom [Yorke] putting on a cassette and saying, 'We should sound like this', and he played 'Dead' by the Pixies on *Doolittle* [1989]. All their songs have got no fat on them; it's all been thought out to not be boring and to be as empty as it can be and *still* be exciting. It's interesting that they reformed and carried on. I think, of all bands, they can get away with it, because they were always in their forties, really. I can't imagine a teenage version of the Pixies. There's just something kind of dark and strange and grown up about them always, so that's why they still sound so good.

I went to the gig in Paris at Zénith [May 2016] and you played 'Creep', and it didn't feel as much of a *moment* as maybe it had in the past. It used to have such a weight behind it when you performed it, and now it just feels part of the set.

Yeah, now we lump it in with 'Paranoid Android' and 'Karma Police', and there's a few songs that people know and are excited to hear, so it's not like there's just one … Which is great.

When *OK Computer* [1997] first came out, did you see people's reactions and think, 'Everything's going to be different now?'

No. I kind of don't really remember the reaction, because we were touring and nothing changed, really.

You said you've never been interested in being the biggest band in the world, that's never been what it's about, but having a record like that kind of makes you that by default.

I remember the venues getting bigger and us not getting used to it quickly enough, and it all being quite stressful. There's an element of that with us still now. I remember clearly being in Aberdeen when *The Bends* came out [in 1995], and getting a copy of the *NME*, and reading a good review and feeling really excited. I remember thinking, 'Look where I am, so far from home, and playing a concert tonight.' That was a good memory.

Magazine are a band you've namechecked a lot. When did you first hear them, and when did you first fall in love with them?

Older sister, again. It's all down to that. I keep thanking her, and she says she had a friend called Dave who gave her the record. So really, it's all down to him. He pushed her in the right direction. It was just one of the few records we had and listened to over and over again. *The Correct Use of Soap* was a really big record.

What is it about the sound or the playing that resonated?

I suppose the songwriting and the ways songs have been arranged, and it was just quite well thought out. I've always been a bit distrustful of the noble savage idea of songs all having three chords and that somehow *means* more, is more sincere, because their music isn't quite like that. It's great music, and it's simple in a way, but it's not just … Miles Davis said that people were always keen to play down the fact that he'd been to Juilliard, and all the jazzers could sight-read music and were able to play in all 12 keys and were all really well trained. And yet, all their reviewers were keen to try and make out that they were somehow playing from their hearts and didn't know what they were doing, and therefore the music was better. Not that I can necessarily tie that in to Magazine. But it's a dangerous thing to talk about, because people like to know that their music is written and played with as little thought as possible, I think. It's a tough call; you've got to get the balance right, because music that's *just* about maths is always awful.

When did you get into dub? I remember the *Jonny Greenwood Is the Controller* compilation that you did in 2007 on Trojan.

My brother Colin, coming back from college with a cassette of Lee 'Scratch' Perry's greatest hits – that was about the only thing we had. And we had a Matumbi record as well. That was my way into dub reggae, I suppose. Plus we have [guitar technician] Duncan Swift who tours with us; he's part of the crew and he listens obsessively to that kind of music. I find that really interesting, that he doesn't need to listen to anything else. I think that means he's listening really closely and hearing things in it that are worth hearing. I remember feeling envious, like I was missing out on something. So when I got asked to do it, that was my excuse to listen to that stuff for months and really explore it, and it was great.

A couple of years ago, this record by X-O-Dus was finally released, Factory's one reggae band. They released one single, but didn't bother releasing the album. It only finally came out a couple of years ago, and it's great – there's a song called 'English Black Boys', which is just fantastic.

There's an image that has grown around Radiohead's studio work, that it's this very tortured, very emotionally draining, difficult experience for everybody concerned. Is that true?
It is by turns really exciting, and there's usually Thom in the middle of it getting very excited and motivating everyone on. And then periods when nothing's happening and it's just not working and it's frustrating … It's like that for everyone with work, I guess. But when it's going well, it's such an exciting and happy time that that gets you through anything, really. It's only torturous looking back, you know?

Can you remember a particularly torturous period? [Laughs]
Yeah. The traditional Radiohead thing is to record something – and again, it's always been like that – we recorded 'No Surprises' and then worried about it, and then re-recorded it, because it didn't sound any

"You hear what you did the day before, and you can't remember it being played, you don't know where the sounds are coming from … that's really exciting."

good, and then re-recorded it again, and then went back to the very first recording and released it. So that's what you hear. It's torturous in *that* way. It's not like you're sitting, looking for a kick drum sound for two weeks; it's more effort than that, and more hitting brick walls over and over again. That's just how it goes.

You wouldn't keep doing it if you didn't enjoy it.
Yeah. Some mornings you come in, and you hear what you did the day before, and you can't remember it being played, you don't know where the sounds are coming from, when you're hearing two or three people playing together and a new sound coming out of the speakers, and it didn't exist two days before. That's really exciting. You've got this thing that's permanently there and you're not sure where it came from, that's really fun.

Glastonbury. What are your memories of the first song in 1997, the gig that is now regarded by many as one of the greatest Glastonbury performances ever?

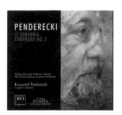

I just remember it being very stressful and the monitors breaking and Thom walking off because he couldn't hear anything, and it just being a disaster. It was like; we can't hear ourselves, we don't know what's coming across. And then I remember him asking Andy Watson, our lighting guy, to illuminate the audience, so we could finally see them. I remember that. You can hear what you're playing, and you hope everyone is hearing each other and that something is coming across, but it was a struggle, yeah.

That must be terrifying! To think, 'There's all these people, and we're headlining …'
… and we're blowing it, yeah. It can happen in live shows; you just don't know what's coming across. You've got no idea. And because it's sounding so bad to you, you assume that's what's happening out front. Maybe it's worse the other way around, when it sounds great on stage and everyone is suffering! We have come off stage thinking it's brilliant, only for our managers to be out front claiming they have nothing to do with us! Famous gig in Bath Moles in the 1990s, playing and thinking, 'That was great!', and literally someone came to our manager Chris and said, 'You got anything to do with this band?' And he said, 'No' [laughs]. And the cock crowed three times. It was terrible. So, yeah. I wonder how bad we could have been? [Laughs.]

Can we talk about your classical work and Krzysztof Penderecki.
He studied electronic music and learned all about synthesizers, and then how to produce things electronically, and then suddenly decided, 'This is all nonsense; I can make all these sounds with an orchestra.' He would never say this, but that's how I've interpreted how he turned his back on all that and went back to violins. His records sound much stranger, more interesting to me than things you can do with electronics. It's all technology, I suppose, computers and pianos, trying to get them all on to a level field and treat them all equally.

But unfortunately taste comes in, too, and this drives me crazy. In an ideal world, you can use any instrument and any sound, and whatever serves the arrangement of the song is all that matters, which is a good, pure motivation. But then sometimes you're recording, say, a flugelhorn, and it just sounds like Burt Bacharach, and you think, 'Maybe this is a bad idea after all', because there are obviously connotations. Sound isn't a pure thing, unfortunately. You assemble these great instruments, and it suddenly starts to remind you of something terrible. And it ruins it.

The smallest rumour of anything happening with the band gets seized upon by people. Does the amount of attention that your work gets make it harder to *do* the work?
Right. I always think of the albums that won Album of the Year in the '70s and '80s: if you have a look at the list, it's really interesting because it's got amazing Rolling Stones records or the Sex Pistols or whatever, but it's also got terrible prog records that have quite rightly been

forgotten. I suppose what I'm saying is no one can make that judgement call until it's far too late, so why worry about it? You just have to assume it doesn't mean anything more important than how it sounds in the room as you're playing it, and how it's sounding out in the speakers when you first record it. That's all you've got to think about.

That's a good attitude.
I hope so, yeah, because otherwise you're excited about your own mythology and it's just awful and terrible. That's when it all goes wrong for bands. We are quite conscious and interested about bands going wrong and falling apart, and how and why that happens, musically.

How have you kept it from falling apart?
Just neurosis, I suppose – just that, mainly, and enjoying it, taking it seriously and enjoying how much pleasure we get when it's going well.

What's the last song we should play? Choice is yours.
How about Sleaford Mods? That would be great.

The First Time Jonny Greenwood Playlist

1	The Numbers	Radiohead
2	Bridge over Troubled Water	Orchester Anthony Ventura
3	Flower Drum Song	Richard Rodgers
4	Fooba Wooba John	Burl Ives
5	Everything's Gone Green	New Order
6	Cool for Cats	Squeeze
7	Wrong Place, Right Time	The Fall
8	Dead	Pixies
9	A Song From Under the Floorboards	Magazine
10	Black Panta	Lee 'Scratch' Perry and The Upsetters
11	English Black Boys	X-O-Dus
12	No Surprises	Radiohead
13	Symphony No. 3 (4th movement): Passacaglia – Allegro moderato	Krzysztof Penderecki
14	Open Spaces (*There Will Be Blood* OST)	Jonny Greenwood
15	No One's Bothered	Sleaford Mods

"I firmly believe that you should use your moral compass, but you should try to avoid following as many rules as possible while using your moral compass."

Josh Homme

The interview doesn't happen in London, as planned, or Paris either, which was the second option; my last chance is here, a shiny hotel in Barcelona, where I'm waiting in the foyer, somewhat desperately jabbing a tour manager's number into my phone. Queens of the Stone Age played the Primavera Sound festival last night, and there's no sign of anyone to do with the band. Primavera starts late in the day, and the final acts don't take to the stage till 3am. The intention is to allow Barcelonians to have their traditional long, late lunch and saunter down to the site in the early evening as the sun sets and the atmosphere gently builds. The reality is that visiting UK and US musicians and audiences still start drinking at midday, as per usual, but just have a lot more time before the entertainment stops. This creates a pretty hyped-up atmosphere, which may have proved too appealing an opportunity to miss for Josh Homme.

I finally locate the tour manager in his suite; he leaves a message for Josh, then we wait for three long hours before Josh finally shoulders through the hotel door. He's a 6 foot 4 inch ginger Elvis, with a deep, rolling, slow voice, a Southern gentleman's manners and a big grin. 'It was a late night last night', he chuckles, while trying to work the coffee machine. 'Sorry for delaying so much. I was up till seven.' He shrugs, looking what I can only describe as wolfishly sheepish, before offering a one-word explanation: 'Ecstasy.'

Matt Everitt: Do you remember the first time you were aware of music as a kid?

Yeah, I do actually. We used to take these long trips in the summertime, driving, and one of the first records I remember was Jackson Browne, *Running on Empty*. The cover is just a road going straight into nowhere, and the entire record is written and recorded on the road in hotel rooms, and in the back of a bus and live. And they're all songs about the road.

The first awareness of music, for most people, would probably be the first single they bought.

The first thing I ever got was a compilation record called *Eastern Front*. When you bought vinyls, they were so physical. The artwork is so compelling. There was an illustration of a guy with a mohawk, and it was live from San Francisco. There were some bands from England, like Chron Gen, and there were a lot of US bands, like Channel 3 and Battalion of Saints. It assaulted my ears – it was really brash punk rock music.

Black Flag is a band you've often mentioned as being really important to you. When was the first time you heard them?

Shortly thereafter – within a month. They had such an influence on me and such an influence on my hometown, because they *actually* played my hometown, and *nobody* ever played my hometown.

Why not? Just too far out?

There was nowhere to play, no reason to go, you know? No money to be made, no gasoline to get in a car. And at the time, the notion of SST [Records] – which was Greg Ginn's label – was that you really could do it yourself: you didn't need to be on the radio; you did not need to pursue the accolades of riches and fame. It was this thing that *you* did, you know? I was so young and I took it as 'This is what you do when you want to pick a religion that's not the other ones.' And so it needed to be that important to you, because they weren't making any money, to my knowledge. So it had to be for the respect of it all, for the religion of it all, and I think that really impacted the whole town at the time.

Black Flag was like this jazz band – whatever punk rock was supposed to be, if you weren't supposed to have long hair? Here they were, they all had long hair! Henry Rollins wore shorts. They kept changing singers but it didn't matter. You could have this revolving cast of people and they could all be important and unimportant at the same time. They could all be part of an amazing phase, but regenerate and continue.

What's a Black Flag track that we should play?

'Thirsty and Miserable'. It's really good.

What was the first gig you went to?

The first gig I ever saw was Carl Perkins, at a place called the Festival. Which was very generically named. It was a single-stage festival at a baseball field in Sand Point, Idaho. I remember hearing 'Blue Suede Shoes' and connecting the dots between him and Chuck Berry, which is someone that I'd also heard recently. And the kind of personal, personable, affable charisma that he had. He had this kind of swagger that was really cool, and it was very friendly.

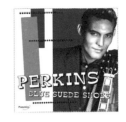

What was your first professional gig? When you first got some money for doing this?
I didn't get money for, like, forever! I mean, you didn't get paid in the desert, you know? That was never a component that was introduced, so it was never part of the dialogue. If you play a free party in the desert, asking for money is quite a dickish manoeuvre. Also, if you drop a hat, someone will pee in it. So my first professional gig? We went to record for the first time out of town, and the person that managed the studio, her name was Catherine Enny, said, 'Do you have a manager?' And we said, 'What is that?' And she said, 'Well, I'll be that.' And her suggestion was to play with Firehose at a place called the Green Door in Montclair. When we played, I think there were four people [laughs]. It went well.

"If you play a free party in the desert, asking for money is quite a dickish manoeuvre. Also, if you drop a hat, someone will pee in it."

When did you first hear Iggy Pop? We're talking about people who, musically, have had a big impact on you.
I would say he is one of the biggest influences on me. I first heard The Stooges when I was about twelve years old, but I didn't like it, and I traded the record immediately. I just wasn't ready for what that was. I was too young to get the subversiveness. And I didn't hear Iggy Pop again until I was twenty. I think, as is the case when you're young, it's so easy to do, to define what we don't like and what we don't want to do in order to build this artistic moat around ourselves to protect and preserve the thing that we're doing.

We didn't have techs [roadies]; we just teched our own gear. It was down to that SST ideal that we took and ran with in a direction that probably had nothing to do with it. It was like, 'No guitar techs! No this! No that!' And I didn't listen to other music. It was part of it.

How can you not listen to music, if you're in a band?
I listened to everything that I'd already listened to. But people would say, 'Oh, you guys sound like Sabbath', and I felt proud about saying, 'I've never heard them', you know? Not realizing that they had infused into

bands like Black Flag and whatever. I was getting the DNA of them through other sources. I started listening to *Lust for Life* and *The Idiot* at the same time, and then I heard the story of their creation and immediately dove into The Stooges and said, 'What?!? What is this?' Then I realized everyone hated The Stooges, and they were dropped, and no one could stand them, and I felt that kinship. And the music and the lyrics – the attitude that it was for girls *and* guys could like it too, if they wanted to [laughs]. Somehow, it was rock that was sexy and scary and real. Songs like 'The Passenger' or 'Neighborhood Threat' or 'Lust for Life' [from *Lust for Life*], or 'Mass Production' off *The Idiot* – just all that stuff.

The first track on the first Queens record [*Queens of the Stone Age*, 1998], 'Regular John' – you've said that was a distillation of everything you wanted to achieve with the band.
Yeah. It was just me and a drummer, Alfredo Hernández – I didn't really want it to be that way, but that's the way it ended up. But I do think that ideas unfiltered are better, because they're not running through these filters and being redirected; they're just right off the tap. And that record is right off the tap: it's one idea, it's repetition and stiffness and trance.

You've mentioned Krautrock and bands like Can being an influence, the metallic repetition. I can see where that comes in.
Well, I've had the same sound man since I was nineteen. His name is Hutch, and he's been a really big influence on me, because when I refused to listen to music, he would try to inject something. When I was writing the first Queens record, I was like, 'I want to do something that is unheard, that's different. I know that's possible.' And so I just got into trance, dance, rock and stiffness, you know? I thought I was on to something, and he was like, 'Have you ever heard Can?' And I was like, 'No.' And then he played me that, and I basically was like, 'Go fuck yourself!'

But there were a few years of a musical gap, because when I first heard The Stooges records and *Lust for Life* and *The Idiot*, it made me want to quit music, because I was young, and I was a little disillusioned by what had gone on, and the touring lifestyle wasn't necessarily for me. And when I heard those records? I was like, 'Well, that's what I want to say. And it's said better than I even know how to say it … So I'm gone!'

I took a two-year break and tried to see if there were other things in life, because I never planned to be a musician. Like, 'Well, that was fun. But no one in my hometown is a musician for a job.' So I took some time away. But then it was great, because you realize, 'I want to say this my way. I don't care if it's been said. It hasn't been said by me and I have my way of saying it too.'

The early mythology of Queens is that you had quite a 'rambunctious' lifestyle. Do you remember the first time that you got into trouble with the law?
Yeah, I can …

What happened?

Well, you know, I'm a lover not a fighter, and I like to hug and hang out, but the first time I was ever arrested? I mean, I've always hated the general set of rules, so I've experienced a little bit of trouble my whole life, you know? And I firmly believe that you should use your moral compass, but you should try to avoid following as many rules as possible while using your moral compass. I've had a few run-ins with the law but the … But I'd rather not get into that.

I wasn't seeking to glorify anything, I was just interested …

Yeah, I don't want to glorify it, either. You know, what you end up realizing is that you, anyone, can get in trouble at any moment. All you have to do is be foolish enough to put yourself in the wrong spot at the wrong time, you know? You get thrown out of one place, and someone takes a picture, and the next thing you know? Branded for life.

The *Rated R* album [2000] was the first record that started to put you in people's faces – 'The Lost Art of Keeping a Secret' and those songs, 'Feel Good Hit of the Summer'. How did it feel when you started getting a bit more recognizable?

It felt unexpected and peculiar. There's no advice that someone could give you that applies to running that gauntlet of flowers and razor blades that is 'starting to do well', you know?

> ## "You, anyone, can get in trouble at any moment. All you have to do is be foolish enough to put yourself in the wrong spot at the wrong time."

Did you deal with it well?

Probably not. I think we were wide-eyed and arms out, and had this attitude that was 'Don't tell me … Show me!' Which is a fun and contagious way to be. And so, I think, instead of sauntering down the hallways of the building of success, we ran down the hallway screaming, 'Arghhhhhhhh!' But I also think, we were from the desert and family guys and, I think, we were *nice* guys … But *loud* guys, you know?

The world you've created for yourself within Queens now seems quite different to how tempestuous it was before.

I think one of the key things to do is not to impose your will on somebody. The true nature of collaboration and positive friction is understanding who somebody is and loving who they really are. Guys like [QOTSA

members] Jon Theodore, Dean Fertita, Alain Johannes, Natasha Shneider, Chris Goss – these are guys and girls that are true individuals, that are pillars of personality. I never wanted to do anything but bask in that light of who each person is. I don't want to change anybody like that. And we've had major moments – recurring, and then dissipating and recurring – when the chemistry of those personalities is explosive, and potentially dangerous to minors and others.

I feel like I've always been the pirate captain that encourages that, and I also understand that things run their course, and sometimes that happens. It's not something to get upset about; it's something to be thankful for, the time that you had. And, you know, you don't harness it. You launch chaos, you know? And enjoy it.

When did you first meet Dave Grohl, who's helped take the band to another level in terms of profile and, more importantly, in terms of bringing his musicianship to the band for a while.
I was nineteen and it was at a place called the Off Ramp [Café] in Seattle, and we knew of each other because he was in [DC punk band] Scream and I was friends with all the guys in Scream – this is just as he went to try out for Nirvana. I was staying at the Wool house – the members of Scream had started a new band called Wool – so Dave really hadn't even recorded yet. When I met him, we just hit it off. Even back then, Dave was telling people about Kyuss. I don't think anyone has been a louder bullhorn for me than Dave, and I don't think anyone's done more without really thinking about it, just saying nice things and being part of each other's lives, than Dave has. We've always been good friends, and we've always had something special that has nothing to do with all 'that'. And we still have it now. It's almost my longest-running collaborative friendship that I've had.

'Sleep Walk' by Santo and Johnny: one of your favourite songs.
It should definitely be played at my funeral, just in case anything happens tonight …

It is a beautiful piece of music. When did you first hear it?
I don't know what age I was. I was in Idaho, in the middle of the woods for the summer – that's where I was every summer. And it was on the radio and I just thought, 'I don't understand what that is'. I didn't know what a lap steel [guitar] was at the time, or a slide. And it sounded like the title: it just sounded like a dream, and it sounded perfect to me. It must have been when I was at least eleven or twelve, because I was already listening to punk rock music, and it was so contrary to what I was committed to, but it hit me in a spot that almost no other music had ever hit me [laughs].

I love those weird recesses in your psyche that are waiting for a song like that, you know? There's something effortless about that song, and its lack of singing means it's about whatever I think it's about.

You're a big Leonard Cohen fan. Can you see yourself like Leonard, sauntering on to stages with a fedora in your eighties?

The real goal in all this is not as much about firsts but lasts. Can your last record be your best record? How many people traverse this crazy, mixed-up circus of a way to live and make their best stuff towards the end? You know, bands peel away and artists peel away or tie a sweater around their shoulders and play some boring acoustic shit for the rest of their lives. But who can make it through all the way and be as cool as Leonard Cohen? You know what I mean? Who can navigate those waters like that? That's the real goal.

You know, the truth is I would love to see how far my wingspan can stretch artistically, and I consume music the way I make music – slowly. I want to enjoy each phase. But I see more phases and incarnations of what I do and it's like staring at a shape in the fog. You see the outline of what could be, and you just walk towards that … And hope it's not the police.

And the final thing: you get to choose the last song that we play. It can be anything.

JD McPherson – he's a blue-collar rockabilly guy. He's a little older; he's in his early thirties, so it's not about dressing like you're trying to be cast in the S. E. Hinton book. 'North Side Gal.' If this song doesn't immediately make you happy and want to jump up and dance, then I'm really sorry about that.

The First Time Josh Homme Playlist

1	Make It Wit Chu	Queens of the Stone Age
2	Running on Empty	Jackson Browne
3	Breakdown	Chron Gen
4	Thirsty and Miserable	Black Flag
5	Blue Suede Shoes	Carl Perkins
6	Hear Nothing See Nothing Say Nothing	Discharge
7	Deadly Kiss	Kyuss
8	Mass Production	Iggy Pop
9	Regular John	Queens of the Stone Age
10	Mother Sky	Can
11	New Fang	Them Crooked Vultures
12	Sing Another Song, Boys	Leonard Cohen
13	Sleep Walk	Santo and Johnny
14	North Side Gal	JD McPherson

"I don't need a producer, I don't need a label, I don't need a budget. If I want to make music, I can make music."

KELIS

K elis is almost the exact opposite of the image that her music has created. The aggressive, militant character that features in a lot of her early songs couldn't be more different from the funny, relaxed, open and totally unintimidating person I meet when I interview her. She's tall, with huge, wild waves of deep black hair and wide Cleopatra eyes, and she laughs – a beautiful, deep, rough chuckle – a lot.

She talks unself-consciously about her career, and I don't think I've ever met a musician who has spoken with such frankness about their dislike of the music industry and described the practical battles they've faced getting their albums released and promoted. Artists almost never discuss the nuts-and-bolts *business* aspect of the music business. But similarly, I don't think I've met a singer who could care less about success. I often hear people say, 'It's all about the music (man)', but with Kelis, I genuinely feel that albums are just the result of something she's been doing her whole life, and would continue doing even if there were no release schedule or record label. There's no bitterness, just a slightly amused antipathy. When she talks about quitting music to concentrate on food – in 2006 she enrolled at Le Cordon Bleu culinary school, graduating as a fully qualified chef – you can tell she means it.

We should just be glad that she changed her mind.

Matt Everitt: When was the very first time you were aware of music as a kid?

My dad was a saxophonist. He would play literally from the time he woke up. We just heard it all day long. My parents bought this really dilapidated brownstone in Harlem, and they began to refurbish it, area by area, room by room. So eventually the whole downstairs two floors were done, and my dad was then banished to the upstairs part that had to then get redone also. But that's where all his music stuff was. He had a Fender Rhodes [electric piano], and all these different saxophones upstairs.

Who did you want to be when you were little?

I thought Sarah Vaughan was amazing. She had this deep, really smooth voice, which I thought was brilliant. Then Betty Carter, and she used to scat; I used to just think, 'That's so good, because then you don't have to remember words!' And Nancy Wilson and Gloria Lynne – all these great ladies. Then Etta James, and it kind of progressed from there.

What was the first record that you owned?

I can't remember the first record I owned, genuinely. I can tell you the first concert I ever went to, though, and that was a Eurythmics concert. I was blown away. Because I grew up in Harlem, I grew up listening to jazz music and to gospel music – that was second nature to me. To see something totally different, I was in awe. Annie was larger than life. And it's funny, because – fast-forward to my career now – I actually got to sit in a room with her and write with her. It was pretty amazing. Here you are sitting with this legend, and she was just really chill.

What about when you first started getting into albums?

It was in high school. First of all, my parents were really strict, so we weren't really allowed to listen to a lot of stuff.

But he was a jazz musician, so surely ...?

Jazz was okay, but with lots of new stuff, my mum especially was just like, 'I don't know what that is. We're not doing that here.' You have to realize, my parents were *jazz*, that's it. Jazz we could play all day long, but I came up in the grunge era, and all she saw was what she thought were very scruffy white people! She was like, 'They're all high! It's not happening!'

Because jazz has a history of people that weren't very high ...

Absolutely – as she's the first one to tell you. But I think this looked dangerous or something. She was like, 'I don't know what that is. We're not doing that' – Nirvana, Pearl Jam, Smashing Pumpkins, The Cranberries and all these things. I went to private school – there were two other black kids in my class – so I was exposed to stuff that I wasn't getting at home, basically. That was the first time I was picking stuff that was new that I wasn't allowed to listen to at home.

What shall we play from that era, then?

Oh, man. I mean, it's got to be Nirvana, 'Smells Like Teen Spirit'.

When did you first hook up with The Neptunes?

I was in high school, and we had constructed a girl group. It was me and just some friends, called BLU: an acronym for Black Ladies United – obviously [laughs]. We would sing and wear horrible matching camouflage outfits. Just all bad. My best friend was friends with this other girl, a rapper, and she was like, 'She's working with these guys. They're out of Virginia Beach. You should meet them, they are kind of "Left", like you.' And I trusted her, because she was such a music person, then I met these guys [Pharrell Williams and Chad Hugo], and they were these two regular, pretty nerdy guys. I met them, and I think the talks about music made sense to me. We wanted to do something different.

The broadness of influences?

I think it was just the fact that we felt boundless. I think it's interesting, because I've been doing this for so long – my whole adult life. I've never done anything else. I signed my first deal when I was seventeen, so it's been 20 years. When I started it, I never had the idea of what this would turn out to be. I never had a plan for fame, or for anything like that. I wanted to do musical theatre, be on Broadway. We just wanted to do something different, and there was nothing to lose at that point. It wasn't like you *have* to make a radio record, or it's got to be a hit. We didn't know what any of that was, so we just did stuff that we thought was cool.

"We just wanted to do something different, and there was nothing to lose at that point ... we just did stuff that we thought was cool."

You mentioned your girl group. We should talk about En Vogue. When did you first hear them?

I was obsessed. Obsessed! Because they were the first – aside from Whitney Houston – girls who felt like me. There was Brownstone, and SWV and all these chicks who we loved, and I sang 'Weak' till I was weak. I loved them so much, but they didn't look like me. But then came En Vogue, and I was like, 'Oh, be still, my heart! Everything is different now.' They were glamorous, and beautiful, and they were all different. I was like, 'I'm the other girl! I'm the fifth member! I want to be in the group!' That was monumental, because they looked like something else. They looked like I could actually be in the group.

1999, 'Caught Out There'. Was that your first featured release?
No. The first song that I was ever on was when I sang the hook for Gravediggaz – part of Wu-Tang [Clan] – a song called 'Fairytalez'. That was the very, very first thing I ever did. I was fifteen, so we had no idea what it meant. We didn't know where music can take you now. I don't think I really understood that. I watched my dad be brilliant, and my dad ended up being a professor at Wesleyan University for music; he was a very well-trained, very articulate, really very talented man, but he never made a dime. So I didn't understand what any of this meant. Doing a song, I was like, 'Okay, cool. Yeah, I've been singing my whole life. It's not like I'm doing something new here.' I had no idea what was happening, and so that was the first thing. The second thing actually was ODB [Ol' Dirty Bastard feat. Kelis – 'Got Your Money'].

That did okay [laughs].
That did okay. Mild recognition, there! And actually it's funny, because right before we did that, Pharrell and I had walked into Elektra Records. I remember [chairman and CEO] Sylvia Rhone was like, 'Too weird. Not doing it. No. Never going to happen.' It wasn't ODB – because he already was who he was – it was me! We were trying to get a deal, basically. We went to somewhere else, and then we went to Virgin and everyone was like, 'It's weird. We don't really get it', then, finally, 'Sure. We'll sign her.'

So for someone who wasn't thinking about that kind of exposure and that success, when 'Caught Out There' came out, how did it feel? Because that tune just went off, didn't it?
Well, yes, it was exciting. Again, still I had no idea what was to come, and, I think, more than anything, it was the issue of now I was a topic of conversation, which I wasn't prepared for at all. There was a mirror being held up to me that I'd never had before.

And now you're famous.
And all of a sudden, yeah, we're having conversations about, like, 'Where does she fit? Because she's black, yet she's screaming' [laughs]. And, 'Is this rock?', 'Is it alternative?' And, 'Yeah, this record is groundbreaking, there's nothing like it, but it's almost too groundbreaking, we don't have anywhere to put her, and we're not willing to put our neck out for her.'

I'm like, 'Okay. What does that mean?' I was already naturally a rebellious person. Not only that, I'm eighteen, nineteen years old? So already I'm in the peak of that, and I'm being told 'You can't do that' and, 'This is too weird. You know you're black, right?' I'm like, 'Thank you. I'm aware.' I had to really puff my chest out. Right now, there's a black community of people who are very eclectic, and open, and very welcoming and willing. But at the time, we weren't told that it was okay. No one said that you could do that. Black girls were not wearing their hair natural and they were not screaming – all these things that they were not doing, and I was doing all these things. Again, I wasn't conscious.

Not a strategy.

No. It's just what I was doing. That's just what I looked like, just what I was. My hair was pink before I ever got signed. So all these things, all of a sudden. In the midst of all that, everything was in disarray. I'd just finished my second album, and everyone from Virgin got fired. Everyone who had been championing me, they're all gone; it just was like, 'Okay, are you going to do this and stand your ground? Or are you going to crumble and cave?' I was, like, push my chest out bigger [laughs].

Obviously, we've got to mention 'Milkshake'. I'm really interested in how it must be to watch something like that become part of popular culture, and popular phraseology.

Again, it's just what we were doing. It wasn't a master plan. It was just, 'Everything sounds this way. We don't want to do that. Let's do something else.' This is now my third record [*Tasty*, 2003], and the same thing happened again: I signed and then everything fell apart. Arista Records folded. I got signed by L. A. Reid, personally, and then he left. And 'Milkshake' had just come out. Here we are talking about 'Milkshake', 12 years later … people hated it! They hated it. We fought for that record. It took over a year to break that record: they would not play it; DJs didn't get it. It was like, I'm not a rapper, I'm not hardcore, I'm not crooning about a man who left. 'What the hell is she talking about? What is it?' No one knew. No one cared. No one got it. We fought like hell.

"Black girls were not wearing their hair natural and they were not screaming … and I was doing all these things."

That's so mad to think about.

Arista got split up, and we were traded. Some people got sent to RCA; I ended up going to Jive, which is traditionally a very pop label. I was put in a situation where I would have never signed there, they would have never signed me, and they didn't love the music and I knew that. But here, 'Milkshake' is out and I'm fighting for this record, like, 'I believe in this record. This is going to work', and Pharrell kept saying, 'It's going to work. We know this record's cool'.

How good did it feel, though, when people connected with it?

It was amazing, but it was terrifying, because there was still no infrastructure to follow it. It finally hit and it was *Wom-bom!* It was huge. It's amazing, I think, because for me, whether it was intended to be that way or not, it was always only the music. There wasn't anything else. I didn't

have anything around that was solid enough to be anything. Everyone's always like, 'Well, what did the label say?' I was never on a label long enough for them to really say anything. I honestly just got to do what I was going to do, and then it got put out.

After *Kelis Was Here*, 2006, did you actually think about just giving up music altogether?
I'm a really extreme person. I think, at the time, I was so fed up, I couldn't see beyond the moment. Again, I'd already gotten so much further than I ever expected or planned. It was like I could take it or leave it.

The musicianship and the musical side of it, no one can ever take that from me. Being famous is not really the relevant part of it. I can make music all day. You might never know it, but I could do it. So I don't need a producer, I don't need a label, I don't need a budget. If I want to make music, I can make music. I was like, 'Yeah, I can walk away. I'm so fed up', because the business of music sucks. It does. That was the first time

"He said, 'We don't really care what's going on with your album, you just sold 1.6 million ringtones.' I was like, I think I hate this guy."

in my life, I think, when I actually had to adhere to a label. That was my fourth album. It was on a label that, again, I did not want to be on. They didn't want me there, either, so it was a very mutual dislike. It was the first time where I really experienced all of the ugliness. The digital stuff had just started, so with 'Bossy', my first single off that album, I had a conversation with my label head, and he said, 'We don't really care what's going on with your album, because you just sold 1.6 million ringtones of "Bossy".' He was dead serious. I was just like, 'What? I think I hate this guy.' I got branded as this furious chick. It was fun, but I really wasn't.

I got angry when *Kelis Was Here* came out. That's when I got angry. It's true – that's when I got angry. I was pissed off. Up until that, I was going with the flow. Everything was cool. Life happens.

You've talked about how you stepped into the world of cuisine. What was the first thing you remember getting right and going, 'Okay. This has turned out special. I think I can do something?'
I don't know that there was a dish. For me, going to [Le Cordon Bleu] school changed my life. My mum was a chef, so I grew up cooking like her. Going to school was monumental, because I stopped cooking like *me*. That was a big deal. I don't think it was one thing, but it was definitely sauce. Everything's better with sauce – I wholeheartedly believe that.

There was a quote from you saying you're good at identifying different notes in food. Is that like having perfect pitch for food?
Completely – it absolutely is. It's so important as a chef, because it's your ears. You need it, so you can find balance in the flavours.

I did want to ask about the album *Food*, 2014, and your first impressions of [acclaimed producer] Dave Sitek.
He's so cool. I love that guy. When we first met I'm like, 'He's a weirdo, in the most fabulous way.' He's so strange and does not care at all. We have a great understanding of each other in that sense. I knew TV on the Radio, but I didn't really know his role; I didn't understand the whole thing. Then when we got in together, I started talking to him. It was the first time that I had a moment like I had in the very beginning with The Neptunes. It was the first time it was like, 'Ahh, great. I can do this.'

What's the song we should finish with?
Let's play Roberta Flack and Donny Hathaway, 'You Are My Heaven'. Because it's great. I think them together, they were, like, the perfect composer–songwriter marriage.

The First Time Kelis Playlist

1	Trick Me	Kelis
2	Spring Will Be a Little Late This Year	Sarah Vaughan
3	Thou Swell	Betty Carter
4	At Last	Etta James
5	Sweet Dreams (Are Made of This)	Eurythmics
6	Smells Like Teen Spirit	Nirvana
7	Truth or Dare	N.E.R.D. feat. Kelis and Pusha T
8	Weak	SWV
9	Free Your Mind	En Vogue
10	Fairytalez	Gravediggaz
11	Milkshake	Kelis
12	Got Your Money	Ol' Dirty Bastard feat. Kelis
13	Caught Out There	Kelis
14	My Favorite Mistake	Sheryl Crow
15	Oceania	Björk feat. Kelis
16	You Are My Heaven	Roberta Flack with Donny Hathaway

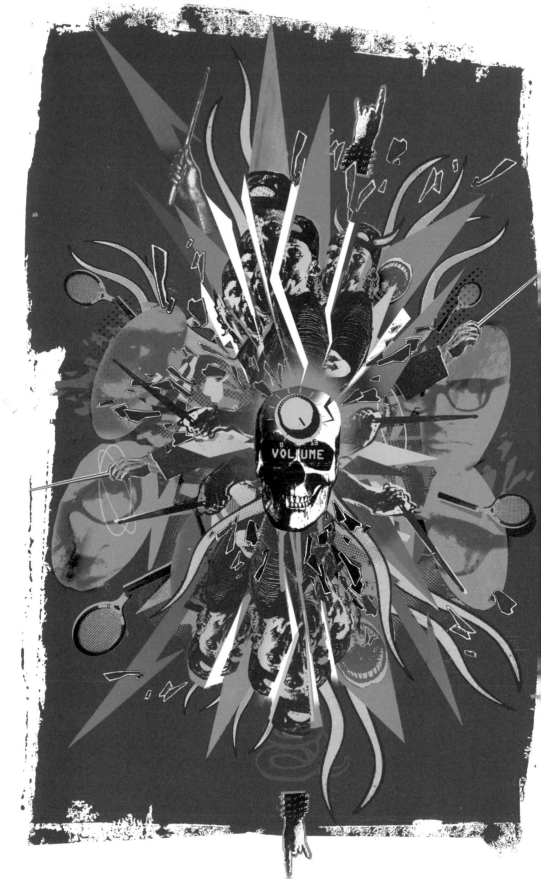

"You get into character, you're up on stage, you're in the moment ... you're with your bandmates ... I'm not quite like that at 7:15 in the morning."

Lars Ulrich

Lars Ulrich has the biggest entourage I've ever experienced. In fairness to Lars – who is one of the nicest musicians you could meet – this is not his fault, but the stars of music-industry-scheduling lunacy have aligned and 17 Metallica-related people are waiting in the foyer. And Lars isn't even here yet.

Metallica are about to release a 3D IMAX feature film to cinemas worldwide, they're doing a world tour *and* a new album is being planned. In attendance are representatives from the band's management, their record label, the press, the movie production and distribution company, reps and PR, a film crew from Metallica.com and Lars's own personal team. We don't have enough room in the lifts to get everyone up to the studio.

I've already endured an extended email exchange with someone from the movie team, demanding to know how many people will fit in the BBC lifts, what floor we'll be travelling to, and how long it will take, so they can build this into the schedule. I've also been told to provide a very specific selection of herbal teas. A machine as vast as Metallica must be run efficiently, but timing the lifts feels a bit much.

However, when you peel back the layers of the promotional onion and meet Lars and his management, they're the most laid-back and charming people imaginable. Lars is friendly, modest, self-analytical and clearly smarter and more charismatic than you might assume a metal drummer to be. He's also philosophical about his band's colossal success, happy to discuss the friction that lies at their core, and his face switches between quizzical and amused depending on the questions. He's also not even faintly bothered about the tea, and couldn't give a toss about the speed of the lifts.

Matt Everitt: When were you aware of music for the first time?
On the top floor of the house that I grew up in my dad had his music room, which was the biggest room in the house. There were a lot of records in there. The earliest I remember was maybe '68, '69 – Miles Davis, Jimi Hendrix, Janis Joplin, John Coltrane, Ornette Coleman, the Stones. Then I started being turned on to a lot of British music. Probably I started listening to rock music maybe around '72, '73: Sweet, Slade, Status Quo, Gary Glitter. In 1973 my dad took me to see Deep Purple, and then I went and bought my first serious record the day after the concert, which was Deep Purple's *Fireball*. Then I was off to the races.

Was that the first rock thing you instantly connected with?
Yeah. If you have one of those 'moments' – as Quentin Tarantino says, 'a moment of clarity' – that's as close as I got to that, at least in music. That was Deep Purple in '73.

Were you ever the guy hanging around gigs to meet your heroes?
I used to want to try to get close to the bands. All the bands in Denmark stayed in the Plaza Hotel, and I would loiter there. This was a few years later, maybe '77, '78. I had the good fortune of meeting Ritchie Blackmore [Deep Purple], Phil Lynott [Thin Lizzy], Ronnie Dio [Black Sabbath].

When did you first fall in love with Diamond Head, because that's a band you've namechecked a lot over the years.
Cut to a few years later, and now I'm living in Los Angeles. Copenhagen is a distant memory, and in my mind I'm on a trajectory to become a tennis player, like my father. The thing that kept me alive as I was dealing with tennis was *Sounds* magazine [British music newspaper]. Every week when that came in the mailbox, that was a highlight. Geoff Barton was writing a lot about the rock scene in England, the so-called new wave of British heavy metal, the Iron Maidens, the Def Leppards, the Diamond Heads and the Saxons, and all that stuff.

    Brute Force was a compilation record that MCA put out in the fall of 1980, and I got that. The first song was 'It's Electric' by Diamond Head. That was another one of those wacky moments: I think I heard that song six thousand times that day, and that was what made me want to be in a band, and form a band, at that time. As that was going on, I was realizing that even though I was a ranked tennis player in Denmark, in Los Angeles, on the street that I lived on, I wasn't even in the top ten, because of the level of competition. The tennis thing kind of dissipated, and Diamond Head sent me in the direction of wanting to be in a band.

The very first piece of music recorded under the Metallica name was 'Hit the Lights', wasn't it?
Yes – first original piece of music. It's always been, I felt, a strong song. It's not like one of the [makes quote signs with his fingers] 'hits' – and I use that word very loosely, by the way.

I think you can say hits.

You can say it; I'll say it in quotes. 'Hit the Lights' was the first piece of music that James [Hetfield] and I wrote together. Obviously, it goes back to day one, and it's been with us and opened the first record [*Kill 'Em All*, 1983]. It's a song we still like playing.

The thing about Metallica is that, at any given moment, we have about 60 or 70 songs that we actually can play. We're not the kind of band that has 18 songs and then we go out and just play those for a full tour. We very easily get a little restless. On the *Death Magnetic* tour, which was the last continuous two-year tour we did, we played, I think, close to 70 songs, and we changed the set list every single night. We haven't played the same set list twice in, I think, over ten years.

'One' [1989] was your first Top 40 single. The world shifted and *got* Metallica, and that single was the start of that, wasn't it?

Well, yeah, in a narcissistic way. We'd like to think that instead of us moving towards the masses, the masses came to us; we stood our ground out in leftfield.

Then came the Black Album [1991's *Metallica*], which did what an album like that is not supposed to do [and sold 20-plus million copies]. How did you cope with that?

You got to remember that we were fortunate, in that by the time the Black Album hit, we were five records into what we were doing. It was a success in what I would call the classic European way: first album; second album; bigger third album, bigger than second; fourth album – each album kind of stepped up. Guns N' Roses came out of nowhere and sold

"We'd like to think that instead of us moving towards the masses, the masses came to us."

a hundred gazillion records. Nirvana came more or less out of nowhere and sold a hundred gazillion records. Pearl Jam, their first record was the biggest. A lot of our peers and the bands that we grew up with in the '80s and '90s, they had their first record be ginormous, so our thing was kind of just step by step. Which was fortunate, because by the time the Black Album hit, we were ten years into it. We'd been around the block a few times, and travelled around the world a few times, and had paid our dues, I guess. In the record industry there is a term called 'legs' – 'This record's got "legs".' It wasn't like it came out and then overnight it sold 15 million. I mean, what was it? Three years. It was the record that kept giving: one of these records like Springsteen's *Born in the USA*; one of those albums

that just has single after single, and all of a sudden you're six singles in and it's three years later.

Twenty million copies? It's sort of like, 'Huh?' It was very cool and we're very fortunate. There were a lot of things that lined up right. It's not just the record; it was also the climate at the time, and obviously a little bit of luck and the way the planets aligned.

'The Ecstasy of Gold' by Ennio Morricone is your opening music when you play live. It's been your opening music for a long time. Why that piece of music? When did you first start using it?

In 1983 we were sent some money from a local promoter-slash-record-guy-slash-entrepreneur-guy who had heard our demo. So we threw our stuff in a U-Haul truck and drove across country and landed in glamorous New Jersey. We walked into his house – Jon Zazula was his name, and he was our first manager for two, three years, and gave us our first record deal and put *Kill 'Em All* out. God bless him. He said that he had the perfect piece of music to open our shows, so he played us 'The Ecstasy of Gold', and that still opens our shows 30 years later.

And you've done a version of it yourselves, as well?

We have done a version of it ourselves, which I actually heard on the radio the other day. I don't think I've heard it since we recorded it three, four years ago. That's quite a funny little instrumental there. Yeah. We've used it in our videos and our DVDs, and we've been in contact with the master himself, Mr Morricone, and he's blessed us. It's been very cool.

I want to ask about [the 2004 documentary] *Some Kind of Monster*. When you saw finished film for the first time, was there that icy moment of, 'This is too much; people are going to see this'? Because, weirdly, it's the thing that opened you up to a whole new audience.

There were some people, especially in the rock world, more than in the film world, who thought that that was too much; it was too transparent. There was a sense, too, of 'I'm not sure I want to know that about my favourite band.' The movie was probably better received in the film world, because the documentaries that really work are the ones that have a story that everybody can relate to. *Some Kind of Monster* is not really a story of a rock band; it's a story about relationships, and everybody can relate to relationships. It's just set against the background of a rock and roll band.

Were you scared of putting it out?

No, because in order to undergo that kind of experience, there has to be trust with the filmmaker, and the filmmakers were Joe Berlinger and Bruce Sinofsky, who we had a long relationship with through the *Paradise Lost* films [a series of documentaries that featured Metallica's music; the first was released in 1996]. So we trusted them, very early on. They didn't come in to film the meltdown; they came in to film the making of the next Metallica record, and then the meltdown started happening. Everything went to hell. They were filming and then, I think, there was one meeting, and it was just like, 'We trust you. Keep filming as all this crazy stuff is going on.' We sort of went along with it.

The way you say, 'The first time I saw the movie' – obviously, the first time I saw the movie, I had already seen the movie a hundred times. Do you know what I mean? Because we were part of the editing. It wasn't just presented one day like, 'Here you go'. What happens in those types of situations, I guess, is that you 'third person' it. I'm fairly thick-skinned. As I sit there and look at double chins and receding hairlines and silly Danish accents, I just kind of go, 'That's just a character. That's not really me.' You find a way to compartmentalize that to the best of your ability.

People have been saying strange things and finger-wagging Metallica basically since we started, so it's something that everybody's always got an opinion on, and we're pretty used to that. I think Kirk Hammett has talked about how he was very uncomfortable seeing himself, but it doesn't bug me that much. You kind of get used to it. I don't know, I just think of something else, become unemotional. Maybe I should have some therapy over that. Maybe we should talk about that in therapy.

"They didn't come in to film the meltdown; they came in to film the making of the next record, and then the meltdown started happening."

As Metallica, do you still feel like outsiders?
Yeah, every day – maybe more, actually. I don't know, it's just part of my DNA. I grew up an only child, and I think the reason that I wanted to be around music, and be in a group, was because I wanted to be part of something bigger than myself. And my three comrades, I think, all have different levels of those same thoughts, and Metallica is a very autonomous entity. The good is we're autonomous and we live in our own world and we can play by our own rules; the bad side of that is we never quite feel like we fit in anywhere, and we certainly do feel sort of disenfranchised. Still, at fifty-two, I often feel slightly outside of the cool kids' circle. Trust me, that doesn't go away as you get older.

The aggression in the records, where does this come from?
You know what? I don't know. I have a saying, 'We've got to step it up!' or 'We've got to fire it up!', so often when we play, especially when we're recording or when we're really in the moment, you know, the old clichés – turn it up to 11! I mean, I guess we turn it up to 12 or 13, or whatever.

I have to be honest with you, this is not something I talk a lot about, because I'm only realizing now, as I get a little older, that there is, I guess, a slight element of a 'character': you get into character, you're up on stage, you're playing, you're in the moment, you're with your bandmates, you're with the audience and, you know, the whole thing is kind of like you turn into a little rock gnome or something. I'm not quite like that at 7:15 in the morning when I'm trying to get kid number three to finish his fruit bowl.

You've played every continent, you've released enormous-selling records, you've released a feature film. You've done everything that a band could do and invented some things that bands have never done before. What ambitions are left?
I suppose we've done a lot. You know, what I think at this point is it's just staying together – longevity, sticking around and keeping buzzing. At the same time, obviously, when you're 35 years into what you're doing, there has to be at least an acknowledgement of the past. We struggled with that quite a bit for maybe the first couple of decades of our career. We were so fearful of repetition, or of not continuing to take it further into the future, that we may have gone too far trying to keep changing it up. And so when [producer] Rick Rubin showed up in our lives about ten years ago, he sat down – and with Rick there's a lot of conversations about your state of mind and all that stuff – and he encouraged us to feel good about our past and to be okay with letting ourselves be inspired by our past, and to let ourselves embrace it and maybe even borrow from it.

"Most of us are borderline civilized people. Yes, I know – BBC shocker! Metallica drummer claims to be somewhat civilized!"

What do you think are the worst preconceptions of Metallica?
That we live and breathe super heavy metal 24 hours a day, and that we have devil horns coming out of our foreheads and all that type of stuff.

I can see the horns.
That's why I have my hat on. I think to a degree maybe more so in England: I think England, a little bit more so than other countries, still has a segregation in terms of the music that's sort of a remnant of the class system, and I think there's definitely a feeling sometimes that the metal kids are looked down upon. So that whole thing about us being the metal guys or the brain-dead stoners that eat metal for breakfast and all that kind of stuff? You know, we're pretty chilled, normal dudes with a very vast outlook on music, from jazz to classical to pop to reggae, and

metal is the heart of rock and we sort of gravitate towards what we play.
But most of us are actually borderline civilized people. Yes, I know –
BBC shocker! Metallica drummer claims to be somewhat civilized!

How have your relationships within the band changed?
We know each other so well; the longest relationship I've ever really ever
been in, other than with my dad, is with James Hetfield. I know most of
the time what he's going to say in a sentence. I know when to push his
buttons; I know when to pull back, or when to give him some space. We
all know each other really well, and we've found a way for it to function
and we caretake that. Being in a band, 35 years in, in your early fifties?
I mean, it doesn't get any easier. Trust me. But you've got to work at it,
and you've got to learn to listen, you've got to learn empathy, you've got
to learn to compromise. We're pretty good at it. It generally functions
well. When people are in high-pressure situations and sleep-deprived
or whatever, there can be some weird energy, but it's momentary.

What's the song we should play to finish? Anything you want.
The last song we should finish with? It's my choice? Goddamn. That does
open it up to quite the possibilities.

Well, everything that's ever been recorded is pretty big.
In all existence? 'My Apocalypse' from *Death Magnetic*. There you go.

The First Time Lars Ulrich Playlist

1	Enter Sandman	Metallica
2	Blockbuster	Sweet
3	Fireball	Deep Purple
4	It's Electric	Diamond Head
5	Bad Reputation	Thin Lizzy
6	Hit the Lights	Metallica
7	The Ecstasy of Gold	Ennio Morricone
8	Metallica	Some Kind of Monster soundtrack
9	Overdose	AC/DC
10	Supersonic	Oasis
11	The Number of the Beast	Iron Maiden
12	R U Mine?	Arctic Monkeys
13	My Apocalypse	Metallica

"People have got an attachment to my image of a tragic artist. I'm not really like that."

MARIANNE FAITHFULL

There are some subjects that are almost impossible to avoid if you're interviewing specific people – an event or relationship that's inexorably tied to them, no matter how hard they twist and turn to shake it off. With Marianne Faithfull, it's The Rolling Stones. She was discovered at a party in London in 1964, aged just sixteen, by Stones manager Andrew Loog Oldham and had a huge hit with Mick Jagger and Keith Richards's 'As Tears Go By', before coupling up with Jagger and co-writing the classic song 'Sister Morphine'. To ask her about it is predictable – to ignore the connection is to dismiss the flashpoint of her career – but to focus on it does her a huge disservice and underestimates her musical output. Marianne doesn't run from the subject, and – perhaps with the wisdom and experience that comes with beating cancer, hepatitis and a heroin addiction – she's happy to muse over the impact of the '60s. But her enthusiasm is reserved for Brecht and Weill, along with contemporaries like Nick Cave, Damon Albarn and PJ Harvey, all of whom have written her songs to deliver in her beautiful, dark style.

Faithfull is warmer and more flirtatious than she appears on the page. Her voice is deep, slow and only slightly torn at the edges – until she laughs and you can hear a lifetime of smoking in a filthy chuckle. For someone who's been making music for more than 50 years, she looks great: her dark cornflower-blue eyes smile out from a chic, blonde mop of hair, and she's still got an aura of cool about her, a mixture of French nonchalance and British couldn't-give-a-fuck attitude. There's a reason why people – including the Stones, Allen Ginsberg, William Burroughs, Francis Bacon, David Bowie – gravitated towards her: they wanted some of her magic, not the other way around.

Matt Everitt: When were you first aware of music as a child?
Very early: my father played the guitar and the country folk fiddle. He had the most beautiful voice. I listened to a lot of classical music, and when I went to the convent at eight, I started to play the piano and then sing. Then at about fourteen, I started to get interested in popular music.

Who were your first musical obsessions at that age?
I liked Elvis very much. I didn't like his later period, but I loved 'Heartbreak Hotel', and I liked Chuck Berry. I bought some awfully stupid shit too: I bought 'Venus in Blue Jeans' [by Jimmy Clanton]. I loved The Everly Brothers, 'Cathy's Clown', and I loved Buddy Holly.

When did you think, 'Music is something that I want to do'?
I didn't. I didn't expect a career in music. I was at school. I was planning to go either to university or to drama school, or to music school to be a singer – a *real* singer. Then I was discovered and all my plans went out the window, and I had a hit record. I'm very glad I did. I think it was a great opportunity for me; I loved it. I've put my heart into it ever since.

What kind of people were inspiring you then?
Just other students, really. You know, a lot of kids got up in those days and sang in tremulous little voices 'The House of the Rising Sun', or 'Babe I'm Gonna Leave You'; Joan Baez was a great influence on me.

When did you first come into contact with The Rolling Stones?
I guess I first heard 'Not Fade Away', that was the first thing, but before that I loved The Beatles. I really liked The Beatles, from the first record on. I still love 'Girl'.

'As Tears Go By' became this enormous hit for you. What's your relationship like with that record now?
Oh, I really, really love it, and I sing it in all my concerts. It wouldn't be right to not sing 'As Tears Go By'. People love that song. It's kept its beauty, and it's kept its lustre. I love singing it; it's mine.

Do you remember recording it?
Of course I do, yes. It was very, very new. I'd never been in a recording studio. It was quite frightening. It was at IBC [Studios, in London]. The way it was laid out, the booth was very high up, so up there was Andrew [Loog Oldham] with Mick and Keith. I was far below. That felt kind of strange. I had no idea what to do.

Did you enjoy not just being a musician, but being a pop star?
I did, yes. I met a lot of interesting people. People I would have never met if I hadn't left school and started touring. I met The Hollies, who were great. All those beat groups, I liked them very much, yeah.

I'm not going to dwell on the '60s London scene, because it has been done to death, although you did say, in retrospect, that the whole period damaged you, personally and artistically ...

I think I'm too hard on myself, and I'm too hard on the '60s. I actually changed my mind. I think it was a fantastic time, and I don't think it damaged me. I think it was just me that brought that in – I brought the element of that. It was my self-destructiveness, it wasn't the '60s. So I've changed my mind. I think, to be fair, that fame can crush people, and I was crushed. I didn't like being in the middle of the goldfish bowl. I could handle my little bit of fame as Marianne Faithfull, it wasn't so bad, but when I fell in love with Mick it became really serious, and I found that difficult. It wasn't that bad, you know. It was great fun.

Love in a Mist, 1967 – that was your last album for nearly ten years. Did you fall out of love with music?

No, I think I really did believe that what the Stones were doing was more important than what I was doing. I started to put my attention and my talent into Mick's music: we wrote 'Sister Morphine'; I helped on a lot of songs; I gave him ideas. I really made that my priority.

"I'm too hard on the '60s ... I think it was a fantastic time, and I don't think it damaged me. It was my self-destructiveness, it wasn't the '60s."

'Sister Morphine' was originally credited to just the Stones, and there was a legal battle. What happened? It's officially co-authored by you now, isn't it?

Well, I got the money. In the '70s I went to [the Stones' business manager] Allen Klein, and Keith wrote a letter to Allen Klein saying that I had written 'Sister Morphine'.

A famously difficult manager.

I rather liked him, you know. There's nobody left like that, those kind of really weird, difficult managers. Allen was wonderful. You know he did pay me. From 1975 I started getting royalties from 'Sister Morphine', but I wanted my credit too. I had to fight for that, and I got it, eventually.

A performance I want to ask you about: 1973, performing with David Bowie. 'I Got You Babe'. If you could set the scene ...

It was in the old Marquee Club in London, with incredible costumes by a boy that was in David's entourage, so it was him that dressed me

up as a nun. It was wonderful. You know, David's a genius; he's a great, great talent. My dress actually was backless, and I was wearing no clothes underneath, so you have to remember that when you watch it.

Broken English [1979] really established you as a solo artistic force. What were your inspirations for the record?

I was listening to the Plastic Ono Band; I was listening to Dr. Hook. I had been listening to a lot of Hank Williams, and the stuff I've always loved and still do, like Otis Redding and James Brown and Sam Cooke.

The country theme surfaces and resurfaces in your career.

Yeah. I fell in love with country music in the '70s. I loved Willie Nelson and Waylon Jennings. I loved being, even for a moment, in a world where everything was black and white, because my own mind is multiple shades of grey, and that's in my records, too. I love the world where men are men, and women are women, and if you leave me I'll kill you, you know? I loved that. It made everything feel secure.

Have you got a favourite Hank Williams track?

Oh yeah, 'I'm So Lonesome I Could Cry'. I mean, there are millions of great songs – 'Your Cheating Heart', but I particularly love 'I'm So Lonesome I Could Cry'. It reminds me of living with Ben, my wonderful punk husband who I fell in love with in about 1975, and we had a great life. The soundtrack was 'I'm So Lonesome I Could Cry'.

"I loved being, even for a moment, in a world where everything was black and white, because my own mind is multiple shades of grey."

There's a parallel between country and punk rock, I think. Country's very raw, it's very anti-establishment.

Yeah. In a funny way, yeah. I found punk very refreshing. I loved Led Zeppelin and all that, but it had gone away from anything I could ever do myself. It had become almost like chamber music. I think that's what they wanted to do. Punk brought it back to the street, and brought it back to your front room.

You did 'Ballad of the Soldier's Wife' in the mid-'80s. When did you first hear Kurt Weill?

When I was growing up, my mother used to play Lotte Lenya records. Then Hal [Wilner – producer] came, that's how I met him. He asked me to perform 'Ballad of the Soldier's Wife' on *Lost in the Stars*, his record

Marianne Faithfull

of the music of Kurt Weill. We became great, great friends, and that has been a very good creative relationship for me, for years.

That whole world of Kurt Weill inspired Bowie a lot, as well.
Yeah, I think people like me or David would be drawn to it first by its decadence. Then when you really start to examine it and get to know it, there's much, much more to it than that – it's not just decadent, but it gives it a wonderful, glamorous veneer, yeah.

***Strange Weather*, 1987: that was the first album you recorded out of the grip of heroin. This was the first album to see you really embrace jazz.**
Yep. Changed my musical character. I was free by then. That's right. Well, I think when I first got off heroin, all drugs, and alcohol, it was a terrible shock [laughs], and I didn't feel at all perky. I felt rather depressed; but I battled on. I really enjoyed my recovery, but I couldn't see myself singing little pop songs anymore. I wanted to go deeper. I wanted to do something else. Hal was a perfect person to do that with. I love *Strange Weather*, I still sing the song 'Strange Weather' on my tour.

What jazz artists inspired you especially?
Well, Billie Holiday first. Let's play 'The Man I Love'.

Someone else you're fascinated by is Bertolt Brecht.
Very much so. From *Lust in the Stars* on, I became more and more fascinated. Hal turned me on to *The Seven Deadly Sins*. Then I was asked to play 'Pirate Jenny' in a production at the Gate Theatre in Dublin, in the early '90s. I found I could sing it very easily. It's quite hard to sing, you know Kurt Weill, a lot of the time, was using the scale that you would hear in the Jewish temple. Really, I think I have a racial connection to that, because my grandmother was Jewish in Vienna.

After, I did *The Threepenny Opera*, which ran for three months. So I really immersed myself in it. The next thing I did was *The Seven Deadly Sins* with Dennis Russell Davies and the Vienna Radio Orchestra, which I think is one of my favourite records. It was amazing recording with them. My father had died the day before, so I was in quite a strange state. I almost regressed to six years old, but it was a wonderful experience.

***Kissin Time* in 2002 brought a whole new family of collaborators, like Blur. When did you first meet those guys?**
Through [Blur bassist] Alex James; it was Alex who sought me out and wanted to make friends. I loved him immediately and we did make friends. Then I met Graham and Damon and the lovely drummer, Dave. Got to know them and hung out, and then we did a couple of things together. We did *Kissin Time*, and then on *Before the Poison* [2004] we did 'Last Song'. I call it 'The Last Song'; Damon calls it 'Green Fields'.

What do you look for in a collaborator? Is it someone that echoes your tastes, or someone that's going to be completely different and challenge you?

No, I look for someone who echoes my tastes, who maybe brings it into a completely different way, but who I can recognize as a great, great writer. I want to work with really good people.

Before the Poison saw you working with PJ Harvey. I feel like there was a certain kinship there?

Yeah, we get on. We still get on very well; we're still very good friends. We talk to each other on the phone. I'm going to see her when I get back to Paris. I love _Let England Shake_. I'm just in love with that record. I like all her records, but this one I'm seriously mad about. I think I met her when she was supporting U2 in America. We fell in love, yeah. There's nobody like Polly. She's one on her own, and very strong. She's not affected by commercial concerns; she could do that if she wanted to do. Man, she could drop out a really hot commercial record, but she doesn't really care. She's going to do what she wants to do, whether anyone likes it or not – of course, everybody does like it. There we are.

Let's talk about the new album, _Horses and High Heels_ [2011]. Was it an easy record to make?

No, no it wasn't. It was superficially an easy record to make. We did a week of rehearsal and arranging, and then we did three weeks of recording, but halfway through I wasn't really happy with it. I was worried about it. It was sounding too American. It was sounding like The Doobie Brothers, or something like that – which might just have been the format, you know, with the two guitars. So I realized we had to get some more input, and that's when Wayne Kramer [from MC5] came in.

"I wanted to make a real pop album, and I wanted it to be happy. I am happy, and I felt I had to spell it out."

Lou Reed makes a couple of appearances as well.

I've always admired Lou very much as a guitarist. I know he's best known for his songs and for his wonderful performances, but his playing is so good. I've always told him that, and this time I felt there was a place where I could ask Lou to put some guitar on, and he did, brilliantly.

Was there a need to shake it up a bit? Move away from jazz?

Yeah, I think there was. I wanted to make a real pop album, and I wanted it to be happy. I am happy, and I felt I had to spell it out. People have got an attachment to my image of a tragic artist. I'm not really like that, and

I tried before on *Kissin Time* to present a much more happy position, but it wasn't really accepted. They didn't like it. I love 'I'm Into Something Good', but the fans didn't like it at all. Too happy.

I suppose people's image of you is going to be an image of the songs you record; the songs you record aren't necessarily you.
No, but just because you record songs that are sad or … I don't know. I think my whole style has changed, too. I'm not slow anymore. I just can do it now, where maybe I couldn't before.

You have talked in the past of retiring. Is this going to be your last record?
No. No! I'm going to take a break. I'm not going to go into the studio for another two years for sure.

The last question: we've had all these firsts, you get to choose the last record that we play.
I think you should play something by Polly. 'Let England Shake.'

The First Time Marianne Faithfull Playlist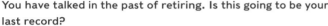

1	Broken English	Marianne Faithfull
2	Heartbreak Hotel	Elvis Presley
3	Memphis, Tennessee	Chuck Berry
4	Cathy's Clown	The Everly Brothers
5	Babe, I'm Gonna Leave You	Joan Baez
6	Girl	The Beatles
7	Not Fade Away	The Rolling Stones
8	As Tears Go By	Marianne Faithfull
9	Sister Morphine	The Rolling Stones
10	I'm So Lonesome I Could Cry	Hank Williams
11	The Ballad of the Soldier's Wife	Marianne Faithfull
12	The Man I Love	Billie Holiday and Chris Spedding
13	Pirate Jenny (from *The Threepenny Opera*)	Bertold Brecht, Kurt Weill, Lotte Lenya
14	Last Song	Marianne Faithfull
15	Let England Shake	PJ Harvey

"We didn't necessarily want to conquer the world. And then we wound up doing exactly that."

MICHAEL STIPE

Michael Stipe was one of the first very famous musicians I ever interviewed and – there's no other way of putting it – I totally bollocksed it up.

It didn't have the hallmarks of a potential catastrofuck. R.E.M. were playing the intimate (for them) Hammersmith Apollo, London, in 2005, showcasing their well received thirteenth album, *Around the Sun*. I was one of only a couple of journalists, so there was no huge media scrum, and I was led into a small, darkened, sweet-smelling dressing room to find Stipe perched on a high stool, like a rare bird. Hands are shaken, microphones are prepared and the first questions go well enough. Stipe is thoughtful, gracious, patient – a little hesitant, but given his reticence for explaining too much about his work, all is going well enough.

I seem to remember looking at my rather serious questions, and thinking I should introduce a bit of levity: 'You rarely publish your lyrics. They're often indecipherable …' 'Yes', he replies. 'Do you ever alter them during a show?', I ask, 'Slip in some nonsense? Just to see if people will attach some huge significance to them? Mess with the audience a bit?'

'Why,' he leans forward, pronouncing every word deliberately as if each was a question, 'Would I do that?' He's staring at me – not angry, but with a look of confusion, maybe even pity. 'These are *my* songs.' And that's it. The interview technically isn't over, but in real terms, it is. I limply ask a few deflated questions, which he answers politely, but his air of disbelief hangs over me like a bad smell. Later that night, I stand blankly watching R.E.M. play a brilliant show, cursing myself for my clumsiness and overfamiliarity.

This isn't *that* interview (are you mad?); it is taken from two others, from 2011 and 2016, that occurred many years later. Michael is still thoughtful, gracious and a little hesitant, but I don't think I fucked these ones up.

Matt Everitt: When were you first aware of music?

It would have been The Beatles. When I was living in Germany, I was staying with a friend and she was making cabbage soup out of her garden for me, and 'Michelle, Ma Belle' came on the radio, and I remember standing alone in the living room thinking that it was really beautiful. I think they were singing in German or French – I don't think it was the English version. But that would be my first memory of music.

Was it a musical environment you were brought up in?

Not particularly. My parents were very specific about what they loved, and they would play it over and over again. I come from an artistic family, but music was not a huge part of my upbringing.

What was your first single? The first record that was yours?

My grandmother took my two sisters and me to Mr Pemberton's record store. We bought an Elvis Presley album from the film *Double Trouble*, and a Disney film called *The Parent Trap* starring Hayley Mills. Among the singles was Tammy Wynette's 'D-I-V-O-R-C-E', and 'I Want to Hold Your Hand' by The Beatles. 'King of the Road' by Roger Miller. I think as a preteen, there were songs – before punk rock radically changed my life at the age of fifteen – on the radio that resonated with me. 'Bennie and the Jets' by Elton John was a huge hit single in the US. I mean, as someone who records music, the production on that song is one of the weirdest ever to make probably the Top 20. And then 'Rock On' by David Essex, which my band went on to pay homage to in the song 'Drive'.

What about the first gig you went to that made an impact?

I saw the Ramones perform at a small club, not much bigger than this room. Edwardsville, Illinois. I then moved on to another part of the country, and they played, I think it was 1977, but they played a small club with The Runaways opening, and I took my father's camera and took photographs, and was blown away by the music. Joan Jett jumped off stage. She had taken some Quaaludes, as it turns out, and she jumped off stage to dance with the audience, and she landed on top of me.

In 1980, the first ever R.E.M. gig – although you weren't called R.E.M. at the time – in Athens [Georgia]. It's a legendary event now. Was it actually any good? What can you remember?

It was spirited [laughs]. Other than that, no, it wasn't probably very good. It was very punk rock. I mean, it was, you know, a bunch of people threw a party and got really hammered and jumped around and slept with each other, and got more hammered and woke up and regretted it.

The myth is that after that first show, every time you played, you'd gather this audience. You made a connection very quickly.

Yeah, I mean, the real punk rockers in our small town didn't like us very much, because we brought a larger crowd of people than any other

Michael Stipe

punk rock band. And we brought people that they didn't really like that much. We actually had some semi-trained musicians in our band, which angered a lot of people who felt like we were not being true to the art scene, or the art ethic. And as a result, we drew more people, because we had more crossover appeal and that caused friction. But we were just pop, pop, pop, pop, pop. We were pop. We were a pop band.

What can you remember from that first single, 'Radio Free Europe'? Were you unbelievably excited to get in the studio?

No, I mean, I wasn't [laughs]. I didn't know the process of recording, and, in fact, it wasn't until the second album that I realized the difference between the bass guitar and the guitar. I didn't know which did what sound. Now, I knew that the bass guitar had four strings on it, because I could count them, but I didn't know that the bass guitar was the one that did the low notes and the guitar was the one that did the high notes. I mean, that's how ignorant I was of music.

What can you remember from your first US TV appearance on *Late Night with David Letterman*, which was '83?

God fucking damn. I remember they told us that after we played our song, Letterman would walk over and he would speak to one member of the band. Peter was designated as the guy who would speak to David Letterman. So we play our song ['Radio Free Europe'], we did fine. We were nervous. Letterman starts to walk over, and I sat down. I didn't know the first thing about television. I know now that my frame ends about here [gestures to his waist], right? But at the time, I knew nothing. I sat down so he could talk to Peter. I didn't know that he was reaching to shake my hand. And I didn't know that by sitting down, I dropped out of frame like a Muppet. So I became, instantly, the eccentric artist

That was the moment!

That was the moment where I became the enigma. And the word 'enigma' has followed me to this day. So that's why I say 'God fucking damn' when I think about the David Letterman show.

What was the track that first put you into the mainstream?

The first R.E.M. song? On some level, it's the insane insecurity and the courage to perform in the first place. From the first show that we ever did, I kind of felt like a huge pop star, just because the people clapped after we would do something and that's a great feeling. But I think 'The One I Love' is a song that came out in 1987, and that went to the Top 20 in the US. And that's when it felt like, 'Wow, this is really, actually serious. This is real.'

It always fascinates me when someone works for a long time and wants something, and then they get what they wanted ...

Well, we didn't know what we wanted. The thing was, we're the band

that had no goals, so the fact that we were making records and touring just felt like this amazing adventure to us, and we didn't necessarily want to conquer the world. And then we managed to. We wound up doing exactly that in some small corner of the universe that belonged to pop music and us.

When did you first feel famous?

I wanted to be famous since I was a teenager. I'm not sure why, but it seemed like the thing to do – and, obviously, well, it worked. But the reality of fame has nothing at all in common with the fantasy of fame, and so I followed my teenage dreams quite naively. And I worked very hard, and I found the right people to work with. I don't know that I'm a great public figure, but I'm pretty proud of who I became, and I'm pretty okay with who I am today.

In terms of *Out of Time* [1991], was there a moment, watching 'Losing My Religion' on MTV for the first time and thinking, 'Okay. We've entered a different world'?

It was exponential for me, in terms of how many people on the street recognized me suddenly – that just went from 4% to 98%. I became a face.

"We had no idea that it was going to keep getting bigger and bigger and bigger, and then eventually start getting ... not as big."

Do you think you dealt with the attention well, in hindsight?

Yeah. It was a slow burn for us, so I had a decade to get used to the idea of it. And at that point, I was pretty grounded. I think you can feel when you're on an upswing, but my art teacher at college, when I was nineteen and twenty – James Herbert – said to us, 'You're only as good as your last painting.' And so, however big 'Losing My Religion' was, or whatever song followed it, we had no guarantee that that was going to continue on an upward trajectory. We had no idea that it was going to keep getting bigger and bigger and bigger, and then eventually start getting ... not as big. All those things that happened.

Someone who's made an impact on you is Patti Smith. When was the first time you heard her, and first time you met her?

I bought Patti Smith's first album [*Horses*] the day it came out in 1975. I was fifteen. I sat up all night listening to it and eating a bowl of cherries. In the morning I threw up and went to school, with the idea in my fifteen-year-old head that that's what I was going to do with my life.

Was that the moment? The ground zero?

That was it. I mean, how lucky, for me, at the age of fifteen, to have a very clear idea of what I wanted to do?

Is there a song off that first album?

'Birdland'. It's about a boy whose father has died, and he imagines his father coming down in a spaceship to take him away to another place. It's a beautiful song.

And then meeting her for the first time?

Well, we laugh now. We're great friends, but I don't think I would be the performer that I am without her, because she's such an influence and such an unbelievable force in music, and now we know her skills as a writer. We first met in 1995. It was the year that her husband passed away. She was, I think, feeling a bit alone in the world, with two young children and not really knowing what to do, and I reached out to her through a mutual friend, Scott Litt. She had had several losses that year, including her husband Fred 'Sonic' Smith, and we became very, very fast friends and very close friends.

R.E.M. is often credited as being one of the bands that took alternative music into the mainstream. Did you look at bands like Nirvana or Pearl Jam and recognize some of yourself?

Never! I never get it when people say, 'They took so much from you' – I just don't see it. When people compared us to The Byrds early on, I had no idea what they were talking about. And of course it was the way that Peter picked the string of the guitar rather than strumming it, but I didn't know enough about music or music history or the sound of The Byrds to make that distinction. So when that flips back around on me and on us? I only recently found out that my voice is incredibly unique, in that people recognize my singing voice instantly. I didn't know that for 25 years of making records. That's not false modesty or humility – I honestly had no idea that my voice was that unique.

What was Warner Brothers' reaction when you first delivered *New Adventures in Hi-Fi* [1996]? It was a very big record, but it was coming off the back of much more accessible albums. Were Warners freaked out?

I don't remember. One of the reasons we signed with Warner Brothers to begin with is because they had signed Neil Young, who everyone in the band was a giant fan of. And Neil Young would go off and do these records that were completely, like, him stretching – really pushing himself in completely stylistically different ways from what he's known for. And the record company seemed to be quite supportive of that, and we were impressed by that. So, *New Adventures in Hi-Fi*: I remember everything about it, but I do not remember the record company's reaction to it. It's my favourite album of our entire career.

Why's that?

It's a great record. You know what? I don't even like rock music. Let it be said. But it's a great rock record. And it captures – and how could we have known it at the time? – it captures a band at their absolute peak as a four-piece. Bill left after we recorded it.

When was the first morning you were like, 'You know, I'm not going to have a shave'? And then, 'You know, maybe I'll just keep it going'? Because it's looking great.

The beard? Three Halloweens ago I went as a failed radical fairy. And to be a failed radical fairy, you have to have a lot of facial hair. Put flowers in it. Way too much glitter, way too much make-up. Overdo the eyebrows. And it worked: people laughed and laughed and laughed, and I had a great Halloween. Then, by the time the next Halloween had come around, my father had died and I was in mourning, and I'd never had a beard before. So I started growing it for the second year of being a failed radical fairy for Halloween, and then I just kept it going. And at some point it became ridiculous.

Do you use much product on it?

Are you really asking me that?

I'm really asking you that, yes.

Okay [laughs]. I wash it with shampoo and I've tried conditioner, but it doesn't condition very well. Rather than Skid Row Santa, I'm kind of

"I don't see any good reason for us to ever perform together again as R.E.M."

going for a Poseidon-slash-Zeus-slash-Brancusi-Matisse kind of appeal [laughs], so I keep it a little trimmed on the sides to show off my beautiful cheekbones. And that's about it, really. I put some oil on it from time to time, but I don't really fuck with it too much.

When did you first think, as a band, 'Our work here is done'? It's an enormously emotional decision to make.

We created this beautiful thing – I've said it a million times, and I'll say it again: we own the triumphs and we own the disastrous failures of our 32 years together, but it's this beautiful thing called R.E.M. and, for me, it was really important that the legacy remain intact. And the only way to really do that and to do it properly would be for all of us to agree that it was time to just stop, and then to agree that we will never, for any reason, come back together. We will not be the band that does that. I don't see any good reason for us to ever perform together again as R.E.M. In Mexico City [the band's final show in November 2008] … it's still difficult for us to talk about. It's a very emotional thing, but, as we performed the encore, Peter walked over and, before 'Man on the Moon', he said, 'I think this is the last time, right?' And I said, 'Yeah. That's it.'

What do you miss most about it?

I miss performing. I miss writing and I'm very shy to write with other people, because I really feel like I'm really a one-trick pony if I don't have Mike and Peter, or Mike, Peter and Bill, behind me, or next to me. I don't know that I can do what I do. So … I'm still not sure that I can do it. But I'm going to try.

What should we end on? It's your choice.

'Harlem Nocturne'. That's a beautiful one, by The Viscounts.

The First Time Michael Stipe Playlist

1	Nightswimming	R.E.M.
2	Michelle	The Beatles
3	Double Trouble	Elvis Presley
4	Let's Get Together	Hayley Mills
5	D-I-V-O-R-C-E	Tammy Wynette
6	King of the Road	Roger Miller
7	Bennie and the Jets	Elton John
8	Rock On	David Essex
9	Roadrunner	The Modern Lovers
10	Radio Free Europe	R.E.M.
11	Birdland	Patti Smith
12	The One I Love	R.E.M.
13	Volume	Pylon
14	Paralysed	Gang of Four
15	Ashes to Ashes	David Bowie
16	Man on the Moon	R.E.M.
17	Harlem Nocturne	The Viscounts

"I can't always say that I've known exactly where I'm going, or how or why, but I've known what I *didn't* want to do. Or where I *didn't* want to end up."

NENEH CHERRY

I t's a difficult characteristic to explain or justify, but some musicians are just cooler than others. Neneh Cherry is cool. It's obvious – she's just cool. She was cool the first time most people saw her on *Top of the Pops* in 1988 singing 'Buffalo Stance', she was cool during this interview about her life in 2014, and I have no doubt she was cool at most points in between.

Cherry's career illustrates her willingness to follow her artistic path instinctively, without worrying about factors like success or what might or might not be described as cool (obviously a cool thing to do). She placed the same worth on massive worldwide success and small-scale underground projects (so cool), and sought out surprising collaborations (very cool). A life spent in Stockholm, New York and London, and her stepfather – the brilliant American jazz musician Don Cherry (indescribably cool) – has provided her with a broad worldview of music that has nothing to do with scenes or genres, and more to do with a journey and building a family of creative relationships.

She has huge corkscrew hair and bright, pretty eyes, and she smiles with her whole face. She laughs more than most people I interview, and is incredibly easy to talk to. She is so bright, funny and positive that when we chat about the huge success of her 1989 debut solo album *Raw like Sushi* it feels like she's never discussed the subject before.

She is – and there's no other way of putting it – cool.

Matt Everitt: When were you first aware of music?

I think my awareness of discovering music for myself happened on a swing. My mother used to hang swings in our house. My stepdad was a music professor at Dartmouth University, so we were living in Vermont. I was on my swing, and I was listening to Sly and the Family Stone.

That's a very cool artist to start off with.

Because my dad was a trip, he used to always go out and buy all kinds of records. He was into the 'world of music' kind of thing, so we also had the first Jackson 5 record – *Diana Ross Presents the Jackson 5*. Those were two records I can remember getting into. It's not my earliest memory of having a relationship with songs; there was always music around me, my whole life, so before then I'd obviously soaked up stuff, but that's a memory of choosing something, wanting to hear it again and again. And remembering the force of swinging to the songs. I was definitely fascinated by The Jackson 5. Obviously, they were kids, but older than me, but there was definitely a fascination with them.

Jazz has played a huge part in your life. Who was the first jazz artist that really made an impression on you?

I mean, the direct connection to jazz, I can draw from it now, from my spine. When I was growing up, the people that were around, like my stepdad, were working with it; they were friends with my parents and stuff, they were people we knew. And, you know, I think it's hard for me to actually look at who I was into then. You know?

"The direct connection to jazz, I can draw from it now, from my spine."

Because they were family friends?

Yes. And I could sense things with my dad. Like, when we'd go to Ornette Coleman's house, I knew he was someone that my dad really looked up to, that Ornette was like a guru for him. And he always used to play a lot of Thelonious Monk in the house, and John Coltrane.

At one point we lived in a building in Brooklyn, when I was two years old, and some of my very early memories are from that – 1966, seeing a cockroach on the floor. We'd been living in Sweden; it was the first time I ever went to New York, but the reason I started talking about it is because Coltrane rehearsed in that building, and Ornette Coleman had rehearsal studios there. I've always liked the story of my mother going, 'Yeah, we used to go upstairs when Coltrane was rehearsing, and he always used to say how sweet you were, and take you on his lap.' That music was like the sound of my upbringing, of my daily life.

A lot of the people that were around were amazing musicians and people, but you have to find things out for yourself, and what I really shared with my dad was listening to records. He would go out and come back with Chaka Khan and Earth, Wind and Fire, and we would sit and journey through the record player, you know? I think, for me, the discovery of the meaning of the jazz happened as I've been on my own journey – joining Rip Rig + Panic, meeting people that were really into Sun Ra, into my dad's music, and thinking, 'Oh yeah, well I know that stuff.'

What were the first records that you bought, the ones where you felt like, 'This is mine. This doesn't belong to anyone else'?
I bought a Donny Osmond record once. Yeah, yeah [laughs]. When I was ten, some solo record of his. That's when everybody that I went to school with was listening to Donny Osmond's *Sweet and Innocent*, you know? But then, when I was twelve, I went and lived with my family in LA, the Compton area. I had my first boyfriend there; I fell in love for the first time. And, culturally, the stack of records that I brought with me from there back to Sweden broke my heart, but it also kept me alive, because I was lovesick. Me and my brother travelled back by ourselves from LA to Sweden, to go and stay with our grandparents – from the sunshine into the dark, cold weirdness of Sweden – and the records that I had with me from that trip were *Songs in the Key of Life* [Stevie Wonder, 1976]; Johnny 'Guitar' Watson, *Ain't That a Bitch* [1976], Deniece Williams, 'Free' [1976], and the Emotions; they became the soundtrack to my existence.

You mentioned Rip Rig + Panic. The first single, 'Go, Go, Go! (This Is It)', is a pretty fierce-sounding record, even today.
It's funny, I listened to it not that long ago, and I was quite happy to discover that it still sounded quite timeless, and that made sense. I wouldn't be sitting here if I hadn't have done that – coming here and meeting Ari Up, Tessa [Pollit] and Viv Albertine from The Slits, and Gareth Sager, Sean Oliver and Bruce Smith, who were coming out of the transition between the Pop Group and Rip Rig + Panic.

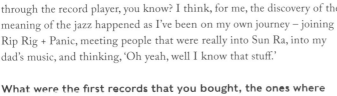

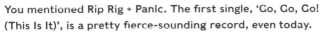

And later, when The Slits were doing this tour here, they invited my stepdad, Don Cherry, to play on the tour, and he took me along, and that's where I met everybody. A few months later I had gone back to New York, and I got this call from Gareth and Bruce and Sean, who were doing Rip Rig + Panic, asking me if I would come and sing. I can remember, I was lying in the bath and I took the call, and I was like, 'Oh okay, I'll just have to think about it.' And I was standing there looking at my mother like, 'This is really weird. I just had this call asking if I could sing.' And I thought, 'Well what can I lose? Shit.' I went back to London – somehow got enough airfare together – and the first track we ever did was 'Go, Go, Go! (This Is It)'.

I can remember Gareth playing me the track – Gareth was the songwriter and wrote all the lyrics – and he showed me how it went. And then I got on the cans and I thought, 'Okay, I don't know what the hell

I'm doing, but I'm just going to let it happen.' I think I was just more determined to not freeze than I was intimidated by the fear. I definitely had the fear, but I thought, 'Well, what the heck!' And that was the first thing I'd ever recorded properly.

I'm not sure what led me, or how I got through it. I suppose, in a way, that's the power of music. I mean, I still feel that thing, when it happens, when you're driven by music – it's like you can be completely petrified before you start and then, as it happens … Face the fear and just sort of go, 'Okay, well, if it's awful we'll just go again.' I think that kind of spontaneity is a wonderful, magic thing.

I have to ask you about 'Buffalo Stance', which came out in 1988. Can you remember people's reaction to it?

I think the wonderful thing with a track like 'Buffalo Stance' was that it was always very immediate. I can remember having a cassette of the rough cut of what I'd done and I was playing it to a couple of people in my kitchen, and they were just, 'Oh yeah, that's wicked!' I think that's the thing with that track: it's always had a kind of fairly direct effect.

Even the process of recording it was pretty immediate, because Tim [Simonen] knew what he wanted to do. So we went in and recorded it with that kind of energy that we had, letting it roll, taking it and capturing it as we went along. It was done in a pretty unself-conscious way. But it's an amazing thing for me to have a few things in my life where I can feel that I have been a part of something that had a kind of magic.

It's not something that you can go back and recreate, but there was definitely something about that track that summed up that time and place. It's also like a synopsis of my journey between fifteen and twenty-five. It just gave me a chance to celebrate that, that little ditty.

When *Raw Like Sushi* came out, did you enjoy that amount of success? Your profile was so high, there was the *Top of the Pops* incident [Cherry appeared while eight months pregnant in 1988], and your world seemed to go quite crazy for a while.

I think that I was able to just ride it, you know? Myself and Cameron [McVey – *Raw Like Sushi* producer and Cherry's partner], we'd built a posse of family, a think tank, a body of people around what we were doing. We were pretty self-sufficient and we were running the office, all of it really, from our little house just off Kensal Road, in London. And so, in a way, we moved into it as a family, you know? I felt really protected. Okay, yeah, I got pregnant. Maybe it wasn't the best time to get pregnant, but I certainly had the most amazing child from it, and once I was pregnant, I wasn't not going to have the baby, so it just had to happen with all the other stuff that was going on. It wasn't planned, it wasn't schemed, but in a way it was amazing. It became like a force, like a kind of protection.

Because I hadn't been out there, in that dimension, as a solo artist. As a woman, I'd always been in bands in a far more bohemian place than where all of this ended up. I felt kind of headstrong. I can't always say that I've known exactly where I'm going, or how or why, but I've known what I *didn't* want to do [laughs]. Or where I *didn't* want to end up.

There is that loophole in the land of being really successful. I've always felt really conscious of that super success that happened with *Raw Like Sushi*; it always felt very temporary. So for me it was like, 'Okay, just get in there and enjoy it, ride it out.'

It's transient, and through all of this, the importance of holding on to that thing was going to get me to where I am now, maybe. People have questioned, 'Why did you give it up?' or 'Where did you go for 18 years?' It's like, 'Well I've been doing lots of stuff, and maybe there isn't lots of product to show for it, but that doesn't mean that it hasn't been important.' I think that my real home maybe isn't in that lane of that very mainstream thing. I feel very at home where I am now, actually.

"As a woman, I'd always been in bands in a far more bohemian place than where all of this ended up. I felt kind of headstrong."

'7 Seconds' brought you together with Youssou N'Dour. At the time, it seemed strange to have a non-English vocal on a pop single in the UK. Looking back now, it's ridiculous to think that, but it was a big deal at the time. When did you first meet Youssou N'Dour and decide to do this song together?

I had a family connection to Youssou. He had two managers who had worked with my dad, and a dialogue happened through that. I had met him a few times at festivals when he was playing with Peter Gabriel in our early days. He was, in his own world, starting to do really well. So we were having this dialogue; there seemed to be a cultural meeting that we felt was really necessary.

Wanting him to sing in [Senegal language] Wolof, and his second language, French – I didn't do anything in Swedish, but I should have, maybe – was part of taking it all and doing something with all the different things that we had. It doesn't matter, does it? When Youssou starts singing in Wolof, you don't think about the fact that you don't understand, because you get it, and I think that was part of the magic of that song. I mean, you could *hear* it, and people obviously did, all around the world, and felt something. America was the only place where they were wanting us to rerecord the vocals and do just English.

Seriously? [Laughter] They tried to get you to do it again?

Yeah, because American radio didn't want to play it: 'No one's going to understand!' We recorded another version – well, Youssou did it all – but

how could it be the same? So, consequently, the States was the only place where that song didn't do what it seemed to do everywhere else, because they did change it. My dad always used to say, 'Don't let them change you. It is what it is.' Didn't work, anyway.

You mentioned it earlier, this idea that you fell out of the public eye. But you work with people all the time: Peter Gabriel, Timo Mass, Christian Falk, Gorillaz. You've never been away, but the perception is that you have been, which is strange.
Well, if people can't see you, and if the product isn't there, you're not in the public eye; it's sort of like you don't exist. So I suppose it's a bit like that. A lot of people haven't maybe seen the stuff that I've been doing.

How did you meet Damon Albarn to work with Gorillaz? How did that relationship come about?
He has a relative that works with him in the studio and stuff, who'd been working at our little studio, and he went over to work with Damon and they started making the album [*Demon Days*, 2005] – I don't know whether he made a suggestion. Damon, who I've bumped into quite a few times over the years, I think said to him, 'Oh, can we do something together sometime?' Anyway, I got a call about it, which was really

"... If the product isn't there, you're not in the public eye; it's sort of like you don't exist."

exciting, and a very rough cut of 'Kids With Guns', and I wrote some things and went to the studio and we did one version, and then Danger Mouse was around when we did the next version. It's something that I'm really proud and honoured to have been a part of. I went for the shows in Manchester, and we did five days at the Apollo Theater in New York.

That must have been amazing.
It was just incredible. Damon has this magic, a way of making everyone there part of it, an intrinsic part of it, and I think everyone felt equally as important to the whole picture of the tapestry. But somehow there was no battle of the egos, you know? It was like Ike Turner and De La Soul, and it was just this amazing thing and everyone felt like they were part of everything. It was a very cool thing to do – to *experience*.

When did you first meet Kieran Hebden – Four Tet – whom you worked with on this new record? [*Blank Project*, 2004].
I actually met Kieran for the first time about two years ago in Norway. I've been listening to him for a really long time, and I adore his music.

I think he's – dare I say? – a genius. He has a very natural relationship to what he does. We talked about working together and it just felt very right, as soon as we sat down and had some tapas.

It's very stripped down, very immediate; your voice is right up there in the mix.

There's no frills at all, and to tell you the truth, that scared me, doing it. It was really natural the way that we did it, and to have Kieran there in the driver's seat, but when we left, I didn't listen to it for about a month.

I did feel really naked. But then I came back to it and was like, 'No, this is the truth', without being like, 'Oh, he was all about making this super righteous record.' But I think it is how it needed to be, you know?

I'm very conscious of how things come together, and why they come together, and really a lot of it is about the chemistry and the people that are around that make that able to happen. Whatever that is, that thing becomes the work, the body of work, the album, the *product* [laughs].

And the last thing – you've had all these firsts, let's do the last. What should we finish the show with?

I'd like to play something off *Science Fiction*, the Ornette Coleman record. 'What Reason Could I Give' – we could take that, maybe.

The First Time Neneh Cherry Playlist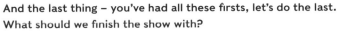

1	Manchild	Neneh Cherry
2	Underdog	Sly and The Family Stone
3	Nobody	The Jackson 5
4	You Leave Me Breathless	John Coltrane
5	Love's in Need of Love Today	Stevie Wonder
6	Ain't That a Bitch	Johnny 'Guitar' Watson
7	Free	Deniece Williams
8	I Don't Wanna Lose Your Love	The Emotions
9	In the Beginning	The Slits
10	Go, Go, Go! (This Is It)	Rip Rig + Panic
11	Buffalo Stance	Neneh Cherry
12	7 Seconds	Youssou N'Dour and Neneh Cherry
13	Kids With Guns	Gorillaz
14	Blank Project	Neneh Cherry
15	What Reason Could I Give	Ornette Coleman

"It was pop sensibility with a punk approach, hip-hop beats speeded up to a house tempo. There you are: that's the formula, kids."

Norman Cook

I've been friends with Norman for 15 years, so I struggled with how to describe him. Instead, I've written about some things that you might not know about the man behind Fatboy Slim.

According to *Guinness World Records*, he's had the most hit records under the most names, and he's played every Glastonbury for the past 18 years but never collects his fee (even when he headlines). I've seen him DJ there in a giant, padded bumblebee outfit, and he once attempted to play the Miniscule of Sound, a phone box–sized tent billed as 'The World's Smallest Nightclub' (the bouncers turned him away, telling him he had to send in a demo mixtape first).

Norman is colourblind (and uses that as an excuse for everything from missing traffic lights, to his choice of Hawaiian shirts, to his inability to operate his laptop). Football is very close to his heart; I've seen few men happier than when Brighton and Hove Albion FC earned their promotion to the Premier League in 2017.

Many people I know have benefited from his generosity: he's helped keep a roof over the heads of more than a few friends over the years, myself included. Also, he's a rather handsome chap – and I'm not just saying that because of the roof thing.

If you visit his recording studio (with a giant acid smiley face on the roof), it's useful to know there's a hole under the carpet in the middle of the room. This is where legendary funk bassist Bootsy Collins repeatedly stomped his foot during a session, cracking the floorboards. If your chair leg falls into the crack, you flip over: 'You've gone into the Bootsy Hole!' Norm refuses to mend it.

This last thing about Norman, you might know: audiences are drawn to him in a way that simply doesn't happen with other DJs. Whether it's his skill, charisma or enthusiasm, people just love him – always have done, always will. He is the original Superstar DJ.

Matt Everitt: When was the first time you were aware of music?
Probably singing in the car on long journeys with my family. Both my parents liked to sing. We probably didn't have a radio in the car in those days, but we would sing harmonies. There was a lot of Peter, Paul and Mary going on. Then for recorded music, it would probably be 'I Can't Let Maggie Go' by Honeybus, which was my dad's favourite tune.

Was it quite a musical family?
There's no history of showbiz or anything; they were more into amateur dramatics. I wouldn't say that they had a hugely great taste in music. My staple diet was Peter, Paul and Mary rather than Bob Dylan. There was an awful lot of Kenny Ball and His Jazzmen going on; a healthy amount of The Beatles, which is good; and also a generous dose of The Carpenters. So it was quite middle of the road. I didn't have a big brother or sister who was into Motown, so I had to forge my own musical identity out of Herb Alpert and the Tijuana Brass. A lot of bossa nova went on in my family, which might explain some of my later Latin influence.

What about the first record that you owned?
The first record I owned was 'Devil Gate Drive' by Suzi Quatro. For me, in those days, she was the cutting-edge, leather-clad rock chick personified. She was the wilder side of life. She didn't take no shit from no one, and she rocked out on Devil Gate Drive. And she played bass as well.

Was this about the time that you started to think, 'I'd like to do that – whatever that is that they're doing, making that noise'?
I would love to say yes. Sadly, it was more to do with The Osmonds. Donny had a piano with light bulbs all around it that lit up when he played, and he had a leather jacket with his name in studs on the back, and I think that's when I thought, 'That's what I want to do for a living'. I'm ashamed to say it, but Donny Osmond was my inspiration.

What was the first album?
My first one was *Black and Blue* by The Rolling Stones [1976] on cassette. The pivotal song was 'Fool to Cry', which, I think, was probably my first introduction to the concept of production. It starts with a heavily affected Rhodes piano, which I just thought was the most warm, sexy-sounding thing I'd ever heard. I'd think, 'How does he make that noise?' That's the first time I was thinking that music wasn't just people playing their instruments: there was this thing called production. Then you get into reverb and delay and everything, which subsequently became my career.

What was the first gig that you went to?
The first gig I went to was Queen. In Hyde Park, 1976. So I would have been thirteen. No idea how my parents allowed my seventeen-year-old brother to take me all the way up to London to go to a free gig in Hyde Park, but they did. That was probably the moment when I thought,

'Right, you can do something with this stagecraft thing. That was my brief flirtation with pomp rock, and then punk rock quickly took over.

THE CLASH

When did you start playing instruments yourself?
I started as a drummer – only for about four gigs. I wasn't the world's best, but you didn't have to be. This was in punk days. Then I was lead singer for a bit, and then I was guitarist, but my first professional gig was on bass, with The Housemartins. I'd previously been the guitarist in Paul Heaton's old band, The Stomping Pond Frogs.

Who were your big punk obsessions?
The Clash. They had the swagger, they had the fashion, they had the politics, they had the tunes. For me, that epitomized everything that was exciting, romantic and awesome about punk rock – not nihilistic gobbing and flirting with Nazi armbands. They had their politics down pat, they had their look, they had their stance, and every time I ever played bass guitar, I always thought I was Paul Simonon.

"That's the first time I was thinking that music wasn't just people playing their instruments: there was this thing called *production*."

How did a love of punk mutate into working with Paul Heaton?
Well, by the time I met him, Paul was riding a scooter and listening to soul music. The first meeting was at a pub; his band was supporting my band. I just thought he was a fantastic front man. We quit our respective bands and started one together. He was wearing fireman's trousers. Paul still, to this day, does tons of things that no one quite understands what the motivation was or what point he was trying to make. But yeah, everyone was trying to be fashionable and new wave, and he just turns up with rubber fireman's trousers on. I fell in love with his voice and his attitude, and he had much better lyrics and was a better singer than me.

Was there that real community spirit in The Housemartins?
Oh, absolutely, yeah. We based a lot of our ideas upon The Clash, and one was that we were a gang and had a dress code. There were certain things that weren't allowed.

What wasn't allowed?
Hats [laughs]. I used wear those French fisherman's hats, and when I joined the band they said, 'There's no hats in this band'. When we first

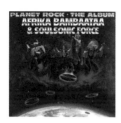

started, it was very anti-fashion, so yeah, basically, you couldn't wear anything fashionable. We would have band meetings about 'What's our stance on this, and what's our stance on that?' I mean, we were against hotels at the beginning. The first proper, major tour we did, we stayed at fans' houses. To save money, but we also thought that was like living some kind of rockstar dream, and if we fell into that kind of mindset, then next thing we'd just be egotistical, drug-addled lunatics.

We've got to talk about 'Happy Hour' [1986], because it was such a remarkable success. For a band with these very strict rules and this code, how did fame and *Top of the Pops* suit you?
We really liked the *Top of the Pops* bit, because we'd all grown up watching it, but the fame bit we weren't so fond of – Paul especially. At this point, we were still denying hotels, and I remember we did [British music TV show] *The Tube*, and they put us up in a hotel and Paul's like, 'I don't want to hang around in hotels with these rich people'. So we kind of went even more staunchly anti-fame. I think Paul's complete anti-fame stance set me up well for later life, because I've never taken it that seriously, though I've since enjoyed some of the luxuries of it, and enjoyed some of the ego side of it. I can always hear Paul's voice going, 'Uh-huh. We don't act like that' [laughs]. He's always there, keeping me in check.

When did you first get into hip-hop?
Going to see The Clash, and then being supported by Grandmaster Flash. I was already a DJ, but it was like, 'What the hell is he doing with the records? How's he making that noise? And why is it making me dance so much?' 'Adventures of Grandmaster Flash on the Wheels of Steel' was a real life-changing record for me. I've based my career on it ever since. The idea of chopping up songs and making other tunes out of them – hip-hop was probably as big an influence as punk. It had its own language, and its own fashion, and its own culture. This is when I was just starting, when I was old enough to DJ in clubs. Until then I'd been a party DJ, then I did weddings, and when I moved down to Brighton when I was eighteen, I could DJ in nightclubs. It was around the year that 'Planet Rock' [Afrika Bambaataa and the Soulsonic Force, 1982] came out, and that record changed my life. It was like, 'What is this weird abuse of electronic instruments, and why do I like it so much?'

That was pre-Housemartins? You'd always had that love?
I was a club DJ playing funk and electro. But in those days we called it 'black music'. It wasn't called dance music or EDM; it was called black music, and I didn't feel, as a suburban white kid, it was my place to make that music. It wasn't until the sampler and the drum machine were invented that, basically, white people could make 'black music'. It just opened the floodgates, from Coldcut to Tim Simenon. And that, for me, was the end of The Housemartins, because all my mates who I'd been DJing with are now making records and they're in the charts with music

that I *really* like, and I'm in the charts with music that I don't really like doing, and I'd much rather be doing what they're doing, please.

What was your first post-Housemartins electronic incarnation?
The first thing I did – which was about three weeks after I moved back to Brighton and thought, 'Right. That was a lovely dream. What am I going to do next?' – was a remix of 'I Know You Got Soul' by Eric B. and Rakim [under the name Double Trouble]. A record company plugger I'd been working with at The Housemartins who knew me as a club DJ, just said, 'Oh, we've got the rights to "I Know You've Got Soul". How can we remix it? What could we do?' And I went, 'Well, isn't it a cappella on the other side? You could spin it.' I did a little demo of mixing it with The Jackson 5, 'I Want You Back', and sent him that and said, 'That's what you could do'. And he said, 'Do you want to go and do it in the studio?' And I did, and so, literally three weeks after The Housemartins, I had this new career as a remixer, and it got to number three in the charts.

"'Adventures of Grandmaster Flash on the Wheels of Steel' was a real life-changing record for me. I've based my career on it ever since."

You've gone under many different names throughout your career. Is that a way of trying to protect a little bit of yourself?
There was a little bit of hiding behind different names so no one really knew who I was. To be honest, it was more about having more than one record out at once. And being signed to one label and not wanting to put everything out on that one label. When I started doing it, I was signed to Island as Freak Power, but it said in the contract I could make records under pseudonyms on independent labels, as long as I didn't do interviews or ever tell anyone it was me [laughs]. So then Pizzaman arrived, and then Fatboy Slim, and the Mighty Dub Katz, all of which I denied were anything to do with me at first. You only got outed if it was really successful, and I could have more than one record out at the same time.

Tell me about that first Fatboy Slim album: 1996, *Better Living Through Chemistry*. It defined a very specific sound, and really helped kick-start a new era of British electronic music.
Well, it wasn't really an album; it was a sort of 'greatest hits so far'. In those days, there was no precedent of dance albums that made any sense or sold any copies. But I think by the time we released *Better Living Through Chemistry*, I had seven singles out as Fatboy Slim, and I remember JC [Reid] and Damian [Harris, of Skint Records] saying, 'Look, if

you just do three more tunes, we've got an album there', and I said, 'Why on earth would we want to release an album?' But it had a sort of cohesion as an album, and it tapped into another punk-like DIY revolution where people were a bit bored of corporate handbag house music, and so we sort of ripped up the rule book and thought, 'Let's have the energy of acid house, but include the beats from hip-hop and then The Beatles that I grew up with.' It was pop sensibility with a punk approach, hip-hop beats speeded up to a house tempo. There you are: that's the formula, kids. Now go out and make a record.

You said that electronic music didn't sell albums, but then you released *You've Come a Long Way, Baby* [1998], which became one of the first big crossover dance records.
I think The Prodigy would get the medal for being the first to make a cohesive dance album that sold outside dance music. When I was making that, I was thinking of it more as an album, but still, I remember having meetings with people about the promotional campaign, and this amount of units, and these territories, and I'm like, 'Just remember what you're dealing with. This is an underground dance thing.' But they saw how that wave was coming in and saw that I could be riding on the crest of it.

Tracks like 'Praise You' and 'Right Here, Right Now' crossed over into the States, and all of a sudden you've got MTV, and you've become DJ-as-pop-superstar. Was it intimidating?
'Intimidating' might be too strong a word. It was harder in America, because they really couldn't get their head around the fact that I wasn't a band. I would get to gigs and the sound man would say, 'Are you in Fatboy Slim?', to which my reply was always, 'No. Do you want to be?'

I did gigs in America where I would play my DJ set and then the audience would be waiting for Fatboy Slim, the band, to come on afterwards; they couldn't understand why I'd played 'Rockafeller Skank' and 'Praise You' when the band were going to come on in a minute and do it [laughs]. Intimidating? A bit, but more exciting. It felt like we were breaking ground. I've always maintained that there's a movement of interesting music that comes out of mainly black, gay America, or just black America, and then comes to England, and bands like The Beatles or The Rolling Stones make a whitened version of it, then we sell it back to the Americans and they're like, 'What is this crazy new sound?'

I've got another first, and it's up to you if you want to answer or not, but when was the first time that you thought your lifestyle maybe was getting in the way of your music? You've been quite open about the fact that you've cleaned up.
There never was a time when I thought my lifestyle was getting in the way of my professional career. My reasons for quitting were more to do with my family and my health. Had it gotten in the way of my career, I maybe would have stopped or slowed down earlier on, but the reason

I got away with it for so long is that being a DJ and making abstract, druggie music is, you know, not necessarily prohibitive to living the life. No. There wasn't a professional thing.

Music is always the soundtrack to your life, and if someone complains that I haven't got a head for figures or remembering footballers' names or anything, well, when it comes to music, I have got a photographic memory: I remember what was playing when I've met every single girlfriend I've ever had. So if you want to do first snog, first shag, then bring it on.

Okay. I want locations, circumstances, and music ...
Taylor Fox – that's the girl, not the artist. She was American. I'd love to meet her again and find out what happened to her. She wore glasses, which made my first snog somewhat complicated, because I didn't know where to put the nose and glasses arrangement. And it was Tina Charles, 'I Love to Love'. Basically, she was singing it to me because I wanted to love and she wanted to dance, so it was sort of role reversal from the song. I just wanted to carry on snogging, and she wanted to dance.

And finally, you get to choose the last song of the show.
'Music Sounds Better With You' by Stardust.

The First Time **Norman Cook** Playlist

1	Eat, Sleep, Rave, Repeat	Fatboy Slim and Riva Starr feat. Beardyman
2	I Can't Let Maggie Go	Honeybus
3	A Taste of Honey	Herb Alpert and The Tijuana Brass
4	Devil Gate Drive	Suzi Quatro
5	Crazy Horses	The Osmonds
6	Fool to Cry	The Rolling Stones
7	Safe European Home	The Clash
8	Happy Hour	The Housemartins
9	The Adventures of Grandmaster Flash on the Wheels of Steel (extended mix)	Grandmaster Flash and The Furious Five
10	Planet Rock	Afrika Bambaataa and the Soulsonic Force
11	I Know You Got Soul (Double Trouble remix)	Eric B. and Rakim
12	Santa Cruz	Fatboy Slim
13	I Love to Love	Tina Charles
14	Music Sounds Better With You	Stardust

"Just because I hear something doesn't mean that everybody is going to hear it. But with *Graceland* ... everybody fell in love with it."

PAUL SIMON

I f you're lucky, there's a moment during an interview where you and the guest connect – not a life-altering, telepathic melding of minds, but a shared reference point or joke. For the guest, it's when they realize that you're familiar with their work and there's no agenda; for the interviewer, it comes when you're able to calm the part of your brain that's screaming, 'THAT'S PAUL SIMON! SITTING THERE! PAUL ACTUAL FUCKING SIMON', and have a conversation with a fellow human (even if they happen to be one of the greatest songwriters in the history of popular music).

In this case, the moment happened a few hours before we started recording, when Paul realized he could choose *any* music from the near-limitless BBC archive to play in the show. He's naming rare tracks by artists as eclectic as The Crows, the Ian Campbell Folk Group and the Ensemble of the Bulgarian Republic. 'Good luck finding these songs', he laughs, looking slightly surprised when I insist there's nothing he could pick that the BBC won't have somewhere in its vaults. 'Cool', he smiles, and I know it's going to be okay.

He speaks like he sings, with that soft, melodic voice, pacing his words with a slow rhythm that rises and dips. He may have had a twitchy relationship with the media in the past – I guess 40 years of questions about a Simon and Garfunkel reunion might do that to a person – but here he's open, funny and relaxed, and 'Artie' comes up in the first five minutes of our conversation.

My lasting impression is that he's quietly proud of the whole of his legendary back catalogue, but, winningly, even more passionate about the music that informed it. 'Could you find any of those songs?' he asks, as the tape starts rolling.

Matt Everitt: When was the first time you were aware of music?
I guess I was aware of it because my father was a musician. He was a bass player, so I could hear him practising. Also, I'm a big baseball fan – I'm from New York, so I'm a New York Yankees fan – and before the baseball game, there was a popular music radio show. And because I used to score the games – we'd write all the names down and indicate whether it was a base hit or an out – I would listen to the end of this music show, because I didn't want to miss the beginning of the ball game. And I kept thinking, 'Boy, this music – I cannot stand this music.'

Finally, one day, the disc jockey said, 'They just sent in a record I got this morning, and this has got to be the worst piece of music that I've ever heard. If this record is a hit, I'll eat my hat.' And he played a record called 'Gee' by The Crows. It was an early R&B doo-wop song and it was the first time I ever heard that, and I was thinking, as I'm making out my line-up, 'That's the first piece of music I've ever liked on this show.'

That's when I remember being interested. Oh no, you know what? When I was in the fourth grade, Art Garfunkel got up and sang at the school assembly. I didn't know who he was. He sang a song called, 'They Tried to Tell Us We're Too Young', and everyone went crazy for it. And I thought, 'That's interesting. Everyone goes crazy. I wonder if I can sing this.' I didn't meet him till two years later.

Was your first single 'Pledging My Love' by Johnny Ace?
That was the second single I owned. The first single that I bought? Oh, nobody would know it. It was an instrumental called 'Back Street Blues'. It was a New Orleans band. I can't remember who it was.

Were you a confident kid when it came to singing? In a lot of your very earliest recordings, some of the vocal inflections are borrowed, but they're very committed vocal takes.
Well, one thing that had a big influence on me was when I was sitting in my room and singing a song that I liked, 'Anywhere I Wander'. I was singing this song and my father – who, as I said, was a musician – was getting ready to put the bass in the car and go drive off and play his gig, and as he passed by my room, he stuck his head in and said, 'You have a nice voice, Paul.' And that really had a big affect on me.

But I started to sing with Artie just when my voice was changing, so I never knew whether my voice was going to crack or not, so I had less confidence. Also, Artie – who was the only other kid in the neighbourhood interested in singing – was famous for having this great voice, famous in the neighbourhood, you know? So I was singing with a guy who had, you know, the 'Great Voice' in the neighbourhood [laughs].

Little Walter, 'My Babe' – what is it about him and that song?
First, I just love the groove. I guess he's my favourite harmonica player. He was a genius, a virtuoso player. That song really had an influence on me. I love the groove of it, and when I came here and I started to sing,

'My Babe' was one of the songs that I used to sing. I think my favourite rock and roll song of all time is 'Mystery Train' – the Elvis Presley version of 'Mystery Train'. I love the title. I don't know where that title comes from, because it's not in the song. I started to research it, and I think that title pre-existed. Those verses and that title may have been around in the blues movement of the '20s or the '30s, and found its way into that song. [Presley's guitarist] Scotty Moore, that lick that he plays, it's just my favourite rockabilly lick. I taught that lick to my seventeen-year-old son. I said, 'You want to see my favourite little blues lick? Here, this is it.'

You once said that you greeted success with bewilderment. Does it still feel like that?

No, it's an evolved version of bewilderment. I look upon it as an enormous piece of misinformation! You know, if you're really serious about what your art is and what you're making, the more opinions that you get from other people – especially if they're excessive praise or excessive criticism – it's just a big confusion. And then you have to spend time editing it later on and say, 'Actually, it was that brilliant' or 'Actually, it wasn't that bad as everyone said.' And then you think, 'Did I really need to spend all this time thinking about somebody else's opinion when it's hard enough to figure out what it is that I'm doing musically without paying attention to people who have no idea what I'm doing?'

So, I mean, that's a downside. The upside of success is, of course, you have enough money to take care of your family, to take care of friends and relatives and people who are in need – to give, you know? The downside of success is fame, which is pretty much toxic.

I want to talk to you about 'Mary, Don't You Weep' by The Swan Silvertones – an important song for you.

The Swan Silvertones were my favourite gospel quartet, and they still rank up there. Their lead singer was named Reverend Claude Jeter, and he had this ethereal falsetto, a beautiful falsetto, and in this one particular song, 'Mary, Don't You Weep', at a certain point he scats a line: 'I'll be your bridge over deep water if you trust in my name.'

So that was in there. At the same time, I was writing this melody, which was also influenced by a song on an Everly Brothers album, *Songs Our Daddy Taught Us*, and the particular song was called 'Long Time Gone' and it had this jump of an octave – and that's in 'Bridge over Troubled Water', this octave jump. But anyway, those two elements. It's not like if I said, 'Here, take this element and take this, and see if you can write "Bridge over Troubled Water" [laughs].' You won't, you know?

Somehow that got tied into whatever strange force that I experienced that made me write this song in a relatively short time, like a night or two. And you know, when I wrote it I said, 'Wow, that's better than I usually write. And I never used those chords before. And that's good … [pauses and smiles] … I'm going to give it to Artie to sing.' Which was probably one of the bigger mistakes I made!

I was listening to the Aretha Franklin version. It's brilliant.
That's what I had in mind, because that comes from black church, and that's what The Swan Silvertones are. But Artie sang it in a choirboy voice, which was also brilliant. Artie's version is as good as the Aretha version, but that's the white and the black versions of the song. It seems to be sung more at state funerals and things now; it used to be weddings.

Anyway, it's a strange song for me, because it became so well known by the version that Artie sang and by the version that Aretha sang, that even though I wrote it, I very rarely sang it. It almost feels like a song that's not mine. It's a little bit strange.

I find it amazing that you documented the split with Artie in song – that you took 'So Long, Frank Lloyd Wright' and 'The Only Living Boy in New York' and you wrote about that split as it was happening. It was a tremendously brave thing to do.
Well, 'The Only Living Boy' is not really about our split. 'The Only Living Boy' is about Artie going off to make the movie *Catch-22*, which he was shooting in Mexico. I mean, we weren't splitting at that point. He was just leaving for an extended period of time, and I was writing a song that said, you know, 'Good luck. Do your best. Have a great movie. Have a great time.' 'So Long, Frank Lloyd Wright' is kind of kidding around and saying, 'Yeah, we're splitting', because Artie studied architecture at school. But no, we didn't split until after *Catch-22*.

> ## "Lyrics always come last with me, whether they come from the groove or whether they come from the chord changes."

You talk a lot about finding a groove on a song musically, and that being, sometimes, the jumping-off point for the lyrics, whereas I assumed that lyrics came first.
Lyrics always come last with me, whether they come from the groove or from the chord changes. On this album [*Stranger to Stranger*, 2016], 'Insomniac's Lullaby' was a guitar piece that was written with the intention of having a song on top of it, but I didn't know what the song was. When I first started to write, when I was living here and with all the early Simon and Garfunkel songs, my process was I would sit with my guitar and I'd play and I'd sing whatever came into my mind, and that's how I wrote. A lot of those songs – including 'The Sound of Silence' and 'Homeward Bound' and 'The Boxer' – became very popular songs, but my playing got more complex. I wasn't really able to play the guitar and sing at the same time, because I was concentrating on guitar moves.

So then I would put the guitar down, record, and then start to write the lyrics. After a few years of that, I got up to the point where, around *Graceland* – or even *Still Crazy After All These Years*, which I wrote on guitar – where I said, 'I'm going to have it be played on piano.' And then I thought, you know, it really doesn't matter who plays what I'm going to sing over; it doesn't have to be limited to what I play on guitar.

PAUL·SIMON
GRACELAND

The source can be different.

The sound can be different, and the source can be different. All I have to do is give a sketch and find the right player. By the time I got to *Graceland*, I'd say, 'I want to do something that sounds a little bit like this. What do you play?' And they'd play something and I'd say, 'That's good. Now could you change the key and play this over here?' So I was more in editing mode. I don't even really need any instruments. I can just have a groove and sing over it.

If I go back to 'Cecilia', that's all 'Cecilia' was: just us pounding on drums and piano benches and stuff, and somewhere in there I heard a minute and 15 seconds of a really good groove and I said, 'Just make a loop of that and I'll write a song over it.'

You mentioned *Graceland*. I'm fascinated by this idea, this moment when a collection of songs connects with an audience far bigger than the audience that it was maybe intended for, and it gains a momentum. Very few records connect that widely. Well, my feeling about *Graceland* was if people like this I really won't be surprised, because I *really* like this. But if people don't like it and they don't get it, I won't be surprised either.

When it first came out, the first people who interviewed me, their big question was, 'Well, you're forty-four years old now. How does it feel to be making pop records when you're forty-four?' You know? They really didn't know what was going on. They were just looking for the angle. It took two, three weeks before people said, 'Wait a minute, this is music from South Africa'. And then when everybody heard it the way I heard it? Well, it was very exciting, but shortly after that happened, the whole political issue arose around it, so it became like a cultural phenomenon – not just musical, but also a political debate.

So that was an exceptional thing to happen in my life and in my career. I did it again when I wrote a musical for Broadway called *The Capeman* [1998]: there I used doo-wop music and Latin music, and I thought, 'This is a really good sound. I really like the way that these two sounds mix.' Well, that was a complete flop! I mean, revisionism now says it was way ahead of its time, but at the time it was an absolute flop.

Just because I hear something doesn't mean that everybody is going to hear it, you know? But in the case of *Graceland*, all of a sudden, everybody heard it the way I heard it and fell in love with it. It's one of the highlights of my musical career and education.

We should mention Roy Halee, working on *Stranger to Stranger* [2016]. Obviously, you trust him; were you like, 'Well, we've done this work before, but he's the right man for this album'?
I've known Roy Halee for at least 50 years. He did the audition tape for Simon and Garfunkel at Columbia. He did all the Simon and Garfunkel albums, and he along with Phil Ramone and Tom Dowd were considered the great engineers of the '60s and the '70s. Halee was an extraordinarily gifted engineer. His ear was so great that he would invent echo sounds, and he'd move a mic an inch and a half and it would make a difference. Or he'd say, 'I really want a deep echo sound.' Like on 'The Boxer', he'd put the drum in an elevator shaft and put the mic way up at the top.

On 'Bridge over Troubled Water', Roy was the first engineer to use 16-track. Everybody was always recording with 8-tracks, but he linked up two 8-tracks so that he had 16 tracks going, but he would use the same machine to link it. Well, on this one day, he couldn't get the exact machine. One was an Ampex and one was something else. So he linked them up, and when he played back 'Bridge over Troubled Water' with the drums, because the machines were just an eighth of an inch off, the drums, instead of coming back like a simple *crash … crash*, it came back *cra-crash!* And he said, 'Listen to this! Listen to what is going on here!'

"A lot of what goes on is an accident, and you hear it and you say, 'I want that sound' … it's like capturing lightning in a bottle."

It's an accident. And that's the way he thought, and that's the way I think. A lot of what goes on is an accident, and you hear it and you say, 'I want that; I want that sound.' You know? And you go for it. It's like capturing lightning in a bottle. That's how records used to be made. And then it became more and more controllable and digitized, and it changed in its quality. If you listen to records from the '50s and you listen to records from today, they're very different in sound. That's why I use sounds from different periods and mix them with very modern sounds.

When we were talking about choosing music for this show, you mentioned 'Theodora Is Dozing' from *Music of Bulgaria* [1955]. You've taken influences from all over the world, but what was it about this piece of music that resonated with you so much?
Well, this album was called *Music of Bulgaria* – it's been released under several different titles since then. In the early '60s New York folk scene, people were listening to this album, and that's where I heard it. I particularly love this one track. I thought it was so beautiful. I think the guy

who played it for me was this American folk musician called Dave Van Ronk – he was a pretty famous guy in New York. Van Ronk was kind of a leader of the New York Bleeker and MacDougal folk scene.

You once said that when you were a kid, all you were interested in was girls, rock 'n' roll and baseball. Has anything changed?
No. The first statement is basically true. I have to leave the girls part out, because now I'm interested in one girl, my wife, and yeah, that's it. I still love baseball: I love to watch it; I'm a fan. I played it when I was a kid so, you know, I understand the game, I understand strategy, and it's a very relaxing thing to watch. Otherwise, I pretty much don't watch television.

Girls, rock 'n' roll and baseball: it's a pretty fine maxim to live by.
Drugs is left out of that. Otherwise it was the same [chuckles]. You know, drugs, sex, rock 'n' roll, but in my case you have baseball in there.

We always ask the guest to pick the last song. Are you going to pick 'Mystery Train'?
'Mystery Train' is my favourite.

Then we'll go out on that one.

The First Time **Paul Simon** Playlist

1	Still Crazy After All These Years	Paul Simon
2	Gee	The Crows
3	Too Young	Nat King Cole
4	Pledging My Love	Johnny Ace
5	Anywhere I Wander	Danny Kaye
6	I Am a Rock	Paul Simon
7	My Babe	Little Walter
8	Mary, Don't You Weep	The Swan Silvertones
9	Cecilia	Simon and Garfunkel
10	Long Time Gone	The Everly Brothers
11	The Only Living Boy in New York	Simon and Garfunkel
12	Graceland	Paul Simon
13	Polegnala E Todora (Theodora Is Dozing)	Ensemble of the Bulgarian Republic
14	Insomniac's Lullaby	Paul Simon
15	Mystery Train	Elvis Presley

"I thought, 'My generation: this is our problem. They're not going to give it to us, we have to take it.'"

Pete Townshend

A friend who has worked with Pete Townshend for years described him as 'The last great rock and roll interview', and he's probably right. The handful of other artists who've had a comparable impact and longevity have retreated into myth-preserving silence or rarely let their guard down. But to ask Townshend about any moment in his life or The Who's career is to provoke him to contextualize, philosophize, self-analyze, adjust then readjust his opinions. In the '60s and '70s he was famous for very long, contemplative interviews in the music press. Not much has changed.

This interview is taken from two conversations – one in 2012 and one in 2013. Both took place at his offices, a short, civilized stroll from Richmond Green in West London. The walls feature modish op art and the remains of a smashed Rickenbacker guitar framed in gold. Nearby there's a classic '60s scooter and a vintage Wurlitzer keyboard: 'That belonged to Leon Russell', Townshend explains, spotting me admiring it. 'He can't have it back.'

Tall, still slender, in a lean black suit, big boots and a red and white gingham shirt, Townshend has a long, oval face tipped by grey stubble, with thoughtful blue eyes winking out from either side of that famous nose. His responses veer between thoughtful introspection, amusement, slight exasperation and genuine anger; he's got the air of a comfortably wealthy university lecturer who might punch you out for asking the wrong question.

I'm not sure if Townshend would do interviews, given the choice, but unlike so many other musicians he sees it as an opportunity to explain himself. Aside from the joy of hearing him analyze his own achievements – not least elevating the very idea of pop music into art – it's great to see him dig with passion into subjects he's covered before, looking for new angles, trying to make sense of his life. Plus there's a story about Keith Moon throwing a TV out of a hotel window – so everything you want in a great rock 'n' roll interview.

Matt Everitt: When were you first aware of music?

Really, really early. My dad was in a swing band; I can just remember the sound of his clarinet. He didn't practise the clarinet like a pop musician; he practised as though he was an orchestral musician, very hard for two or three hours every morning. That was probably my first exposure.

Was it seeing him perform live that planted the seed in your mind that you wanted to be a musician?

Not really. What made me want to be a musician was a little bit more trite. I was at a show, aged about eleven or twelve. I was on the Isle of Man, up in the balcony with my short trousers and my smart holiday blazer, and these two pretty girls came and sat, one on either side, with their big dresses and cleavage. One leaned across me, tickled me under the chin and said, 'Oh, what a cute little boy.' The other said, 'So which one do you fancy?', pointing at the band. I thought, 'I like this game.'

When were the first stirrings of your love of rock and roll?

We were on the Isle of Man again, and my father had the right to go to the chain of cinemas that were owned by the people that employed him at the ballroom. We went one Saturday morning and we saw a rerun of a Bill Haley thing, probably 'Rock Around the Clock'. Me and my friend, Graham, sat there – we were eleven – saying, 'This is really great, isn't it?'

'Man of Mystery' by the Shadows was your audition piece for Roger Daltrey in 1962. Was that the first time you met him?

I was in my last term at school, and down the corridor comes swaggering Roger Daltrey in tight trousers and a draped jacket looking like a cartoon Teddy Boy. 'You', he says. 'I hear you play guitar. Do you want to join a band?' The only conversations I'd had with Roger prior to that was when he was threatening to beat the shit out of me. It was his thing. So I'm thinking, 'Hey, this is interesting. Yes, I think I would like to join a band.'

One of the first big Who singles, 'I Can't Explain', is you essentially articulating the feelings of a generation of postwar kids. Did you always want to be a spokesman?

Only after that record was released. I wrote it about the kind of things that young people feel: I see you across a crowded room; I wouldn't say that I was in love with you, but I would love to come and talk to you, but there's no point because I know that I couldn't explain if I did. After it had become a hit, we were at the Goldhawk Club in West London and we'd played the song four or five times, and these kids came backstage and one of them, led by now famous 'Irish Jack' Lyons, who's a mod, said, 'We want to tell you something: we want you to write more songs like this.' I said, 'What do you like about it?' He said, 'We like the fact that it … that it … erm …'. I said, 'That you can't explain why.' He said, 'That's it!' I realized then that all I really had to do was get hold of what it was that they wanted to say and put it into words.

'My Generation' is part of The Who's identity. Can you remember first trying to document that feeling of isolation from society, and wanting to kick against it?

I'll tell the story about what triggered me writing 'My Generation'. It was two things. One was being pushed out of the way in the Express Dairy by a woman in a fur coat, when I was in my flat, in Belgravia [in London]. 'Get out of my way', she said. I thought, 'Hold on a minute, I'm first in the queue. Get to the back of the queue!' She just pushed me out of the way. I thought, 'Well, yes, I'm young and I look like an idiot, but actually I'm a songwriter.' The other thing was I'd always wanted to convert an American hearse into a low-cut gig-mobile. I'd managed to get hold of this Packard hearse. One day I went out and it had gone. When I investigated, the command had come from the Queen Mother to have it removed, because it reminded her of her husband's funeral or something. I remember thinking [shouts loudly], 'You people can't fucking well do this! [Shouts even louder] You're going to push me aside in the fucking Express Dairy and take away my fucking car. Fuck all of you!'

Then I calmed down a bit, and I thought, 'My generation: this is our problem. They're not going to give it to us, we have to take it. What is there to take? Nothing that they have, we want. We have to draw a new line, we have to make a new divide.'

"You people can't fucking well do this! You're going to push me aside in the fucking Express Dairy and take away my car. Fuck all of you!"

It's the blues, isn't it? Like, I'm not being treated properly. I haven't got a public forum so I have to express myself in the one way that I can. Were The Who a blues band?

Yeah, but the comparison is an uneasy one. There's this spoiled-brat eighteen-year-old being adopted by these two Kings Road white boys, Kit Lambert and Chris Stamp, who want to manage a pop group and they install me in an apartment in fucking Belgravia. It's not a Louisiana porch and I'm not starving. But it triggered a new way of approaching pop music. Art has to have a function. It has to do something. It has to effect some kind of movement or change to be worthy of the word 'art', otherwise it's just decoration. A lot of pop music is just decoration.

Today, in the West, young people are having to reposition themselves again. It's such an interesting echo for me, because I can remember how hard it was, how much effort went into just deciding that I was going to write a song like 'My Generation', which, if it goes to number one, the police, the Royal Family and MI5 are going to come and imprison me!

It felt very similar to what those girls have done in Putin's Russia [anarcho-punk band Pussy Riot] – it felt as radical. Of course, what actually happened was that it was completely dismissed by the establishment!

Henry Purcell, the composer, is someone you've noted as being an influence on your songwriting. When did you first hear him?
Around the time of 'My Generation'. I was living with my manager, Kit Lambert, who was Constant Lambert's son. Constant had been the artistic and music director of the Royal Ballet at Covent Garden, and his favourite composer was Purcell. One of the pieces he loved to play was a suite called 'The Gordian Knot Untied'; I was very, very struck by it. There's a piece called 'Chaconne', which is profoundly sad and moving, but at the same time it has what we call in music suspensions. A normal chord or a minor chord, that's all I knew; then with Purcell, suddenly I was in a world of suspensions. I got into baroque music, and into orchestration. That was when the pretentious Pete popped up and started to think, 'I can write an opera!' In 1965, The Who had barely had a handful of pop hits, and I'm thinking, 'Well, this is going to be over soon. What am I going to do when I grow up? I'm going to write operas.'

Tommy [1969] was your first rock opera. Do you like the term 'rock opera' or is it a bit of a weight around your neck?
It's both, really. Rock opera, yeah – it was a bit of a gag. It was Kit Lambert that urged me. In a sense, the thing with him was that he knew that there was no snobbery. Music is not the place for snobbery, ever. As po-faced and pretentious, as outrageous, as audacious, as complex as any music is, it's still supposed to entertain. It's still a part of show business, and it's still just music. It's still just the division of time; a piece of music, if it's three minutes, four minutes, or if it's four weeks long, it's still just time divided – it's nothing much more or less.

For some people, The Who are synonymous with hotel rooms being trashed on tour. People like those stories, but personally, after a while I'd find it distressing.
I suppose, yeah, it was sometimes. I don't want to be hypocritical, I don't want to pretend that I wasn't a part of it, I just felt it was something that we had to do in order to survive the road. It's very weird now: when we have a tour, I very much doubt I'll have a bad day. I'm travelling first class all over America; I'm going to stay in a fabulous hotel to rehearse in Florida. But go back to when this started, and it was just dire – getting on a plane which could catch fire in the air and half crash, half land, or on buses that would get caught in snowstorms in the middle of the night.

Not only that, The Who weren't even particularly long-haired, but you'd go into a hotel room and all the businessmen would turn around and kind of go, 'Hey, look at the poofs. Look at the queers.' That was America then in 1967. Finally, you'd think, 'Today, we're going to fight back.' What do you fight back at? You take it out on the television set.

The other thing was that Keith Moon, who led a lot of these adventures, was just so funny, and it made it bearable.

I remember once we were going to Atlanta airport; we were halfway there and our driver was going, 'We're not going to make it, we're not going to make it.' Keith said 'Oh my god! We've got to go back! We've got to go back!' 'But we're going to miss the plane, Keith!' 'No, no, no, we've got to go back.' We all thought that he must have left drugs in his room. So we drive back to the hotel, he runs up to his room and comes out holding the television set, throws it over the terrace, and it lands in front of the car. He gets back in the car and goes, 'I nearly forgot!' We missed our plane, and we practically missed the gig for the sake of a gag.

It is a contradiction: you're this very analytical, intellectual, sensitive songwriter, but you're also someone who enjoys sliding across the stage on your knees in front of 20,000 people.
Do you think that they do contradict each other? I think you can be a particular kind of person, you can be brash, funny, you can be shy, but if you're a human being, when you start to dance, take alcohol, flirt with somebody, start to jump up and down, kick a football around, your body chemistry changes. That's all that happened to me. That became part of my stage persona. Then that also gave me the confidence to have some of that grit off the stage. I wouldn't say that I was necessarily shy, but I wasn't particularly confident. I talk about myself as a manic-depressive: I had these big mood swings, and I couldn't understand why.

"Music is not the place for snobbery, ever. As pretentious, as outrageous, as audacious, as complex as any music is, it's still supposed to entertain."

I now look back, and I think it was just to do with the fact that my body chemistry is such that when it's at rest I'm quite depressed – I don't mean necessarily mentally or spiritually depressed, but I'm quite slow. I think that's what makes me addictive and compulsive by nature. I'm trying to get something from my body all the time that gets me up, that gets me free, that gets me released.

Your battles with alcoholism are no secret. At one point, I think you said you slept with a bottle of St-Rémy brandy. When did you first realize that that was becoming a serious problem?
When it became a serious problem in my life! I think alcohol becomes a problem for the problem drinker when it stops working. For me, brandy was a wonderful medicine, and then it just stopped working. I would

drink gallons of it and nothing would happen. It didn't make me feel better, it didn't relax me, it didn't lower my inhibitions, it didn't make me laugh, it didn't make me funny – it just did nothing. When that happened, I really panicked and realized that I had built up a tolerance.

The tragic early deaths of Keith Moon, in 1978, and John Entwistle, in 2002, didn't stop the band; the band kept going.
The *brand* kept going. The Who is a brand now. I think Roger Daltrey and I, we're a duo, an uneasy duo. I think he feels very differently about this to me. He still feels there's a band, and I think that's because it's his band. He started it, in a sense. He was the guy who first brought in John Entwistle, he then brought me in, then he brought in Keith.

Today when I talk about The Who as a brand, I'm talking about the fact that I wrote the songs; I'm not just a songwriter, I'm also a publisher. I carry this archive with me, and when I die it will just go into a folio, and it will be somebody else's business – but today it's mine. I feel that the music carries the iconic idea of The Who.

When Keith died, the band was pretty much in stasis, nothing very much was happening: we weren't playing very well, we weren't touring, because Keith was so ill all the time. When he died, instead of just moving on to something else, I went back to restart the band, and I don't know that I should have done that. When John died, it was at a time when we were only doing a tour in order to help John financially, and I felt, 'Well, he's gone now, so I don't have to do the tour.' Then I thought, 'This is not about me, it's not about John, it's not about our money, it's not about any of us – it's about the audience, it's about everybody that's put this together.' It was just easier to say yes. We carried on. From that, making that decision – because Roger didn't feel he could make it alone – I learned something about duty and I learned something about doing what's right, and not just what it is that I fancy doing at the time.

[In 2003 Townshend was arrested after entering his credit card details into a child-pornography website. He claimed he'd used the card as part of an investigation into the online porn industry. No illegal images were found on his computers and he was cleared. He accepted a caution as he didn't want to take the case to court, saying he lacked the strength to face the ordeal, believing that he himself had been abused as a child.]
My arrest in 2003 came so quickly after John's death, and I was in a real pink cloud. I was thinking, 'John's died: it's terrible, it's sad.' But I got his cut, in a sense; Roger and I got his cut of the tour, and we were planning to do this big campaign to help an organization called NAPAC, the National Association for People Abused in Childhood – in other words, not children that had been abused, but adults who were still having trouble with the fact that they were abused as children. I had the money to do that, and the next thing that happened is I get a knock on the door in January of 2003, and just thought, 'I know the way it's going to be seen

to be'. In the book [Townshend's 2012 autobiography *Who I Am*] I've written about that and I've explained, and I hope that anybody that has any doubts about me and about my intentions will read it, and then they can make up their minds. I don't think the book should draw a line – I hope it doesn't. I hope it starts a debate, because I think that not everybody's music, not everybody's journey, is like mine.

When did you first realize that your work in The Who would stand the test of time?

As a teenage boy, I could see how the function of the pop song was going to change, how our music had to do something else. We needed to draw a line under the past and move forward, we needed a new set of values. I realized that what we were looking at was a change in the function of the music. The Beatles, The Rolling Stones, The Who, The Kinks would change everything else as well: fashion, the way that we felt about art, movies, radio, everything. And it did; it changed everything.

And the final question: what's the last song we should play?

'Three Steps to Heaven' by Eddie Cochran. It's the first time that I ever heard real acoustic guitar. He recorded his guitar so beautifully; he had his own studio and he made his own records at home. It's another reason I love it: I've always had a home studio. It's my favourite song of all time.

The First Time Pete Townshend Playlist

1	Baba O'Riley	The Who
2	Rock Around the Clock	Bill Haley and His Comets
3	Man of Mystery	The Shadows
4	I Can't Explain	The Who
5	I Gotta Dance to Keep from Crying	Smokey Robinson and The Miracles
6	Young Man's Blues	Mose Allison
7	My Generation	The Who
8	Heatwave	Martha and the Vandellas
9	The Gordian Knot Untied: Chaconne	Henry Purcell
10	I'm Free	The Who
11	Save It for Later	Pete Townshend
12	Eminence Front	The Who
13	Real Good Looking Boy	The Who
14	Three Steps to Heaven	Eddie Cochran

"I think that it's a great thing for everyone to be a pop star, for a short period only ... it is dangerous if you start believing it."

Peter Gabriel

Peter Gabriel didn't remember the first time we met. My old band was working at his beautiful residential recording studio, Real World, near Bath, in 1995. He wandered into the kitchen while we were eating hangover breakfasts and happily chatted. He wasn't slightly bothered that the band had been behaving like total idiots in his musical sanctuary – ransacking the wine cellar, stealing his rowboat and inviting local kids over for parties. I also remember him saying he was off to Euro Disney that morning. 'Nice! When are you coming back?' we asked. 'This afternoon', he grinned, as with immaculate timing we hear the loud *whop, whop, whop* of a helicopter landing on the lawn outside the kitchen window. And out he went, hopping in the helicopter, off on his day trip to Paris. That was when I realized: Peter Gabriel is a pretty cool guy.

He's also funny. His image from Genesis and on through his hugely successful solo career and his current role as a humanitarian and pioneer of creative technology is of a meditative, slightly solemn and composed Serious Artist. But he is a very charming, very bright, very tall, very self-deprecating musician. He's obviously passionate about his work with the Elders – a group of statesmen, peace activists and human rights advocates – but he wears his achievements lightly. He's tall (it's quite a surprise, hence I'm mentioning it again), with a neat goatee beard, cropped silver hair and smiling eyes. He gives thoughtful answers in a soft, steady voice, happy to let his answers drift in odd directions – 'Sorry, senior moment', he chuckles.

After the interview I explained my Real World connection, and apologized for my band's behaviour and our guitarist spilling a can of Coke over his state-of-the-art mixing desk. 'Oh, that's fine', he smiles. 'It was much worse when The Libertines, and Shaun Ryder and Black Grape visited.' Like I say, Peter Gabriel is a pretty cool guy.

Matt Everitt: The first thing we always ask everybody is when were they first aware of music as a kid.

My mum's family were all musical, so Christmases were full of songs and different people playing piano, particularly. My mum still plays 'Buttons and Bows' [Dinah Shore, 1948] – that was probably the first melody. I grew up around music, and church music had a significant impact.

I loved some hymns – not all of them, but when they were good, they were fantastic. And I remember at school we used to scream our hearts out with the right hymns. I would come into the chapel with my bells hidden under my trousers. That was my musical-accompaniment skill.

When did you first find music that belonged to you?

I grew up in what then – I don't think now – was a quite repressive educational system, but at the public school there was a snooker room, and there was a record player there. That was such a release. I would put on Otis Redding and John Mayall blues records, and there were a few of us that would just zone out. And at that point, I started connecting. I love drums. As a small boy, I got very excited when we went to a hotel and there was a band playing. I would sit behind the drummer, in awe, thinking, 'You know, one day I will make more noise.' Because it was physical, you know? And you could hit things. And sometimes they sounded good.

What was your first gig? You saw Otis Redding live, didn't you?

Yeah. I don't think it was my first gig, but it was the first one that blew me away. I think, to this day, that is the best gig I have ever seen. I was seventeen, and I went with a girl I had a crush on to the Ram Jam Club in Brixton [in London, 1966], and I think there were maybe fewer than ten other white faces there. He came on and it was just one of those extraordinary moments when the sun comes out in this superlative performance. I remember reading a bit from [legendary concert promoter] Bill Graham, who has seen a lot of performers in his time, and he said, 'No one, but no one, compared to Otis.' And anyone who was lucky enough to see him do his thing? When the band were firing? It was unbeatable.

What was the first recording that Genesis put out?

First release was a track called 'The Silent Sun', and we hassled Jonathan King into production. And the excitement of seeing our name in print, in [British music newspaper] the *Record Mirror* – I think it had the lowest circulation, which is why Decca could afford the ads. It was only in an advert, but to just see it there blew us away.

When you released that track, did you feel like you were on the start of a long path, or was there a naivety still?

We were definitely naive, but there was a passion for songwriting. We had dreams at that time of just being songwriters, not bothering with all this silly performing stuff, with lots of artists recording our songs. Of course, not one artist was really interested! I think there was an

Italian female singer who recorded one song early on, but she was certainly the exception. So we realized, pretty soon, that the only way that we could get our songs recorded was to play them ourselves.

How do you feel about those early Genesis recordings? They have something which people find endlessly fascinating.
I have my favourites within that period, things like 'Supper's Ready' [1972] or 'The Lamb Lies Down on Broadway' [1974] – not all of it, but there were moments that really felt like they connected. They're clearly the work of young people, but there's still a passion and a charm sometimes, if you like that sort of thing. And I am well aware that a lot of people don't [laughs].

'Solsbury Hill' was your first solo single, the first single to be taken off your first solo album [*Peter Gabriel*, 1977]. It straightaway established you as a solo artist who could be both commercial and also still very experimental.
It is a weird time signature – some people trying to cover it afterwards have had trouble – but, at the same time, it felt quite natural. And it had a different sort of movement. You know, as an ex-failed drummer, it's still rhythm that hooks me into a lot of tracks. And that was the 'attractive' track from the first record that actually got me on the radio. And at that time, I was very conscious of avoiding the Genesis area of music with which I had been associated, because I didn't want to do 'Son of Genesis'.

When did you first find yourself drawn to what would become known as world music?
When I left the music business, left Genesis, I thought I was going to do something else entirely. I really didn't find anything better. I tried, gardening and making babies. Both planting seed, but, um . However, I started doing songs again with a poet friend called Martin Hall. And

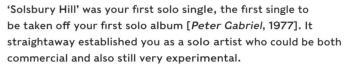

"You know, as an ex-failed drummer, it's still rhythm that hooks me into a lot of tracks."

again, we couldn't get them recorded, so I ended up having to sing them myself and sort of got sucked back into it. I was a little disillusioned with the business. In a way, the success that we sought was a prison. The more successful you got, the more you would know where you were going to be two years from now. Anyway, I was in the countryside and I had a shortwave radio. One of the things that I noticed, which you find in the lyric of 'Here Comes the Flood' [1977], is that as the night came down,

the radio waves would appear miraculously on shortwave, because you couldn't get very good signal in daylight, I don't know why. Probably someone will explain to me or tell me I am just deluding myself.

It is very romantic, though. I like that.

Well, it was something about the space and the emptiness of the darkness allowing things that don't happen in the busyness of daylight, and that's stuck with me. Anyway, I would explore these many, many stations. And there was one Dutch radio station that played some interesting stuff. It had been playing the soundtrack of a Stanley Baker African epic called *Dingaka* [1964]. The rhythms and the voices stuck out for me, and I thought, 'Oh, there's something I should explore here.' And that was a sort of moment, but then I found a few other people that were similarly getting interested in the sounds of other countries, and players and incredible singers from other countries. It was so hard to find: there were maybe two record stores in London that carried this sort of material; except for cultural events, festivals, it was virtually impossible to see a lot of these artists. So I proposed we start to try and get a festival together that would allow us to feature a lot of these extraordinary players, singers, writers, drummers – and that became WOMAD.

First one in '82?

Yes, '82. So I was hustling in '80, but it had taken a couple of years to mature. It started with The Drummers of Burundi, but we had a strange mix of people – Echo and the Bunnymen, Simple Minds, Jon Hassell, and the Sabri Brothers – who were qawwali singers. It was more a mix of world music and what later became known as indie. There were a lot of experiments. Part of the aim was to get all sorts of musicians from different backgrounds to try working together, which hadn't really happened before then. And then we had some of these fantastic musicians going into schools and working on building instruments and masks. We had a really good kids turn-out as well. So it felt a little different from the other festivals, sort of family orientated. Multicultural festivals are very trendy, very common now, but at that time they weren't.

When did you first become politicized? You worked with Amnesty International, the UK Labour Party, and songs like 'Biko' [1980] were hugely political. It is a difficult thing, for musicians. It's very easy to get wrong, bringing politics into art.

I think the Amnesty tours were life-changing experiences for all of the artists. There were two of those, one in America, which U2 had fronted, then the Human Rights Now! tour, which I hustled people for and managed to get Bruce Springsteen to front. We had Sting, Tracy Chapman, and we went around a lot of places. I think that invitation had come partly from doing Amnesty benefits before, and also from writing the 'Biko' song, so, in a way, that was a moment, when I was feeling my way into writing material about the real world. Tom Robinson, who I knew at

Peter Gabriel

the time, he was very good in encouraging me, because I thought, 'This isn't going to be taken seriously, coming from me'. And he said, 'If attention and money move in the right direction, who cares.'

It was good advice. That song changed all sorts of things for me, and led to the creation of Witness.org, which uses cameras for human rights. Now, probably about a third of my work time is related to these sorts of activities, although not directly to a political party. I think we are at a very interesting point, because in the mobile phone we have a device that is transforming our world faster than anything we have ever invented. It's going to turn health care, education, politics, money, all sorts of things absolutely on their head. Instead of the people being on the bottom of the heap, top down, it is going to be exactly the reverse of that.

I think there are extraordinary opportunities to connect. What I would love to see is a world in which there are brilliant mappings – everything is mapped, recorded, so you can navigate either issue by issue or by Google Earth, and see what's going on in the world. That's layer one. Layer two, storytelling: you can zoom in here; anyone can tell their experience, see news reports of an incident, see contextualization, stuff all around it, but allow for people always to have the right to express their own experiences in their own voices. And online campaigning: there are people like Change.org; they started with a few thousand, they've now got millions of people around the world who sign petitions.

"Although national governments are very necessary, I think they will become much like record labels in the music business: they will become less powerful."

These are the sort of numbers that politicians have to start looking at. Then, the hope would be, high-level groups might be able to call up presidents and do high-level interventions. In my ideal world, you would connect all of these elements together, and start to see local and global power, all connected. That is at the expense of national governments. Although national governments are very necessary, I think they will become much like record labels in the music business: they will become less powerful, and less the centre and the arbiters of what happens.

If you look at the setup of the United Nations, the Security Council, so many things that should happen are blocked by one or two countries – Russia and China quite often. And though they reach this impasse, I think there are ways now that we could lubricate things to happen independent of some of that structure. Sorry – it is a long-winded answer, but it is my current passion.

In '86, the album *So* made you a phenomenally huge star. When you started making it, were your first intentions to make something that would connect so immediately with people?

I think everyone thinks, 'Oh, you must have known that "Sledgehammer" was a hit'. We recorded the album, and Tony [Levin – bassist] reminded me of this, he said they were actually ready to go home, the taxi was booked, and I said, 'Well, there is this one other thing that I've got, which maybe we could try and see if we can get something happening.' And that was 'Sledgehammer'. So it was very much an afterthought. But we knew then that there was a hell of a groove. The only thing that I was conscious of at the time was a sort of concession to a more commercial approach. Gail [Colson], who was my manager at that time, persuaded me: 'You're always hiding behind your album sleeves. Why not get a nice photo on the front.' And we did that. And, you know, we actually had women in the audience [laughs]. Which is a wonderful thing.

Then, all of a sudden, recognition is going to go through the roof and you're going to lose a certain part of your privacy.

Yeah, but then you soon get old, bald and fat, and you don't look anything like the picture! It was my pop star moment, which I thoroughly enjoyed. I think that it's a great thing for everyone to be a pop star, for a short period only. Because it is dangerous if you start believing it, or living there.

Kate Bush is someone who you have worked with many times, way back to 'Games Without Frontiers' [1980]. You worked with her again on *So*. When did you first meet her?

I remember hearing 'Wuthering Heights' and thinking, 'That is very interesting'. Then when I came to do 'Don't Give Up' … In fact, because it was set in America, and related to depression, Dolly Parton had been the first thought. In a strange way I think it would have worked. She

"I said, 'Well, there is this one other thing that I've got, which maybe we could try …'. And that was 'Sledgehammer'."

wasn't interested at the time, but she ended up asking me to do it on her TV show, but it was when I was touring and I couldn't do it. I am a big Dolly fan, but it would have been a very different thing. When I was moving back towards our fairer shores, I was thinking it needed a voice that was nourishing and maybe had some frailties to it, and Kate was an obvious choice. I didn't know if she would be interested in doing it. She came down and was very nervous at first, and then absolutely nailed it. And, you know, that song, particularly, has had extraordinary stories of stopping all sorts of people – including quite a few well-known people – from killing themselves. And I think it is very much down to this reassurance and feeling of love that you get from Kate's voice.

Is there the desire to release more records?

Yeah, absolutely. The trouble is, because I have kids again, I want a proper family life. Being a workaholic musician, as many are – I am trying not to do that. And I now do some technology stuff, and this benefit stuff, and music? There's a little less time for it. But I will carry on writing songs until I drop. That has always been a passion, and there is a lot more for me to learn. And I would love to see, in the same way you have these talent shows for singers, I would love to see songwriting featured on one of these big TV shows, because I think there could be an audience if it was done right. It would shift the focus a little bit, because I think that the artists that often have long life are those that write interesting stuff.

What is the last song that we should play?

Right, well, I could finish where I began with Otis [Redding] and 'Change Gonna Come'. Even though it's Sam Cooke's song, Otis takes it to a different level for me. And it's thoroughly miserable and thoroughly hopeful, which, maybe, works for me too.

The First Time Peter Gabriel Playlist

1	Sledgehammer	Peter Gabriel
2	Buttons and Bows	Dinah Shore
3	Have You Heard	John Mayall and The Blues Breakers
4	The Silent Sun	Genesis
5	The Carpet Crawlers	Genesis
6	Solsbury Hill	Peter Gabriel
7	Extract	The Drummers of Burundi
8	Biko	Peter Gabriel
9	Heroes	David Bowie
10	Mirrorball	Elbow
11	Don't Give Up	Peter Gabriel and Kate Bush
12	Flume	Bon Iver
13	Listening Wind	Talking Heads
14	Change Gonna Come	Otis Redding

"We'd look at one another and say, 'That's pretty damn good ... you people are wrong, and we're right.'"

ROBBIE ROBERTSON

S ometimes an interview is scheduled so quickly that you don't get time to worry about the importance of the person you're speaking to. This is what happened to me with Robbie Robertson in 2011: hurried emails, hastily booked studios and me scanning the press release for his new solo album, *How to Become a Clairvoyant*. This was a man whose band became a legend virtually on the release of their debut album *Music From Big Pink* in 1968; a band who represented an authenticity and craftsmanship that stunned the pomp of '70s rock; a band who played as tightly and fought as ferociously as brothers. That band was The Band.

Robbie and I are crammed into the last vacant studio in the building. There's no room for his management or PR team, so we're sat elbow to elbow and face to face. He's dressed all in black, with deep black hair that tousles around a high forehead. He's got a gentle face, and he's wearing black-rimmed glasses with a slight purple hue. He looks a little like David Lynch's beatnik baby brother.

But it's his voice that I remember the most. His speaking voice is smooth and gentle, rising and falling like he's singing a melody half cosmic guru and half Snagglepuss. He's easy to chat to, funny, enthusiastic and more than happy to tell stories. He's fiercely proud of what The Band achieved and the musical ethos they applied to their work. There are no dewy-eyed reminiscences through lilac-tinted spectacles, just an honest statement of fact: yes, we were *that* good.

After the interview, I do the research I should have done beforehand; I rewatch The Band's 1978 concert film, *The Last Waltz*. Legendary guests line up to sing alongside the group: Bob Dylan, Van Morrison, Eric Clapton, Neil Young, Joni Mitchell, Neil Diamond. And there's Robbie, the man I've just spoken to, in his early thirties back then, grinning in the middle of the storm, deep in the moment with his brothers, playing one of the greatest gigs of all time. A member of The Band.

Matt Everitt: When were you first aware of music?

I was first really connected to music on the Six Nations Indian reservation, where my mother was born and raised. I grew up between Toronto, Canada and the Six Nations reserve. On the reservation, it seemed that everybody played an instrument. And so, probably eight, nine years old, I was looking into all these different instruments, and the one that looked the sexiest to me was the guitar.

What was the first record that you owned?

I think it was 'Rip It Up' by Little Richard. The sound of that record just killed me back then. 'Rip It Up' on one side and 'Ready Teddy' on the other. My first real addiction to music came from when I heard Carl Perkins sing 'Blue Suede Shoes', and I thought, 'He plays an electric guitar, and he writes the song, plays the guitar solos, sings them: that's my kind of guy.' I thought you could be more ambitious on the guitar than just strumming. Elvis broke open the door, but that was already becoming a little bit obvious to me. I've always had this issue: if the crowd's running that way, I want to look in a different direction.

What was your very first band, The Hawks, like?

My first band was … not that good! I was probably thirteen, and it was my own band. All the guys were older than me, and it was a good experience of learning that it was not only your responsibility to sing the song and play the song but to figure out what other people should be doing, too. It taught me that if nobody does that, you don't improve, you don't go anywhere, and you can't depend on other people to figure that out for you.

"I've always had this issue: if the crowd's running that way, I want to look in a different direction."

Would The Hawks be your first professional band?

I had another band called Robbie and the Robots. I was in another band called Thumper and the Trombones. Then I was in a semi-professional group called Little Caesar and the Consuls, and then I caught the attention of Ronnie Hawkins and the Hawks. By then I was fifteen.

When you started playing with the guys that would go on to become The Band, was there quite an immediate sense of 'We have something special here'?

I felt very strongly about what Ronnie Hawkins and the Hawks were when I first experienced their music. I thought that they played faster and more violently than anybody else, and it was really exciting to me as a young boy at that time. And then I wrote a couple of songs that Ronnie

Hawkins recorded when I was fifteen, and that's what really kind of pulled me into it. They were all from Arkansas, but they were playing a lot up in Canada because they made more money there. One of the guys wanted to go home and be with his family, and so I was the first Canadian in the group. Between Ronnie Hawkins and Levon [Helm – drummer] and myself, we started hand-picking the other guys that ultimately became The Hawks, which became The Band. And when all of these guys were in the group, we felt like we did have something.

When did you first meet Bob Dylan? Actually, what were your first impressions of him?

When I first met him, I wasn't sure what I thought, because we were a group looking to do our own thing. So this was a bit of a detour, it seemed. But we had a reputation of being a really good band, and he was trying to find a really good band. I was trying to figure out whether he knew what that was – meaning he was a folk singer; used to playing with just himself on the guitar and the harmonica – and when you have to figure out everybody's playing together, whether he knew anything about that. And he didn't! So this was a struggle in the beginning. It didn't happen immediately. For a while, it was up in the air whether this was a calling for us or not. And in the very beginning, everybody was telling him, 'You've got to get rid of these guys. They're ruining your career.'

There's the myth around what happened: the screaming, the shouting, and going electric. Did you really feel persecuted?

Yeah. Well, when you play all over North America, all over Australia, all over Europe, and every night, people boo you and in some cases throw stuff at you? It eventually sinks in that they don't like us, you know? But we were on a mission, and in the beginning we were all like, 'We don't know if we like this music. We don't know if this is where we should be.' But then it was fascinating, it started to strike me a different way, like, 'There's something going on here. There's a musical revolution taking place. I think that we've got to see this through.' The more that I knew about Bob's music and him as a person, the more we became really good friends; it was like we were war buddies going through this together.

Certain things bring you closer together, and this was one of those things. But we came through it alive, and by the time we got to England when we were doing this, we were doing it good. We'd listened to those tapes, and we'd look at one another and say, 'That's pretty damn good. I'm sorry, you people are wrong, and we're right.' That was a very bold statement at the time. And it turned out that the world came around.

What about recording that first Band album, *Music from Big Pink* [1968]? Was it an easy record to make?

It was an easy record to make because we had done our homework, and we had figured out what we wanted to do musically. And it had nothing to do with what we had done with Bob Dylan and the live concerts, nothing to do with what we did as The Hawks, and nothing to do with when we played with Ronnie Hawkins. This was a complete change of mood, and what it really turned out to be was a culmination of all the musicalities from our journeys on the road that we had gathered. We were gathering gospel music, and blues, and mountain music, and R&B and rock and roll, and that record was like putting it all in a big pot and mixing it up and making a new gumbo of music. And when that record came out, people said, 'What is this? Where did that come from?' You know? And I was, 'What are you talking about? This is what you do when you're really serious about making a musical statement.'

We'd already been together for seven years when we made that record. We'd been woodshedding and honing our skills, and that was our idea of what this *was*. This wasn't about getting some cute guys together and getting some guitars for Christmas and starting a band, you know? This was serious with us. So when we made that record, people would comment on it and look at it like there was something extremely mature and timeless about it. And that was because we weren't born yesterday. We really, really went into this trying to do something so emotional and paying respect to all these musicalities that we had gathered.

"Over a period of time it starts drifting, and it starts coming undone from what it originally was. And you can't go back."

It seemed like quite a tumultuous band to be in: lots of strong personalities, lots of very talented people. Did it become difficult to keep up that level of creativity?

You know, it didn't feel that way until real success set in. And also, at a certain point, we were growing up. We were really young – we were acting like we were grown-ups, but we were really kids. When we were playing with Bob Dylan, I think I was twenty-one, and when we made that album, I think I was twenty-three. But we had a lot of depth in our musical understanding, because we were reaching for that constantly.

Do you think success was bad for you?

There was success, and then when you grow up, somebody would get married, so you're not in the same huddle as you were together. And then someone else got married, and then somebody's having kids, and then over a period of time it starts drifting, and it starts coming undone from what it originally was. And you can't go back. You have to accept life as it comes at you and in the different directions that you grow. And you do grow in different directions, you know – that's just the way it is.

The Band wasn't 'the guitar player' and 'the singer' and some other guys. This was a group. That's why it was called 'The Band', because it really was that. Everybody had a very particular part in this movie; everybody held up their end to such a degree that if one of those cylinders wasn't working as strong as the others, everything was out of kilter. And that delicacy would really weigh on you. As time went on and people became more reckless in their lives, and whether it was from alcohol or drugs or lifestyle, those things really played into it. Because it was a delicate balance, it would never feel like what we were trying to reach for.

One of the relationships that's been a constant in your life has been with Martin Scorsese. What was your first meeting like?

I first met him after he did *Mean Streets* [1973]. I recognized something in that movie. I felt very strongly about his storytelling and about his use of music. The next time I met him, he was in the middle of making *New York, New York* [1977]. We set up a meeting to talk about this idea of a concert film. He was squirming and nervous and uncomfortable. He was in the middle of shooting a movie, and when you're in the middle of shooting a movie, you're not allowed to go and shoot another movie!

So he was saying, 'I don't know. This is all of the stuff that I love. I've got to do this. I've got to figure this out.' Then we set about figuring out how we could do this, and that's how we landed on doing it on Thanksgiving Day [November 25, 1976] in San Francisco, which was where The Band did their first concert as The Band. They would be taking off the Thanksgiving weekend, right? So he could say [to his producers], 'I guess I'll just go out to the country and rest up for the weekend', and he actually went off and did this. And when the producers of the movie he was doing heard about this, they were outraged, but it was too late. The concert was done. So it all worked out and really felt meant to be.

Can you remember watching *The Last Waltz* for the time?

I'd seen it hundreds of times in bits and pieces, but I can remember the first time that we saw it with a real audience. It was the first time that a music film like this had ever been shot in 35 mm. It was breathtaking. And I thought, 'It's amazing that nobody's done this before'. The reason they hadn't done it before is because the Panavision cameras that they were using can't run for hours like that: you shoot a scene, you reload, you put a new battery on, you do all of the stuff you need to do. And the director of photography, Michael Chapman, said, 'These cameras are going to melt! They're not meant to run like this, and I do not guarantee that we're going to make it!' because that concert went on for, like, five hours. But we got through it, and it was like the stars were aligned.

What was the first movie score that you composed?

Well, it wasn't about composing for me. It was about understanding the effect that music had on film and film had on music. I appreciated it, and there were movies that had scores to them that I thought were amazing

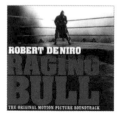

– like the score that Alex North did for 'A Streetcar Named Desire' [1951] – but I don't score movies in a traditional way. I don't read or write music to begin with. That's a drawback ...

So then the next thing is Martin Scorsese asks me to help out with the music on *Raging Bull* [1980]. And so I worked on that music; I suggested some songs that would be used within the story in the background, because there was no score for that movie. We were using this [Italian composer Pietro] Mascagni music, but just in the streets where Marty grew up in Little Italy – there's music seeping out of windows, there's music in the street. They would go to these clubs – Webster Hall and the Copacabana back then – and I did the music that was being played in those places. The experience of working on *Raging Bull* was so powerful that I ended up really becoming drawn to this, but not in a traditional way. I'm interested in breaking the rules and doing things in a completely different way, and that's why every time that I work with Martin Scorsese, it is a different challenge, it's a different movie.

Your first solo album [1987] gave you a massive hit with 'Somewhere Down the Crazy River'. What took you so long?
I wasn't thinking about doing that. I didn't know whether I ever wanted to make a record again. I was exploring other things, and so before doing that, I worked on *Raging Bull*, *The King of Comedy* [1982], and I did score *The Color of Money* [1986], which bled over into me doing that first solo album. There were a lot of other film projects, a lot of acting things, and I came to the conclusion that I wasn't passionate about that. I got a little bit spread thin, and I thought, 'Oh my god, this is just exhausting'.

And there was a period of time in there, too, where I wanted to not be the parent that was always away, you know? I wanted to stick around the house and just hang out with my wife and kids. Then somewhere around 1985 I finished working on those films, and I thought, 'Okay, now I want to start writing songs.'

When did you first meet Eric Clapton? You've been friends for a long time.
We first met after *Music from Big Pink* came out, at a mutual friend's place in Los Angeles. I didn't know it, but he was a huge supporter of *Music from Big Pink*: he said it changed his life, he was going leave Cream, all of this stuff. And I was like, 'Whoa, hang on there a minute', you know? 'Don't throw the baby out with the bathwater.' But he said, 'No, I'm just completely intrigued with the subtleties and the emotion in this music.' I had been wailing on the guitar with Ronnie Hawkins, with The Hawks, with Bob Dylan, and when I first started doing that, it was unique, I was unusual. Guitar players would come from all around just to check out what this guy was doing, and then by the time we were recording *Music*, everybody was catching up with that – Eric Clapton and Jimi Hendrix and all these other guys. So I thought, 'Okay then, the jig's up. It's time to go in a different direction.' And that different

direction for me was being influenced by people like Curtis Mayfield, his guitar playing.

It was the opposite of how loud and busy you could be. The subtleties to it broke your heart, you know? It gave you chills. And I thought, 'That's what I'm admiring.' Steve Cropper, the way he was playing on those Otis Redding records – very little stuff, but it meant so much. Miles Davis, too: other guys would've been playing 30 notes in five seconds, and he was playing one note. And that one note just went right through you. So I just went wholeheartedly in that direction and said, 'This is about playing the song. This is not about jamming.' It had a big effect on Eric, and we've been friends ever since.

We've heard all the firsts; the last thing to do is ask you to choose the final song we'll play. You mentioned Curtis Mayfield, 'People Get Ready', before we started the interview.
Curtis Mayfield came with such extraordinary gifts. There's a song on my record [*How to Become Clairvoyant*] called 'When the Night Was Young' that is inspired by Curtis Mayfield – the chord changes, the way I'm playing on it. The depth in those kinds of things just completely goes back to an origin, and the origin for all of that – because that was the sound in the air at that time – was the sound of Curtis Mayfield and the Impressions singing 'People Get Ready.'

The First time Robbie Robertson Playlist

1	The Weight	The Band
2	Rip It Up	Little Richard
3	Blue Suede Shoes	Carl Perkins
4	Diddley Daddy	Ronnie Hawkins
5	Long Distance Operator	Bob Dylan and The Band
6	Like a Rolling Stone (from *Live 1966*)	Bob Dylan
7	A Streetcar Named Desire (score for the film, 1951)	Alex North
8	Whispering Grass (Don't Tell the Trees)	The Ink Spots
9	Tears of Rage	Bob Dylan and The Band
10	Bell Bottom Blues	Derek and the Dominos
11	Somewhere Down the Crazy River	Robbie Robertson
12	On the Nature of Daylight	Max Richter
13	Axman	Robbie Robertson
14	People Get Ready	The Impressions

"Like most of the Faces stuff, and a lot of my solo career stuff, it was worked out in a pub."

ROD STEWART

There's an idea that the further you get in life, the more you become a caricature of yourself: we simplify the more subtle nuances of our personality for public purposes. It's easier to get on with life when you're not parading 70 years of experiences before all and sundry, but in Rod Stewart's case, it's easy to let the caricature totally obscure the real person.

The clichés are almost endless: the blondes, the skin tight leopard-print trousers, the nose, the hair (more of which later), footballs being hoofed into crowds, 'Sailing' and a booze-soaked bonhomie. But Sir Roderick David 'Rod' Stewart, CBE, has one of the greatest, most expressive voices in music, with apparently effortless skill in interpreting other people's material. Stewart himself never felt the need to impress upon people his incredible credentials, so people often shortcut to the celebrity, not the singer.

He's immediately pally and laugh-out-loud funny – complimentary one moment and piss-taking the next. He'll happily chat about his past, but with a triviality that maybe doesn't do him justice. The Faces weren't simply a shambolic bunch of lucky mates who wandered out of the pub and into the studio, they were instinctive musicians who combined folk, rock, blues and country with real finesse, but Rod seems happy to let the boozy myth take centre stage.

He looks staggeringly good for a man in his seventies, sharp in a modish tweed jacket, white shirt and club tie. He's tanned, with mischievous eyes and that famous hair, massive peaks and spikes of blond and platinum tints, part '70s rock star and part '80s St Tropez bouffant, like a lion's mane with highlights.

He lights up when he talks about the music he loves, but spends little time on self-analysis or framing his artistic legacy. But even with such an important back catalogue, maybe the nobler (and cooler) thing to do is just let people have the image they like, and get on with being Rod Stewart. And it has to be said, he wears it well.

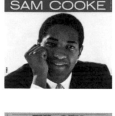

Matt Everitt: When were you first aware of music?

My family were big Al Jolson fans, they used to play Al Jolson music – this will make me sound really old – on one of those things you wind up with a trumpet! I must've only been two. And then they took me, when I was about six or seven, to see *Jolson Sings Again* [1949]. So, Al Jolson!

Was it an instant feeling of 'That is exciting, I want to do that'?

Not necessarily. That was in my subconscious. And I still appreciate Al Jolson for what he did as a singer: I mean, he would get up and sing before 3,000 people without a microphone, which is quite incredible.

What about the first record you owned that was yours?

The first one I actually bought was *Chuck Berry on Stage*, live at Tivoli Theater. There's something about vinyl. It's precious, isn't it? It's like an extension of your body, almost. So that was the first album I bought.

What was your first live music experience, seeing a rock and roll band live for the first time?

I was probably about eleven or twelve, and my big brother, Don, took me to see Bill Haley and His Comets. I remember being up in the balcony and it was literally bouncing up and down. He only played for 20 minutes. He played 'Rock Around the Clock', 'Rip It Up', 'Shake, Rattle and Roll', and 'See You Later, Alligator'. Everybody was going mad. It was the first time I'd ever seen Teddy Boys, you know?

You saw Otis Redding live as well, didn't you? Was he the first soul singer that you fell in love with?

I think that was probably Sam Cooke. When I first got my job, we used to have these little transistor radios, and I heard 'Cupid, draw back your bow …'. And that just influenced me straight away. But my first live soul music was Otis. He had some presence on the stage because he was a big man. Booker T. [Jones] was on the stage, Martha and the Vandellas, Sam and Dave – they all came on and did 20 minutes.

Was that when you started to think, 'That's what I want to do'?

No, because I had already been bought a guitar, years before that. My dad bought it. I'd been going down to Brighton Beach; I was a beatnik. I'd started playing guitar and people listened, so I thought, 'Well, I must have something'. I didn't pursue it any further for quite a while, though.

Tell me about the blues scene in London in the early '60s. It seemed such a vibrant mix of people, like Long John Baldry, who you sung with. Can you remember first meeting that crowd?

Yeah, because we have to pay homage to [British blues harmonica player] Cyril Davies, [British jazz and blues trombonist] Chris Barber and [British blues musician] Alexis Korner, because if it wasn't for those guys, we may never have discovered Muddy Waters, Howlin' Wolf, Jimmy

Reed and all those because – they brought the Chicago blues to England, really. It was electrifying. The Marquee Club and the Ken Colyer Jazz Club [in London] – it really was a small amount of people. And it was just in London, Manchester and Stoke, where all the good clubs were.

Did it feel like you were part of a burgeoning British movement?
Very much so, and I'll tell you a story. When I was with [blues singer] Long John Baldry's band, I saw he had an album cover, Muddy Waters' live album, *At Newport 1960*, and I asked him if I could borrow it. He said, 'No. Mick and Keith have got it at the moment' [laughs]. And he said, 'I only kept the cover to make sure that they brought it back.' Then he said, 'When it does come back, I think The Yardbirds want it.' So I said, 'Well, after The Yardbirds, can I have it?' That's how tight-knit it was.

Can you remember performing with Jeff Beck for the first time? [Stewart joined The Jeff Beck Group alongside Ronnie Wood in 1967.] Did you see him play and just think, 'He's a bit good'.
Well, Ronnie and I were both out of work. I'd been fired from the Hoochie Coochie Men, Long John's band. Jeff said, 'Do you want to join my band?' And we said, 'Yeah, well, that'll work.' It was casual in those days – no contracts. I cannot remember the first show, though. Can't remember the first gig. I remember the first gig we did in New York, at the Fillmore East, when we were on the bill with the Grateful Dead. And this is – I don't know if you know about this, but it's this time where I was so nervous, I didn't come out. I sang behind the amps, and I didn't come out. And we absolutely wiped the floor with the Grateful Dead. They couldn't follow us on. I remember that show! Brilliant, that was.

"I was so nervous, I didn't come out. I sang behind the amps. And we wiped the floor with the Grateful Dead."

Your first solo album, 1969, *An Old Raincoat Won't Ever Let You Down*, was quite a folky record. You've got 'Dirty Old Town' on there. Have you always loved folk music?
I fell in love with folk music because my dad had already bought me a guitar and I didn't know what to do with it. It was a little pre–rock and roll, it was the skiffle era. So then I discovered Lonnie Donegan, and then through him I discovered some of the great folk artists. And with the help of Bob Dylan's first album – he sung about Woody Guthrie – I get Woody Guthrie albums, and I get Ramblin' Jack [Elliott] albums. And then I fell into place. I had a guitar, and these are the songs I'm going to sing: 'Cocaine Blues', 'San Francisco Bay Blues'. So I was in love with folk music before I was in love with soul music.

Every Picture Tells a Story, '71: that was your first number one album. Was that record as much fun to make as it sounds?

Oh yeah, yeah, it certainly was. You know, 'casual' isn't a strong enough word to use when you have a drummer like Micky Waller – bless him, he's no longer with us – turn up to play on 'Maggie May' without a full drum kit. He said, 'I couldn't get my drum kit in my car, because I had to bring the dog.' When we did 'Maggie May', there were no cymbals on it at all. We dubbed the cymbals on afterwards. You know, we didn't have any high expectations. Once you become successful, you start thinking, 'Oh, Jesus, got to top that one; got to do something even better.' But then it was just, 'Throw it together!' and it worked.

I've got to ask you about the Faces. Can you remember their first gigs? Again, are we talking about a band that has that chemistry and enjoys each other's company musically?

Yeah, it was – it really was. It was a love affair between all of us, and I hope they agree or else I'm going to look really silly. I do remember the first show. We played for American airmen: it was one of those massive airplane hangars, and the audience just sat round the outside not know-ing what to do, no one came on the dance floor. After we'd played an hour, we just all packed up. I think this may have been when the drinking started, you know? If we're going to have to do this every night, we better get drunk. But we enjoyed each other's company, so it didn't seem such a hardship that the Americans weren't responding. They certainly did a little bit down the line, a couple of years later when we broke in America.

"You know, we didn't have any high expectations ... it was just, 'Throw it together!' and it worked."

If we're talking about the Faces, we have to talk about 'Stay with Me', one of those songs that's woven into the fabric of rock and roll. What do you think people love so much about it?

I don't know. It's an honest piece of rock and roll. But when, a couple of years ago, I played the Hard Rock Café in London, I played 'Stay with Me'. I haven't got Woody in my regular band, but once he walked on and started playing? No one can play like him. It's just spot on, you know? I do hope we have a Faces reunion pretty soon. I'm all up for it.

Those performances sound so full of life – not over-rehearsed, not overplayed. 'Stay with Me' has got that feel to it. It wasn't a first take, but it wasn't something you'd recorded loads was it?

No, it was worked out like most of the Faces stuff, and a lot of my solo career stuff, it was worked out in a pub. We'd go in there, and go, 'What about this riff? Yeah, that's good. Let's go back in the studio: you play and I'll sing it.' That's how a lot of the stuff was born – in the pub.

In your autobiography, you mention Freddie Mercury a lot. You speak about him really, really fondly. What was he like?
He was a gentleman, and I've got so many stories. The one that I love is about when me, Elton John and Freddie were together and we were going to form a band called Nose, Teeth and Hair [laughs]. And we were quite serious, I think. Freddie was a dear, dear man. I didn't know him extremely well. I wouldn't call him one of my closest friends ever, but he was a good, good acquaintance.

"Me, Elton John and Freddie were together and we were going to form a band called Nose, Teeth and Hair."

I'm just trying to imagine what a night out with you, Freddie Mercury and Elton John would be like.
Oh, my god. Only the strong survive.

In 1975, *Atlantic Crossing*, the album, made you a really big international star. I mean, you were big before, but this was a different level of fame. How do you think you coped with that? Because there's no rehearsals, no practice you can have for being at the centre of that much attention.
No. I had sort of got used to it a little bit with *Every Picture Tells a Story*, but in the interim, I'd fallen in love with a very famous Hollywood film star, a Swedish actress called Britt Ekland, so that really did put us both in the spotlight. I think that's what changed, and I think that's what really annoyed a lot of music critics. Two things: a) I was going to live in America, because the taxes were so ridiculous in this country; and b) I was going out with a Hollywood film star, so the critics hated it. It was all, 'Rod's gone to Hollywood, he's gone all Hollywood', you know? So it wasn't the greatest period in my life. On reflection.

I mean, in my heyday, let's say, the paparazzi weren't as intrusive. There were no camera phones, the internet didn't exist, so you had a certain amount of freedom. Thank goodness, because the things I used to get up to … Good Lord have mercy! [Laughs.]

I was going to ask you about that. You've been quite frank about your indulgences, but a lot of musicians lost their way in the '80s. There was a lot of drugs, a lot of booze: a lot of people went into rehab. You emerged pretty unscathed, didn't you?
Yeah, yeah, thank goodness. I've never really been a druggie. I've never

bought any drugs. I say that in the book quite frankly. It was always a social thing with me. It never interfered with my marriages or my friendships, or my music, or my children. You know, I've always played football, so, Saturday night? If there's a game on Sunday morning, you won't catch me out! I always think football's been somewhat of a saviour for me.

So, genuinely, it helped you where others fell by the wayside.
Yeah.

Football was your saviour!
Yeah, I'm still playing at the age of 68, in an over-fifties league [laughs]. That is an addiction, football, I tell you.

Something I'm always interested in with big stars who have these big hits like yourself: when you've got a song like 'Sailing', what's your relationship like with that track?
I like to give the audience what they want, and quite honestly, I don't get tired of singing any songs. There was a period in the early '80s where I was getting tired of 'Da Ya Think I'm Sexy?', but it's like a national anthem. Around the world, people just love it, and they sing it, and I do it. And if they love it, I love it. You know, we're there to entertain. That's all we're there for, you know. And I want to entertain; I want to give the audience what they paid for.

"You know, we're there to entertain. That's all we're there for. And I want to entertain; I want to give the audience what they paid for."

We talked about _Atlantic Crossing_, and you mentioned Booker T. and the MGs: you worked with them on that album didn't you?
I believe I may have been the last person to ever sing with the Booker Ts, because we lost [drummer] Al Jackson shortly after. [Bassist] Donald 'Duck' Dunn is gone. So there's just Steve Cropper and Booker T. left. But that was a great honour, a really great honour, to work with them.

Yeah, I'm trying to think of the track we did together. It was a Bee Gees song; it goes like this [sings], 'You don't know what it's like to love somebody, to love somebody …' ['To Love Somebody']. We did that song. I don't know what happened to it. That was Rod Stewart and Booker T. and the MGs. Now it should be the other way around: Booker T. and the MGs with Rod Stewart!

'Downtown Train' didn't so much re-establish you, because it's not like you were on your arse sales-wise, but it opened you up to a whole new audience. Had you always loved Tom Waits, or did that one song speak to you in some way?

I was aware of Tom, I think, in 1989 or '88, but that may have even brought my rock and roll audience back a wee bit. But I've loved the guy's work ever since. I've got a track on this album [*Vagabond Heart*, 1991], and he apparently said, 'I'm so glad Rod has done one of my tracks again, I can put a new roof on the house!' I think he said 'Downtown Train' paid for a swimming pool at his house [laughs].

What's the best thing about being Rod Stewart?

Oh, so many things. I enjoy my fame, I really do – you will never find me complaining – but the best thing about being Rod Stewart? I have a seat for life at Celtic Park, and so do my two sons.

Finally, we ask all our guests on this show to pick the last song.

I think I should finish with a song from the new album [*Time*, 2013]. This is a song I wrote about my kids, and it's called 'Pure Love'.

The First Time Rod Stewart Playlist

1	Every Picture Tells a Story	Rod Stewart
2	I'm Sitting On Top of the World	Al Jolson
3	Memphis, Tennessee	Chuck Berry
4	See You Later, Alligator	Bill Haley and His Comets
5	Cupid	Sam Cooke
6	Try a Little Tenderness	Otis Redding
7	Country Line	Cyril Davies
8	Up Above My Head	Long John Baldry and The Hoochie Coochie Men
9	I Feel So Good (live, from *At Newport* 1960)	Muddy Waters
10	Let Me Love You	Jeff Beck
11	Man of Constant Sorrow	Rod Stewart
12	Cocaine Blues	Ramblin' Jack Elliot
13	Maggie May	Rod Stewart
14	Stay with Me	Faces
15	To Love Somebody	Rod Stewart and Booker T. and The MGs
16	Downtown Train	Tom Waits
17	Pure Love	Rod Stewart

"The whole way I've been brought up to sing all of my life is that it's really about emotions."

Sinéad O'Connor

As I'm writing this I'm watching a video of Sinéad O'Connor from August 2017. She's sat alone in a motel room in New Jersey, crying, and she looks exhausted. She's talking about her fight with depression, her loneliness, how much she misses her children, and her suicidal thoughts. O'Connor filmed the 12-minute video herself and posted it on Facebook. It's heartbreaking to see any human so obviously deeply unhappy. The footage provoked a huge outpouring of concern and love for Sinéad from her fans and people who share her battles with mental health.

In it she says, 'I hope that this video is somehow helpful. I know that I am only one of millions and millions and millions of people who are just like me, actually, that don't necessarily have the resources I have in my heart and my purse. Mental illness is a bit like drugs: it doesn't give a shit who you are. Equally, what is worse is that the stigma doesn't give a shit who you are.'

I'm struck by the bravery it took to open up to the world and share her desperation like that. Anyone talking openly about their experiences with depression is helping to break down that stigma around mental health, but doing so when you're that famous? And knowing the media attention that could (and did) follow? I felt as much admiration as I felt sympathy for what she was going through.

I interviewed her in 2012, and she remains one of my favourite guests ever. She swore spectacularly and spoke eloquently. She was passionate, hilarious, honest and interesting, and she didn't stop bloody talking for about two hours. I thought she was great. I still do. I hope she's okay.

Matt Everitt: When were you first aware of music as a child?

One of my very earliest memories as a baby is John Lennon, but I didn't discover it was John Lennon until I was older and saw him on telly. A tiny baby experiences the world mostly through their ears, you know? They can't see much. My mother was very much into music, and I remember hearing this voice before I became conscious of anything else in the world. It wasn't until I got to six, seven, eight, nine that I began to put a body to the voice and see that it was an actual person. Before that I thought it was this disembodied being that used to sing around my ears [laughs]. She was particularly into *Shaved Fish* [a 1975 compilation album by Lennon and the Plastic Ono Band].

Would you call it a musical upbringing?

Yeah, very. My mother and father were extremely musical in different ways, but they did come together when they both sang – light operas and all those terribly awful things that people should be shot for. You know, those awful bloody *H.M.S. Pinafore* things? They had all of those albums. My father is strictly classical, whereas my mother had a very broad range of taste – anything from Johnny Cash to John Lennon right the way through to *Porgy and Bess*. She was mad into musicals.

But I also had an aunt, my mother's sister: at the time when I would've been eight, nine-ish, she was sixteen. She had Down's syndrome, but she was no different to any sixteen-year-old in that she was addicted to music, and she had managed to get her father's record player off him. She'd just lay on the bed like every other sixteen-year-old with her record player, and she used to call me up. She did this thing with me, which to this day I always do with my children: she would make me read every single word inside and outside on the record sleeve.

And she would make me touch the sleeves and touch the photos; partly because she was Down's syndrome, she had this thing about the sensuality and the touching of stuff, but I thought that was a fantastic way to experience records as well as listening to them – you valued them, and what the person had put on the sleeve, and how they made it look. It really taught you to look and get a sense of the human being who was singing these things. I still do that. I can't really listen to a record without studying the sleeve and looking at the person for hours. I put them on my wall and look at them and wonder who they are and all of that stuff.

This would've been the early '70s, so it was before punk – it was even before Bob Dylan, really, in our house. I was mad into Alvin Stardust. She got me into him as well, 'My Coo Ca Choo' – we loved that record.

What was the first record that belonged to you?

It was an Elvis record, which I got when I was about eight, an Italian double album of Elvis called *Il Re del Rock 'n' Roll*. I liked black leather Elvis. I was freaked out by opera Elvis later: I didn't get that. I liked 'Jailhouse Rock' Elvis. I was addicted to all those terrible Elvis movies, even though they were awful. He was always so fascinating to watch.

I never fancied him or anything, but you could observe he was beautiful – but he was far too beautiful to fancy. He was beyond sexuality, really.

That was my first record. The next record I got was Dire Straits' first album [*Dire Straits*, 1978], which was quite some years later. I remember actually working for the money to buy it, so it felt more mine, too.

When you first started writing songs, who were your heroes?

By then, Bob Dylan had really become my obsession. I was first exposed to Bob Dylan when my brother Joseph, who is three years older than me, came home in 1979 with *Slow Train Coming*. We had in Ireland at that time a theocracy, really; it was a very religious country. Unfortunately, it was infected with the worst kind of religious music, where you kind of really felt sorry for God for having to listen to it! The uncoolest people on Earth were basically making religious music. But then my brother came home with *Slow Train Coming*, and that completely changed my life and set entirely the course of the rest of my life and career and what I wanted to be as a person and an artist.

We saw Bob Dylan as this quite prophetic, angelic being. It's similar to John Lennon – there are certain people in the world where you look up and know there's a God, or a spirit world, whatever you want to call it. It doesn't matter what they say or what they do or wear or anything else; it's actually how they look and just their presence and something about them. There was something for us like that with Bob Dylan.

As Irish kids we were moved by Dylan because he was this very flawed character. Even the sound of his voice was quite flawed, and he was crackly and he wore filthy clothes, and he smoked and he had done

"We saw Bob Dylan as this quite prophetic, angelic being. It's similar to John Lennon – there are certain people in the world where you look up and know there's a God."

drugs, and he told everybody to piss off and he was grumpy. He wasn't at all goody-goody, but not only that, the religious music he was making was funky and sexy and cool. I was obsessed with him. I never listened to anybody else for years. I'm still like this with Bob Dylan: I have one iPod that's just Bob Dylan; that's all that's on there. I have another which is just Curtis Mayfield. If I start listening to Bob Dylan, I can't stop for a year; I can barely listen to anybody else. I was like that even as a teenager.

But alongside him there were others: David Bowie was a huge one. I remember seeing David Bowie on Marc Bolan's TV show [British TV series *Marc*, presented by T. Rex's lead singer Marc Bolan]; I remember

distinctly being a very small child seeing it and just being blown away. I loved Marc Bolan, but obviously he just didn't have the kind of gravitas that people like David Bowie had. David Bowie was like a creature from another universe – that's exactly what he was.

Quite literally in personality at the time, as well as music and looks [laughs].

In Ireland, they were inclined not to publish a lot of his interviews, because he was talking about a lot of controversial matters ahead of his time, particularly bisexuality. And I remember we'd be asking our parents, 'What's a bisexual?' We'd be told, 'Be quiet. Be quiet, have your crisps.' So they were inclined to shut him down in terms of they didn't want to print his interviews, but they did show his music.

I just loved how he used his voice. When I go back to listen to my first record, I can see certain areas in which I probably stole the odd little phrase and things from him. Obviously, his lyrics were fantastic, but he often made these noises with his voice: he would say a word and then at the end of it would be a *Hrrrgghh, hrrrgghh* … The way he would use a word, even if it was just, 'Spiders from Maaa-haaaa-aaars' – that was a huge thing, because in Ireland nobody thought of ever saying anything interestingly. And they certainly didn't say it with a whole lot of make-up on and one green eye and one blue eye, telling everyone that they liked to have sex with men and women [laughs]. He was a huge companion, I would call him, throughout my life. The first time I ever had sex was to *Let's Dance*, which is the most fantastic record. Well, it was the whole album. It was terrible, because his parents would be in the next room, and they'd think we were real innocently listening to David Bowie. I've loved that record ever since.

Someone else you've mentioned is Curtis Mayfield. When did you first hear his music?

A couple of miracles happened that would've changed the course of my life. First there was *Slow Train Coming*; previous to that, there were a few stragglers that broke out of the British charts into the Irish charts. It was at the time that the Desmond Dekker song 'Israelites' went to number one, and around the same time, Toots and the Maytals' '54–46 Was My Number' – these branched out over to Ireland, which is unheard of. This is how I began my love of Jamaican music, and my relationship with Rasta music, in particular, even though they weren't overtly Rasta tunes. Then, of course, later, there was Althea and Donna, 'Uptown Top Ranking', and that was all before I left Ireland. When I came to London, then I got involved with Rasta people.

What was wonderful was when you listened to Toots [Hibbert], he was like this big child, and there was this great defiance in what he was saying; he was taking this quite heavy thing that had happened to him and was making something quite defiant out of it. There's a calling in Irish voices – a certain yearning, if you like – but I think Toots had this great calling in his voice. In a way, that's what reached out, right across the bloody Atlantic, and even landed in Irish houses. Whatever way he sang, it doesn't matter what he's singing. Even now I love him. I don't necessarily always like his lyrics, and I don't always necessarily always like the song, but I don't care because I love him.

My experience with theocracy was it dictates to you what the Bible says and it makes sure that you're too busy feeding yourself to find out for yourself. What I loved about the Rasta guys is that they were taking scriptures and putting them into records, so that suddenly I began to learn a whole load of scriptures that I never heard of before. They gave me this whole interest in learning the Bible, and I began, then, to have this very passionate lifelong interest in unravelling what is actually in this book that people have misinterpreted in order to oppress my people.

What's a song that would best illustrate that?
My favourite was 'Fire Fe the Vatican', the Max Romeo tune.

"It's not about notes, and the minute you start thinking about the notes you may as well pack up and go home."

We are talking about firsts, and we have to talk about your first massive international hit, 'Nothing Compares 2 U'. What's your relationship like with that song now?
I love it. I love the song. People always imagine I must be sick of it because I suppose some people do get sick of their 'hit'. I always joke, there's no point in people saying 'hits' — let's face it, remove the 's'. But I love it. I never sing a song that I can't emotionally identify with. The whole way I've been brought up to sing all of my life is that it's really about emotions. It's not about notes, and the minute you start thinking about the notes, you might as well pack up and go home. Without doubt, every single night I kind of do the Stanislavski method of singing. It's called bel canto, the manner of singing which I've studied, but it's a little like the Stanislavski acting method: you have to find emotional stuff inside of yourself that you can use. I mean, 30 years later you've got to be able to sing the same damn song every damn night and find something inside yourself emotionally. But I'm always able to find it.

I always think of my mother, which is why I had the little tear in the video. My mother died when I was seventeen, and it wasn't long after that I was making the video and the song. I think I'm similar to millions of people who love the song: we're all people who associate the song with loss of some kind, whether it's a break-up or whatever. So, still, when

I sing I think about my mother, but I don't get sad about it. I'm talking to my mother, that's my little minute that I spend with my mother, just letting my mother know that I'm thinking of her and that I love her.

I'm fascinated by what it must be like to be not just the voice, but the face as well. Sometimes songs become more than pop songs; they become cultural moments, and then you're in the centre of this whirlwind of attention. How does that feel?
It's very confusing. I think I coped just by smoking a lot of weed! I don't know if I have really coped with it, to be honest. There were good things, but I was so young, and at that age you don't really have a strong sense of your own identity anyway. But there were great things, all my dreams were coming true. If I hadn't gotten rescued by music, I probably could've ended up in a bit of trouble. But then you see you're on a conveyor belt, but it's other people taking you along this track of what they want you to be, and what they want you to do. They want you to be a pop star and they want you to not say this, or to say that, or to wear this or to not wear that, and you stop seeing yourself reflected back at you in anyone that you know. I always say, people are like mirrors; our friends and family are like mirrors. We see ourselves in them. If you don't have them, suddenly you've got all these new people who are not reflecting back at you who you really are, but who they want you to be. You don't realize that what they want you to do is pay their mortgage. You think they're being really nice and everything, but no, they're not. It's a bit of a head fuck.

You did a beautiful rendition of a Bob Marley song ['War'] on *Saturday Night Live* [3 October, 1992], a big American TV show, and during the end of the song, you tore up a picture of the pope. And then you were, for many people, evil incarnate!
And I was wearing Sade's dress. She may not know this, but when I came to England in 1985, I went to a rock and roll auction and I bought a dress for 800 quid, one of Sade's famous white lace dresses that she had made for stage, and I was wearing it on *Saturday Night Live*. And my daughter now has it and she's going to wear it for her wedding dress [laughs]. I've said to my daughter, 'This is a dress for women to cause trouble in'. So we must thank Sade for the dress and the inspiration.

What do you remember from the fall-out of that? A few artists stood behind you, and a lot of artists didn't.
I don't really remember anything, except for one funny thing: when we came out of NBC, myself and a girlfriend of mine were there, and a bunch of young fellas were waiting. What they didn't realize was myself and my friend, Ciara, were the top sprinters at school – we could do 100 metres in 11.2 seconds, the two of us both. So these fuckers decided to collar us outside NBC Studios, young guys. They threw a load of eggs at us, thinking we'd be scared, but they picked the wrong bitches. So the two of us ran after them and they got the fright of their life. We caught

about three of these guys in the corner of some alleyway and just made them apologize, basically. By the end of it they were like, 'We're really sorry. We're very sorry. We understand now.' And that was the end!

In 2011 there was utter furore, utter chaos surrounding …
Oh, me advertising for boyfriends [in a column in the Irish *Independent*].

Which I thought was kind of funny. People didn't seem to get the joke. Do you regret being so honest in public?
God didn't make more than one of us for nothing. We're here to communicate with each other, so I don't have any problem with doing what God put us on Earth to do. We're here to help each other and talk to each other. Some people want to cause trouble, you know what I mean? But you can't let that stop you being you.

The final thing is we have to choose a song to finish on.
Curtis Mayfield is my other big hero, he sang my favourite song ever in the world. My favourite song ever about Jesus is a Curtis Mayfield song called 'Jesus', which is on an album called *There's No Place Like America Today*. It's actually kind of longish, but hopefully you'll play it anyway. That would be what I choose. It's beautiful.

The First Time Sinéad O'Connor Playlist

1	4th & Vine	Sinéad O'Connor
2	Mind Games	John Lennon
3	My Coo Ca Choo	Alvin Stardust
4	I Got a Woman	Elvis Presley
5	Sultans of Swing	Dire Straits
6	Gotta Serve Somebody	Bob Dylan
7	Let's Dance	David Bowie
8	Troy	Sinéad O'Connor
9	54–46 Was My Number	Toots and The Maytals
10	Fire Fe the Vatican	Max Romeo
11	Tomorrow Is a Long Time	Bob Dylan
12	Nothing Compares 2 U	Sinéad O'Connor
13	Chase the Devil	Max Romeo
14	It Doesn't Matter to Him	John Grant feat. Sinéad O'Connor
15	War	Bob Marley and The Wailers
16	Jesus	Curtis Mayfield

"I used to say, 'We're all the same, really ... under the skin', and then I thought, 'Well, no, we're not. I'm more talented than you ...'"

Terry Hall

For almost as long as I can remember music, Terry Hall has been a presence in my life; not like The Beatles, Bowie or the Stones, who exist as these vast cultural concepts – unreal characters with mystical talents – but more like a cool next-door neighbour, whose music you hear drifting over the fence from childhood, or the big brother you look up to, who occasionally pops home and leaves a record or two for you to obsess over. In fact, my older stepbrother was obsessed by The Specials, so I would hear them constantly. I'd delicately browse those brilliant, monochrome 7-inch covers in his singles box, and I'd spot the band's own 2 Tone record label logo and chequerboard design carefully inked on his college folders. My stepbrother was cool, so The Specials were cool.

And then the video for 'Ghost Town' totally changed my life.

For me, in 1981, pop music was Shakin' Stevens, then The Specials loomed into view, crammed into a Vauxhall Cresta, careering round a sinister and deserted inner-city landscape under watery dull-grey Midland skies singing about a 'Government leaving the youth on the shelf' and 'No job to be found in this country'. I was nine years old. One minute my only concerns were Fizz Bombs sweets and *The Dukes of Hazzard*, the next I was witnessing the decline of the entire nation and the wholesale abandonment of my generation.

It blew my tiny mind.

Hall still has the same look he had in that video: deadpan, hooded eyes with slightly satanic eyebrows, carrying a vague sense of menace and the amused air of someone who has seen the joke coming before anyone else. He talks in a slight staccato, with an occasional stutter, but he's got a great – if bone dry – sense of humour and immaculate comic timing. Listening back to the interview, I hear myself laugh a lot. He doesn't.

Matt Everitt: When was the first time you were aware of music as a kid? Can you remember?

Pinky and Perky, *Torchy the Battery Boy* [UK TV series] or Édith Piaf. Yeah, one of the three. I'll throw Paul Robeson in as well. We had a stereogram. Those are the only records I remember. My dad used to play them. Sunday was 'Record Day', after he'd had a drink.

What about the first piece of music that was yours, that you went out and bought?

It could have been 'Fire Brigade' by The Move, or 'Johnny Reggae' by The Piglets. It was in the late '6os that I started noticing records, when I was about ten, and by then I'd started listening to my sisters' stuff. They were older than me; they'd started playing early reggae, soul and Motown.

Were you one of those kids that would listen to a record again and again and again and immerse yourself?

I was quite solitary, and there was very little to do. There was little on TV, and you had a pencil and some paper – that was the extent of what you had in your bedroom. My older sister left home and she put her record player in my room, which meant I could listen to records, and that's pretty much all I did from the age of thirteen – David Cassidy, David Essex …

All the Davids.

… you can never go wrong with a David. Roxy Music and T. Rex, but I didn't really have any heroes. The first person, I guess, would probably be David Bowie – another David, but different to David Cassidy. I remember reading an interview with David Cassidy in *Blue Jeans* or *Jackie*, and he refused to do a photo session because he had a spot. I thought that sounded like a brilliant job. It's like, 'How'd you get to do that job where you can refuse because you've got a spot?'

What was the first gig you went to that made an impact on you?

It would have been Pink Floyd at Knebworth [1975].

People normally say 'Tavares at the local venue' or something!

I'm not like those sort of people. Around that time, and I couldn't really get my head around it, but I went with a lot of older people, we went down in a van, and the first act or so was Linda Lewis. And I remember being at the back and thinking, 'God, she's so small', because I was at the back of the field, but trying to work out how she was so loud, being so small, and get my head around a PA and stuff like this.

What about the first moment when punk hit you?

So many people who formed bands around that time saw the Sex Pistols and The Clash together, and I did in Coventry. And you know that story: 17 people there and everybody formed a band the next day, which pretty much *was* true. I didn't really like the Pistols' music that much – I liked

The Clash; it was a bit more thought-out – and I never liked bands like The Damned. It felt a bit silly to me. Then I saw Patti Smith in '76 or '77, and she was just absolutely brilliant, and then Richard Hell, and then I started listening to a lot of New York new wave punk, which I really preferred. It just felt a bit more musical, and less about how they looked.

When you joined The Specials in '77, what were your first impressions of them as a collection of people?
Hmmm. They were all right. They're not the kind of people I'd, like, hang around with. They were a bit dull and lifeless. I was the youngest member. At seventeen, eighteen, a gap of two years feels like a gap of ten years, right? So I had my own friends outside of the band, and they did too, and we got on okay. We were just trying to suss each other out, musically, what we were all about.

Was it quite obvious to you early on, in those first rehearsals, that there was something there, something ... special?
I think so. We did a tour with The Clash, and I think it was at that point where we felt like something was happening. Because it was really

"We made demos, and they always seemed to end up in the wrong hands. Like Pete Waterman's."

difficult; it was so easy to get gigs, around the Midlands, but beyond that, you couldn't really fathom it all. And we made demos, and they always seemed to end up in the wrong hands. Like Pete Waterman's. He funded a demo that we did. Yeah, he wanted to manage us.

I didn't know that. Great careers that might not have been!
Yeah. What? His. We'd known Pete since the early '70s. He used to DJ at the Locarno in Coventry. He came to a rehearsal and he said we needed to project more. He said, 'What you need is, you need to wear black, and then something on top of the black, a piece of metal or gold or something to draw people in.' Umm, yeah. Cheers, Pete. See you in a bit.

What were those first Specials gigs like? You've said it was like the Magnificent Seven riding into town, a nice analogy.
It was. It was brilliant, especially when we'd sorted ourselves out and we had our direction. It got a bit gang-like: there were lots of bands emerging that felt gang-like, like Dexys [Midnight Runners] and UB40 – our own separate little gangs. It was quite nice, especially going abroad and stuff. In New York, we had photo sessions there, and people couldn't work

out whether we were in the Marines, or if we were gay. They couldn't really work it out – it didn't look like a band. It was good fun.

When 'Gangsters' came out [1979], the first Specials single, was there that moment when you think, 'I'm connecting with people who maybe aren't part of my scene'? It was a big single.
Yeah, it was a big hit, but even at that point I couldn't work out what we were doing it for. I couldn't work out where we were going to go with it, or what was going to happen. You're just so immersed in it, you just got on with it, and the size of the band became apparent when we started touring abroad, really. Even here with *Top of the Pops*, we still lived the same sort of life, so day to day it didn't really change.

When 'Ghost Town' went to number one [1981], you became instantly recognizable as a group, and as an individual. You don't strike me as the kind of person who would really find that 'showbiz thing' a particularly comfortable place to occupy.
No choice, really. It depends on how you deal with it. People used to come up to me and I used to say, 'We're all the same, really. We're the same under the skin,' and then I thought, 'Well, no, we're not. I'm sort of more talented than you and better looking, and everything really.' And from that point on, I could handle it a lot easier. I didn't deny it. That was the weirdest thing, denying that you're popular. Coventry was a very

"It was a big hit, but even at that point I couldn't work out what we were doing it for."

weird place to grow up in, to even think about being on TV or radio or anything. You never left Coventry, really. You worked in a factory and you stayed there, like my parents and everybody that I pretty much knew. Even to go out of Coventry to London was 'passport time', so that made you deny what you were, and sort of apologize for being successful. But once you dropped that, it was okay.

A lot of The Specials' material is politicized. The whole idea of the band was politicized. When did you, as a young man, start being aware of social issues, injustice ...
I think when I was fifteen, and I was asked to leave school because we were playing up and messing about a bit, but we weren't invited to take any exams. And they fed us out to markets and stuff to do work experience, where we'd earn 10 quid a week – which was a lot of money then – but you realized that somebody had given up on you already. And you're fifteen. This thing that was meant to look after you had given up on you.

When did you first think, 'I've gone as far with The Specials as I can?' Was there a moment you thought 'I'm done with this'?

When we were hitting each other on *Top of the Pops*. That was a sign. But it got really out of hand, and we really didn't get on at all. We were from very different backgrounds, and I think they became a lot clearer with more success. People would tend to do this with their money or that with their money, and you have no real common interests. Then you were forcing yourself to be together a lot: you go on an American tour, and you're on a bus with people day in, day out, and you don't really like them. And they don't like you. And it's really hard. I just felt like I was the only person who could see the problems, and everybody else was just content with getting on with it, but I just didn't want to live like that.

Telling the rest of the band was difficult, but it only became difficult when our record company made me aware that it became difficult. It never felt like I owed anybody a living, but when the record company worked out how much revenue they were going to lose, and they were trying to offer me money to stay with the band, I just thought, 'This is so horrible'. It was hard to tell the band, but by that time I'd worked out that me and Lynval [Golding – guitarist] and Neville [Staple – singer] were going to form another band. The only reason to form that band was as a reaction to The Specials.

Listening to 'The Lunatics (Have Taken Over the Asylum)', the first Fun Boy Three record, it was different to what people were going to expect.

Yeah, we said, 'Let's leave instruments at the door. We don't need instruments. Let's just hire some stuff in when we get into a studio, like a percussion box, and if there's a piano, let's play that.' We booked the studio, told our record company that we had an album's worth of material, and we've probably got ten hits … And we didn't have one thing. They were like, 'Great. Get on with it!' So we just sat in a room for the best part of a year and made this record, and Bananarama came in.

The Colourfield's first album [*Virgins and Philistines*, 1985] – Bobby Goldsboro was the inspiration for that. Who is he?

At that point I'd had all these names, like Bobby Goldsboro, Terry Jacks, Jack Jones and Andy Williams, in my head, but I never really listened to them, because they didn't come into my circle, really, but at the end of The Fun Boy Three everything got so loud again and so brash, and the record company was louder and demanding, and so it was time to end that. I wanted a quieter time, and so I moved into the country, and that was my first breakdown. I just had a mental breakdown and I refused to take my duffel coat off for 18 months, but that was quite good. It was a bit indie, Glasgow, Pastels-y.

So I started the band with Toby Lyons, and we went back and started to listen to a lot of what would be called easy listening and I got really obsessed with it, and with the look. All of a sudden you could go to

Austin Reed and buy an outfit and look like David Hunter from [British TV series] *Crossroads*. Everything just felt a bit grown-up: you didn't really have to race anymore, and you weren't part of this thing where you had to get hit records if you choose not to. That's why I chose that.

What's the track that sums up where you were at that point?
It'd be Terry Jacks and 'Seasons in the Sun'.

Do you feel this pull and push away from music, but also the wider music industry?
I'm okay as long as I feel like I'm in control of stuff. That's not about being a control freak, because I'm not at all, but for my own sanity, being in control of stuff, just generally, is a much better thing. You know, I can come and talk to you, because I control it: I made my own way in; I'll make my own way home. Do you know what I mean? It's all right.

I haven't got anybody telling me that I've got to go here or there. It's the same with gigs now. When we tour now as The Specials, we don't feel like we're a part of the music business, we're just our own little entity. It doesn't feel like a pressure.

When did you first think it was time to get The Specials back together again?
It's honestly linked to me getting better. I got ill again about six or seven years ago, and I started on some medication, a cocktail, which is really good, and really made me want to do stuff and get up in the morning. I started thinking about people I'd worked with, and then I thought about people like Brad, our drummer, and Lynval, who I really got on with, and then we didn't see each other for 20 years, and I thought, 'Let's just get back and say hello, how are you doing?' We arranged a meeting with all seven of us, and it was interesting to see how people had changed or not, and we decided maybe to try a rehearsal, and it became apparent that we wanted to do something, but we didn't know what, really.

Here's the thing: the weight of expectation for something like that. You're messing with people's lives, people's musical memories. That's a difficult thing to face up to.
Well, it was until I saw the Pixies reforming and playing at Brixton [Academy in London, 2004]. I thought they did it brilliantly. They just turned up and got on with it, and there was nothing great going on apart from their *stuff*, and that gave me a boost. And then I saw Patti Smith doing something. And when we did our first gig in Newcastle, it just felt like a real celebration of something. It was hard to work out what it was, but there was a definite connection between the band and the audience; we'd grown up together, and it was such a really lovely feeling.

It's hard because it's like, 'Do you go through the motions?' Who knows. But if you go on stage and you're sincere about what you're doing, then it's okay – I think it's really okay.

And obviously it felt good enough to keep on doing it?
Well, yeah. We did about a thousand dates or something. We've come to a natural pause now, where we've played pretty much everywhere, and so we're just having to pause now and see what's good to do next.

What about you? What else are you up to?
I've started writing again, which is good. I've stopped taking my night-time medication, which means I can get up and work again. I've noticed a big difference in me: I'm so much happier these days. So I've started thinking about writing again, and I don't know whether it's for a record. Actually, I've started painting as a form of therapy. It's another tool to communicate with people, because I find it really difficult sometimes, and I feel you can do that much easier through a song or through a painting.

Why is it harder for you, do you think?
I don't know, but it is. Why does it have to be your voice that does it sometimes? Can't you make something out of clay and say, 'This is how I feel', rather than trying to explain it and not getting anywhere with that?

You get to choose the last song. It can be anything.
Well, I think the last song I heard was actually last night, and it was on my iPod, and I was in bed, and it was Jeff Buckley, 'Grace'.

The First Time Terry Hall Playlist

1	Gangsters	The Specials
2	Who's Afraid of the Big Bad Wolf	Pinky & Perky
3	Non, Je Ne Regrette Rien	Édith Piaf
4	Sometime I Feel Like a Motherless Child	Paul Robeson
5	Fire Brigade	The Move
6	Johnny Reggae	The Piglets
7	Kooks	David Bowie
8	White Riot	The Clash
9	Blank Generation	Richard Hell
10	Ghost Town	The Specials
11	The Lunatics (Have Taken Over the Asylum)	The Fun Boy Three
12	If You Go Away	Scott Walker
13	Seasons in the Sun	Terry Jacks
14	Thinking of You	The Colourfield
15	Grace	Jeff Buckley

"I was trapped in a small town. I could see my destiny, and it wasn't exciting. I wanted to get out."

TRENT REZNOR

Trent Reznor is an intimidating man. His work is intimidating: his band, Nine Inch Nails, have sold millions; he's won Oscars for his soundtrack work; and he's been a music and tech consultant for Apple. He looks intimidating, in black jeans and black V-neck T-shirt, with military-cropped black hair, and a determined expression. He even sounds intimidating, speaking deliberately and assuredly in a cavern-deep voice that wouldn't sound out of place in a disaster movie. In short, even before this interview has begun, I'm intimidated.

Unlike most of the musicians in this book, I hadn't met Reznor before we were introduced only a couple of minutes before the interview. He's an undeniable physical presence, with a broad chest and biceps that look like Volkswagen Beetles jostling in traffic. Then there's his history: the anger of NIN's early output appeared to have been siphoned directly from Reznor's psychological distress and fuelled by well-documented, epic substance abuse. But it becomes instantly apparent that the man is very different from the myth.

Reznor is calm, thoughtful and polite, with a tendency to gently mock himself during our chat. This isn't to say he is frivolous about his art – he clearly thinks a lot about the best way to express himself musically and do authentic, meaningful and *interesting* work – but he's also pretty funny. I'm not sure how much of himself he revealed, he's guarded in the way that some very smart people are, studying his environment and assessing the conversation as it unfolds, but as the interview progressed I could feel him relax slightly.

If you watch old interviews with Reznor, you can see he's always been like this – personable, urbane and slyly funny. But seeing footage of him perform in concert, screaming and hissing into the microphone, neck veins throbbing, eyes tightly shut, drenched in sweat, you just think, 'Is that even the same guy? How can someone psychologically exist in both states?' Now, *that* is intimidating.

Matt Everitt: When were you first aware of music?

I was raised by my grandparents, and my grandmother insisted I take piano lessons when I was five years old. I don't think it was the highest priority on my agenda back then, but fairly quickly I started to enjoy it, and then I could tell that it came naturally to me. I learned practising equals the reward of getting through that track or a piece of music, and I think I started to identify with it as something that became part of me.

Did you have many records? Was it a musical environment?

Yeah, my dad played in a bluegrass country rock band, and there were always records around. Things like the Eagles and Poco. I used to listen to the [Jimi Hendrix Experience] *Are You Experienced* record quite a bit.

What about the first record that you owned?

I grew up in a small town in Pennsylvania, and it had a five-and-dime type of store that had a variety of everything and there was a small record section. And I remember, for some reason, buying The Partridge Family's *Greatest Hits* record, and that was a *big deal.* That was mine! That wasn't my dad's music. Some good songs on that record, as I recall, too. You know, the first concert I'd ever seen was the Eagles in 1976 with my dad.

What was that like?

It was more people than I'd ever seen in one place! And some people were … [whispers] smoking marijuana. It was exotic and it was great. I was being urged to become a concert pianist, and at some point around puberty, a rock influence came in there. I was pretty good back then. Being at one with an instrument and being able to feel like you're in control of it and watching your hands do something you couldn't believe you can do, I enjoyed that, but it didn't feel like the endgame for me.

I was trapped in a small town where I could see my destiny, and my destiny wasn't New York City and it wasn't exciting and it wasn't on a movie screen. I wanted to get out. I felt like I didn't belong there and there wasn't anything to do, and so I had to imagine my way out of that place. I could see my reflection on the TV when it was turned off and I'd stand with a yard stick and I'd picture myself on stage, you know. And I kind of always knew I wanted to do what I ended up doing.

When you started forming bands and playing in bands, who were the kind of people that you were looking up to?

Initially, in high school, if you got a band together, you just learned other people's music, and then hope to play a high school dance. I didn't know what was beyond that – maybe you could play a bar someday? But the only bars that would hire music in that area were after cover bands that would play what was popular at the time, so we started forming cover bands. Got some friends of mine, I'm talking about fourteen, fifteen years old, young and no idea what we're doing – [Deep Purple's] 'Smoke on the Water' for two hours, you know? [Eric Clapton's] 'Cocaine'.

Later I got out of high school and I started playing with some older guys, and they were actually really good players, but it was still primarily a cover band that would play a bar circuit. About around that time – and this would've been '83, '84 – I was out of high school, brief career in college for computer engineering as something to fall back on. You know.

If this music thing doesn't work out, you've always got that?
Yeah, that was it. I didn't want to let my grandparents down, but I had a revelation in college: I was taking calculus one day and I realized there's people that really like to do that, sit and work on calculus problems, and I thought, 'I *can* do this, but I don't love to do it.' I really loved to make music, and at that time of my life I was too afraid to actually write music. Cleveland was the closest real city to where I was. It had a cool music shop that sold exotic keyboards and synthesizers you couldn't afford. I got a job working there and started to become a keyboard player for bands that were playing original music. The synthpop explosion was very exciting to me. I was a keyboard player and obsessed with technology.

The exotic nature of a synthesizer that could make all these different sounds but was attached to a keyboard that I could play got me into sound design. Hearing Human League – with a drum machine! That just felt like magic. I loved the idea of rock music that wasn't based on

"I was cleaning toilets in a recording studio so I could get time at night to teach myself engineering."

the archetype of Led Zeppelin or The Beatles or guitar/bass/drums. That synthesis of things felt like a really fertile and exciting time to be around. At a point in my life, early twenties or whatever it was, I was thinking, 'There's something brewing, and I think I can be a part of it.' It took me a few more years before I had the courage to sit down and really write.

When I got to college and I had access to college radio station – a library of vinyl – I couldn't believe it. I was in there trying to tape everything. It was a lot of stimulus. I think that's when I got around to actually writing. I was cleaning toilets in a recording studio because I knew I could work at night or I could get time at night to teach myself engineering and have access to a studio and try to see what I had to say.

The myth is that you started working on what would be Nine Inch Nails demos at the studio, and then the demos got sent out, everyone loved them and you got signed.
It wasn't quite as simple as that. I mean, that's kind of the Cliffs Notes version of it, but it really came from realizing that what I wanted to do

wasn't going to happen by playing out in bars in front of people. I wanted to take the time to figure out what I had to say as a writer and also nurture the idea of Nine Inch Nails – but it wasn't called Nine Inch Nails yet – what my thing was going to be. And what did it feel like? And what did it look like? And what might a name be like? And what is it about? And what did the picture look like? And all those things. I wanted to form it into something that felt like it had an identity.

I mean, you're essentially starting a brand – not to speak in marketing terms, but you *are* doing that when you create a band. And it has a 'feel' to it; it has an aesthetic, an art direction and all those things. I wanted to let it reveal itself to me, what it was, and that took some time. The main hurdle was trying to find out what I had to say.

It's finding your voice.
That's exactly what it was. And it revealed itself in a strange way after the first few songs I attempted to write were terrible. They were bad because it was me trying to sound like The Clash, you know? Trying to sound like somebody that I'm not. I can't speak with authority through that voice.

I'd been writing lyrics in the form of phrases and stuff that comes out of me in moments of anxiety or rage or some form of cathartic need to get this out of my system. And I thought I could never show those to anybody because that wasn't a construct: that was guts, and that was me, and I wasn't that interesting. I wasn't a larger-than-life character, and I certainly didn't want you reading how I felt, unfiltered, about anything.

"I wanted to take time to figure out what I had to say as a writer and also nurture the idea of Nine Inch Nails."

But when I did finally get around to it, I knew there was something that had power to it, and it was an honesty that I hadn't achieved by faking it the way I had been. I had a friend that was a manager, and we thought, 'Let's just try to get a 12-inch deal with a European label and figure out what this thing's going to be.' Nobody really was interested. One label said yes. All the labels I liked, they all weren't interested. Which is funny, because those are the recordings that went on to become *Pretty Hate Machine* [Nine Inch Nails' 1989 debut album]. So we took the one deal we were offered, a pretty bad label, but it got us started.

The Downward Spiral in 1994: David Bowie's Low is the record that you've associated with that album. What's he like?
Oh, Dave, you mean? [Laughs] I remember playing something on my answering machine, a message from him saying, 'I would love to tour

with you'. It's unmistakably his voice. And I remember playing it for as many people as I could. *Downward Spiral* came out: it changed the trajectory of the band. I handed that album in – that was our second proper album – with an apology: 'I don't think this was the hit album that you wanted, new record label Interscope, but it's a record that I have to make and I feel great about it. But, you know, good luck trying to sell this one.'

And then, to everyone's surprise, as *Closer* took off, we went from being a theatre-type band to sold-out arenas all through the States, and touring for two and a half years pretty much solid. And my life getting kind of upended in every way. Everything changed and I wasn't really equipped to deal with it. Anyway, at the end of that, towards the end of that cycle, I was pretty burned out. Bowie rings up and says, 'I want to do a tour, and the only band I could think of doing it with would be you guys. It's all I would love to do.' Of course.

Yeah, let me just check my diary ...
'Yes. Let me think about – Yes!' So we did an amphitheatre tour in the States for probably six or eight weeks. We were bigger than he was at that time in the States, and he had just finished the *Outside* album that, by his own admission, wasn't what anybody wanted to hear, necessarily, but it was something he felt he needed to get out of his system, and he was just going to play music primarily from that. There was no way on earth I was going to have Bowie open for me, so we made the show make sense, where we would come out and play, and then he comes out and joins us, and his band joins everybody, then my band leaves and I stay with his band, and then I leave and his band continues.

Every single night was, 'I can't believe this is happening.' I've met a number of people that I've admired; when you meet them, it's tough for someone to live up to what you've projected them to be. I'm aware of that every time I meet somebody that's a fan. But Bowie exceeded it – just in terms of being a gentleman and a smart guy and somebody that would say something to me and think about it. I remember him saying, when we first met in person, 'You guys are going to blow us off stage, because we're not what people want. My hits? I just can't play them. I have to play the new album.' And I thought, 'I don't know if I could do that.' But it made sense in the big picture, and I admire his courage.

What I've admired about him as an artist is his ability to seemingly fearlessly throw out something that isn't broken. You know, here's a construct or a character or an album or a sound, and not milking it for three records or four and saying, 'Well, what's the next thing?', Madonna-style. He makes something great and then, 'I'm done'; now it's the next thing. Regardless of how successful it was, it was still the courage involved of going out there and having faith in your vision.

Where did you first hear Johnny Cash's version of 'Hurt'?
[Producer] Rick Rubin's a friend of mine and someone that's been around in key moments of my life. He rang me up and said, 'How would

you feel about Johnny Cash covering "Hurt"?' And I said, 'Well, I'd be flattered.' And I didn't really think much more about it, because it didn't mean it was actually going to happen. And I remember not long after that, a CD shows up in the mail. And I put it on and it bothered me: it didn't seem right; I wasn't in the mood to hear it. And it felt like ... that was *my* song, and that was one that felt like it really came from inside. It was like eeing your girlfriend making out with someone else, you know? It just felt uncomfortable. I just pretended it didn't happen. I didn't *dislike* it, but it felt invasive. And then not long after, Mark Romanek, who is also a friend and worked on a number of videos for me, a great, great director, sends me a video, says, 'You've got to see this new video I did for your version of "Hurt" with Johnny Cash.' As soon as I put it on, now it wasn't my song anymore. You know? Now I got it, and I started tearing up. I got goosebumps, and even thinking about it now I just got goosebumps. And I just felt honoured to be involved in it.

And it came at a time when I was really dipping my toes in the water of writing again after taking time off and getting sober and addressing some real issues in my own life – severe enough that if I *didn't* have a career, it was okay if I could just like myself and feel good about myself someday. I took a few years off and I was just starting to get back into seeing if I had anything to say, and did I need drugs to write. Which, of course I didn't, but the fear in you is looking for any reason to validate what you did. And this came at a time when I really felt like, 'Wow. I did something good here'. Even though it was a strange thing that happened in my bedroom, writing something down, on the other side of the world – and now this guy *got it*. My friends came together and made a video for him, and it's weird how it all worked out. That's a long-winded way of saying it was what I needed, and it's a flattering experience.

We have to talk about film music. What was the first film that you could remember seeing when the music really hit you? It's fine if it's *The Jungle Book*. It doesn't have to be pretentious!
That would have been a great answer. When I fell into scoring films in the '90s, there was the terrible movie soundtrack that was just a collection of songs that someone figured out they could co-market for the worst reasons. I had a moment with one of my heroes, David Lynch, with *Lost Highway* [1997], where I got the call and he came to New Orleans where I was living, and we worked on sound design for that film and a little bit of scene scoring. But it wasn't until [David] Fincher's *The Social Network* [2010] that I got thrown into it, and I really enjoyed the process. But, to answer your question, I watch a lot of films but I don't dissect them into thinking about the music that much. And I kind of like that I don't do it.

I think a lot of the music in films is pretty boring, really – particularly Hollywood films. I think a lot of what comes out of there could be from a sample CD. It just performs a purpose that manipulates you to feel a certain way, you know? What was fun about working with David Fincher was what he wanted the music to *do*. It felt like I was colouring out of the lines, because he showed me a rough cut of the film. Fincher calls – and I've always admired him and we were acquaintances at that point – [adopts Fincher impersonation] 'Hey, I'd love for you to do my next film. It's about Facebook.' I mean, how could that be exciting? I hate Facebook. But I read the script and I knew if he was interested in it, there was something good about it. And when I read the script, I thought, 'Okay this is an excellent script. But what would music sound like for that?' You know? Sweeping, epic battles? I can imagine that. Serial killers stalking prey? I can probably do that.

Nerds arguing in a courtroom? I'm not sure what to do. And he showed me a cut of the film, and it was really just smart people talking – clever dialogue. And I think the smartest thing that Atticus [Ross] and I did – he co-wrote the music with me – was to just really get inside his head and say, 'Why is it that you're asking us to do this?', first and foremost. And what he sent back to us, it didn't seem like the safe route. It felt like the music could actually be a key part of making this film, to colour it the right way, and give it an attitude. And it's not the safe route. It's about taking chances, and it's about bending rules of cinema and trying to make it more adventurous. That's what was really attractive for us, and the process of working on it was very creative and rewarding.

The First TIme Trent Reznor Playlist

1	Head Like a Hole	Nine Inch Nails
2	Are You Experienced	Jimi Hendrix
3	It's One of Those Nights (Yes Love)	The Partridge Family
4	Rock and Roll All Nite	Kiss
5	Get Down, Make Love	Queen
6	Never Let Me Down Again	Depeche Mode
7	Hot on the Heels of Love	Throbbing Gristle
8	Dig It	Skinny Puppy
9	Never Understand	The Jesus and Mary Chain
10	Closer	Nine Inch Nails
11	Scary Monsters (and Super Creeps)	David Bowie
12	Hurt	Johnny Cash
13	Hand Covers Bruise (*The Social Network* OST)	Trent Reznor and Atticus Ross
14	Everything	Nine Inch Nails

"You either get in and see what it is, or you stay out and wonder what it is."

Wayne Coyne

'Come in! Come in!' Wayne has opened the door and is enthusiastically ushering me into his hotel room where we're doing our interview. He's wearing a slender, grey three-piece suit, a battered but smart-looking white shirt open at the neck and no shoes. 'Yoga!' he exclaims, seeing me spot the foam mat on the floor. 'You must do yoga! Do you do yoga?' (I don't do yoga.) 'Yoga is great for your joints! Keeps you young!' He grins at me and says it again, apropos of nothing, apparently just because he likes the sound of the word. 'Yoga!'

Having spoken to Wayne a few times over the years, I can confirm he is just as lovely as he appears in every interview you've ever read, and you won't find many people who'll disagree. Speaking to him is to listen to his thoughts whirl directly from his brain out his mouth. He's unguarded, charming, friendly and – I mean this as a huge compliment – a bit like a five-year-old boy in the body of a fifty-six-year-old man. He's wide-eyed and excitable in conversation, and he's got an endless enthusiasm for what cool stuff might happen any moment now. In fact, there's a lot about Wayne that makes you wish you were a kid again.

At the Glastonbury Festival a couple of years after this interview, I spotted a figure dressed in a bright green, furry frog onesie with a pink-and-yellow striped tummy and giant neon blue horns on its head. The frog wanders over and pulls down its hood to reveal a mass of grey hair, a face covered in multicoloured, sparkly glitter and eyes that look like collapsing black holes full of stars. Obviously, it's Wayne. 'Great to see you!' he beams and gives me a hug. We chat for a while about the festival and then he's off to get ready for The Flaming Lips' performance that night. Watching the show later, I witness confetti cannons, people dressed in superhero costumes, strobe lights, lasers and Wayne himself rolling out into the audience in a giant inflatable hamster ball … And that was just during the first song.

I've taken up yoga.

Matt Everitt: When was the first time you were aware of music?
I had four older brothers and an older sister, and my mother liked music
a lot, so she played the record player a lot. I remember these kids shows,
one of them was *Captain Kangaroo*, and they would play this song
'Puff (The Magic Dragon)' by Peter, Paul and Mary. I would hear it all
throughout my life and I could connect it back, because when you're
really little, in this song you're the kid, and it's not about imagination –
the dragon is real. But as you get older, you realize that, little by little,
he grows up and he leaves the dragon, and it's crushing.

I remember, when The Beatles first played on [US TV variety show]
The Ed Sullivan Show, I remember us trying to get home so we could see
The Beatles on TV. The big bang: before this there was no music, and
now there was music. My mother really loved Tom Jones, and when Tom
Jones first hit, he was really young, and he's got his hair and he sings
these overly dramatic romantic songs. You don't think that you're really
influenced by these things, but sometimes I'll see a Tom Jones picture
from that time and he wears a suit a lot like I do, and he has *hair*, you
know what I mean? So these things connected probably to the joy that
my mother would have from listening to that.

You saw The Who live in '77?
Yes, and this was still with the stellar line-up. People say by then they
were burned out, but on this night they certainly were not. My brothers
would play *Tommy* [The Who's 1969 album, composed as a rock opera],
but it's not the same as this communal experience. Back then they even
had giant lasers and things. It's one of these movie moments that remains
in your mind: sitting at the top of this arena, and them doing 'Listening
to you, I get the music …' ['See Me, Feel Me'], and it probably went
on for ten minutes, and it felt like the arena was going to just collapse
because everybody was stomping their feet, and it was so loud, and then
we *wanted* it to collapse! We felt, like, this complete surrender.

**So, when you started playing in bands yourself, was that
something that was very important to you, to try and have that
connection with your audience and make it an experience?**
I never felt like I really had something to offer you, you know? To me it
was always, 'I'm really just glad to be here doing my thing. I hope you
like it, and I hope it works out.' As The Flaming Lips, we realize people
like our songs, but early on it's really just a desire to do it. You form a
band and you think you'll play through the summer and it'll all collapse,
and you would go back to working at a restaurant. I honestly felt that
way until just a couple of years ago: 'Well, we've been lucky but it's bound
to fall apart, the wheel will fall off any minute now.' A couple of years
ago I started to think, 'Oh, I guess I shouldn't worry about it anymore.'

It's going to be 30 years next year that we've been together, and I
just sort of thought, 'Aw, geez, why worry about it anymore?' I still worry
plenty about it being worthy of the audience's time and money and all

Wayne Coyne

that, but we may as well just present ourselves, do whatever we want and hope that we can get away with it.

'She Don't Use Jelly' [1993] was the first breakthrough for The Flaming Lips?

Oh, totally, yeah, yeah. We first put out a little EP that we made in Oklahoma City – just made it ourselves. There was enough of a circuit, I suppose, a scene, that you could go and you could play to 20 people at this little venue and then you could drive and you could play it to 20 people in this little basement somewhere, and that all felt as though that would be enough for us, you know? In the beginning we were very satisfied that people seemed to like us, and we weren't having to work in restaurants. We worked at restaurants up until probably '93 or '94. It is very difficult for people to make money, and so we would play shows and make some money here and there, but we still would all work. We'd been going since 1983 and 'She Don't Use Jelly' doesn't 'happen' till 1994.

That's a long time.

And this is really the secret to The Flaming Lips' longevity: you get to do these things for a while and sort of sit there and explore them. By the time we were having this hit, we had done the 'underground thing' a while and we enjoyed it, but we were curious about other things. We wanted to have a hit; it just becomes curiosity, because you've already satisfied a lot of other curiosities. So we made this song, without any

"To me it was always, 'I'm really just glad to be here doing my thing. I hope you like it, and I hope it works out.'"

intention or without even a record company coming in and saying, 'If you did this or that, this would be great.' But when we did it, even when we first recorded it, I could see mainstream people getting that. A lot of our songs have a kind of strangeness to them, but this had just enough of a hook that people could be like, 'I want to hear that again', you know?

We played a very long tour opening for a forgotten group called Candlebox that was selling probably a million records a week at the time. Grunge was reaching its worst heights. This group was becoming huge, huge, and we were playing hockey arenas with them as this tour went on, for three months. We would play this song to their audience; they would hate everything else that we played, but we would play this song and they'd be like, 'Oh, we like that one'. You can stand on the outside of it and you go, 'Well, I wonder what it's like to be, you know, on MTV all the time, or to be played on the radio', and then suddenly we were.

Luckily, this record didn't sell millions of records. It was popular enough that we could go around and play that song for quite a long time, and, of course, money flies in the door pretty quick, you know? There was a sense that if this went on for a while, our lives would be completely changed, and that's a stressful thing. I mean, for a group like us that was really just about recording music and thinking about music and creating music and creating an identity and playing shows, you're suddenly into this other realm where you have to talk about yourself a lot.

I suppose I'd call that the beginning of 'belonging to the world' a little bit. The world gives you this popularity: you can't really just go out and get it; they have to like you. We didn't have any clue as to what to do to become more popular. I think we were so set on just doing our trip.

The Soft Bulletin was that breakthrough record. What is it, do you think, that works so well and made people click with you?
We started making it in 1997 – it came out in '99 – but I think it was a really lucky bit of timing, because Mercury Rev, who are dear friends of ours, were having success with *Deserter's Songs*, which has similar themes, similar sounds, because all of us were recording with [producer] Dave Fridmann in the same studio at the same time. I think we fell into this trend of emotional, ethereal, spacey American music, and Mercury Rev was the big deal, then suddenly we were a little bit of a big deal.

But *The Soft Bulletin* has something about it, because people come up to me and talk about a song like 'Feeling Yourself Disintegrate', and 'Race for the Prize', and they'll inevitably be talking about the death of their brothers or their mother, or something that struck them in the zenith of thinking about how great life is.

It's saying, 'We have this epic adventure awaiting us, but it's not easy, it's not going to be without some struggles', you know? And I think everybody knows that; there's a subconscious knowledge of 'Yeah, we're all going to get into that.' And I think when people hear *The Soft Bulletin*, without it being said, in there is the message, 'I'm with you out there. I can see you starting your journey, and I'm with you on the other side, but I can't do it with you. But the music can do it with you.'

Somehow music gets in there and connects all these things and lets you know you are alone, but everybody is alone in the same way and somehow they've made it, and you will make it; somehow, as long as the music plays, there's a feeling that it will work, or it's worth believing.

I was going to ask you about your first trip. The preconception for people who maybe don't know a lot about The Flaming Lips is that it's a druggie band.
The main thing I think that happens with the idea of drugs and art and music is that you're just willing to try something; you're willing to go for it. And a lot of people who are artists, they're sensitive to things. But the dilemma with being sensitive, too, is that you just want to sit in the corner. Kind of like me: a lot of times I just want to sit in the corner

and draw pictures and write music; I don't really want to go out in the world and say, 'Look at me!' So there's the quagmire of being the isolated, sensitive dreamer who has to confront the freak that makes you want to go out in front of everybody

And that's usually associated with this other dimension of your personality that says, 'I'm just going to go for it!' And when you say that, a lot of times that applies to everything in your life. It doesn't mean I'm just going to try to be a rock star: I'm going to try to make my art, I'm going to try to have sex, I'm going to do drugs. It doesn't have any limit.

For me, it was really never like that. There were a lot of things in my life that I wasn't trying to get from being in a group. I felt like I already had a magical life living with my older brothers and sister and their friends. I think my younger brother took LSD when he was twelve years old. But back then it seemed very normal. I mean, it seemed like everybody would be taking LSD by the year 2000 – we'd be living in space, taking LSD, listening to The Beatles.

In the mid-'70s there was not anybody – in our circle, anyway – that knew the limits yet. Everybody was youngish, the oldest people around us would have been in their early twenties, and everybody was of the belief that if you didn't take drugs, you were an idiot, you know? You just weren't into what life is now, which I really regret now, because my father was a very hard-working, normal guy who could not understand this part of it. He was proud of the idea that you get up and you earn your living

"I'm with you out there. I can see you starting your journey ... but I can't do it with you. But the music can do it with you."

and you work hard and you're kind to people, and there's an element of that lifestyle that my older brothers and their friends embraced, but it wasn't about working anymore. The dynamic of everything changed and nobody knew what was right and where to go. So I would take drugs when I was young, fifteen, sixteen, but I would always be too scared of the more freaky drugs. I mean, I still like drugs that get you up and keep you awake and having fun, but I don't like the long, long trip of LSD.

I believe I'm lucky that my mind is addicted to my art and my music, and if I'm away from it for too long, I do have a reaction, I think, a little bit like a drug addict, where it's like, 'I gotta do that!' There are times when we do so much music. I mean, we'll literally have played ten shows in a row and we'll get home, and I'll go back in the studio, that same day, and be like, 'I still want to do this!', and people are like, 'My god, man. Don't you just want to watch TV or whatever?' I really don't.

Now I realize that nobody wants to live that way all that time – I may want to [laughs], but nobody else wants to. I realized that when I would take drugs there would be some moments when I really liked not being so obsessed or so driven. Then it would get to a point where it'd be like, 'Well, yeah, but I want to go back and make music now.' But we don't take drugs when we make music. I think that's probably one of the main things that is different with us. We don't drink and we don't take drugs when we're doing our thing.

It's not great for creativity, generally. I think people think it is.
Yeah, it's not at all. I think people have to explore a little bit about drugs and about their state of mind, and it's not easy. Some people will realize that they have a personality that is so intense that they'll get addicted; other people will try them and that won't happen. It is one of life's great risks, but I think you don't have that much of a choice. You either get in and see what it is, or you stay out and wonder what it is, you know?

"My mind is addicted to my art and my music, and if I'm away from it for too long, I do have a reaction ... a little bit like a drug addict."

And if you're lucky, maybe you get into it and you're around some really cool people and some cool things happen and you find a good way to have fun and explore yourself. I mean, to me, it really is about experimenting with yourself; that's what I think is the greatest thing about it – you get to kind of not be so self-aware and you get to say things and do things that, once you sober up, you'll be like, 'I'm glad I did that, because I'd never do it if I was thinking straight.'

You've talked about loving *The Wizard of Oz*.
There's a really, really great reissue of *The Wizard of Oz* soundtrack, the outtakes and all these things, and there's a recording of 'Over the Rainbow' – I don't think it's in the movie – and even though Judy Garland is acting, she's crying. Because it's about longing: it's really not about fantasy; it's really about this other world that she wants to be in so bad. Once I heard it, I started to cry. When we were growing up, this movie would play every Easter, and we would watch this movie every year. It became seared in my mind, not just from it being a fantastical movie that's fun to watch, but this music! And when I heard this one recording, it was emotional and it had this longing, and we began to play it live after that. This is before we had songs like 'Do You Realize??', and we'd play it at the very end of what sometimes would be a very chaotic,

punk rock, freaky, druggie jam – at the very end of the night we'd play this, and people would literally cry. I would cry when we'd be doing it.

Because we've been a band for so long, you really get to explore who we are right now. And there would be times when we would really want to explore being a heavy, druggie, sonic group and it'd all be about sound and power. And we got towards the end of that and started to think, 'I want to hit these people with some emotion', and we would do those things, like singing 'Over the Rainbow'. That's the greatest moment of playing in front of people that we would ever feel, because it was like some electricity was going through us, just some melting of our minds.

What's the last song? What should we go out on?

At the end of every Flaming Lips show we always try to play Louis Armstrong's version of 'What a Wonderful World'. It's like drinking moonshine after drinking whiskey; it takes over. To have a guy like Louis Armstrong, as old as he was, and all the horrible, racist things that he had been through to get to play music in America when he did, and he *smiles*. He decided to say, 'When I'm standing up there, I'm going to smile, and that's going to be part of my deal.' And I do that, because I thought, 'I like what it says to people.' It doesn't say, 'Look at me, I'm an idiot'; it says, 'Despite all that we know about the world, all this pain, all this war, we can still stand here and smile and say what a wonderful world.'

The First Time **Wayne Coyne** Playlist

1	Race for the Prize	The Flaming Lips
2	Puff (The Magic Dragon)	Peter, Paul and Mary
3	I Saw Her Standing There	The Beatles
4	What's New Pussycat?	Tom Jones
5	Peace in Mississippi	Jimi Hendrix
6	See Me, Feel Me	The Who
7	Search and Destroy	The Stooges
8	Breathe (In the Air)	Pink Floyd
9	She Don't Use Jelly	The Flaming Lips
10	Opus 40	Mercury Rev
11	Over the Rainbow (*The Wizard of Oz* OST)	Judy Garland
12	Do You Realize??	The Flaming Lips
13	What a Wonderful World	Louis Armstrong

"Suddenly it was like all the things that normally I'm hung up about don't matter – past, present, future."

WILKO JOHNSON

Wilko Johnson's manager issues this statement on 9 January, 2013: 'I am very sad to announce that Wilko has recently been diagnosed with terminal cancer of the pancreas. He has chosen not to receive any chemotherapy. He is currently in good spirits, is not yet suffering any physical effects and can expect to enjoy at least another few months of reasonable health and activity.'

Just under two weeks later, Wilko's manager agrees that I can interview Wilko about his illness and his farewell tour if I can go to his home near Southend-on-Sea.

All week I've been preparing my questions and watching *Oil City Confidential*, Julien Temple's 2010 documentary about the band Dr. Feelgood. Live footage from the mid-'70s shows show a threatening-looking gang onstage at the Kursaal Ballroom in their birthplace of Southend. They're dressed in grubby suits, with their fringes stuck to foreheads and speedy glares. Singer Lee Brilleaux looks like he's eyeing up the next skull to break a bottle over, and to his right is Wilko on guitar. Marching about the stage all in black, jutting his jaw back and forth, he looks like a skinny rooster, chopping out rhythms that are half classic R&B and half punk, way before punk even existed.

Now I'm on a slow train, rattling through Romford, Wickford and Rayleigh, on a dry and bitterly white-cold morning, looking through my questions for Wilko, and the only thing I can think about is; how do you interview someone about their life, when they know in a matter of weeks they're going to die?

Matt Everitt: When were you first aware of music?

When I was very young, there was a programme on the television, something about Robin Hood. The theme music they used was 'Greensleeves', and I remember being absolutely fascinated by this melody and I would always go around saying that was my favourite song.

I didn't take much notice of music at all when I went to the grammar school, where they really put me off classical music because we had this idiot, his method of teaching music was to dictate at breakneck speed the explanation for all the Enigma Variations. It wasn't until I started hearing The Rolling Stones that I was really turned on to rock and roll.

The minute you heard the Stones you were like, 'I have fallen in love with this!'

This was a time when The Beatles were very, very, very big. In fact, I went to see The Beatles at Southend Odeon. I say, I saw them – you couldn't hear them. There was just this screaming, to which I was contributing, you know? Seeing The Rolling Stones on the television, on [British TV show] *Thank Your Lucky Stars*, they looked so outlandish and you knew that your parents would not dig them at all, and this was a large part of the attraction. But it also led me on to find out about the American music that they had derived their music from.

When did you first fall in love with the blues?

Off the back of the Stones' success, the record shops in this country started getting filled up with blues records. Suddenly hearing the absolute power and feeling in this music. I dug into John Lee Hooker and Howlin' Wolf and all of them! I can remember taking the day off school to get the Stones' first album. I looked in the second-hand singles box and found this Johnny Kidd and The Pirates record, 'A Shot of Rhythm and Blues'. This Mick Green character [Johnny Kidd guitarist] intrigued me, so I started to try and copy him, and I really based all my guitar style on him.

When you started playing with Dr. Feelgood, was it pretty obvious early on that as a unit you had something really muscular, really different, really aggressive to offer?

The whole thing started by accident. When I was eighteen, I had what we called a junk band, a skiffle group. We used to play on the seafront on Canvey Island, and I can remember one day these boys coming up to us – much younger, thirteen, fourteen. Normally, you wouldn't consider such kids, but one of them, he had a very vivid personality. He was very keen on what we were doing, questioning us, and this was Lee Brilleaux [Dr. Feelgood singer]. He was an impressive person; he just had this nervous vibration about him, you know? Penetrating.

A little while after that, I went to university, and I actually stopped playing. Time went by. I finished university, I went out to Kathmandu, as you did in those days. When I came back, I was thinking, 'Blimey, so now it's about time I go and get a proper job', and I'm walking down the street on Canvey Island and who comes towards me but Lee Brilleaux, who is now nineteen years old, and he was a solicitor's clerk. Lee's telling me this junk band of his had evolved into a rock and roll band, and that the guitar player had just left. He was obviously angling for me to ask, and I was waiting for him to ask me. And then later on that day, Sparko [John B. Sparks], the bass player, comes knocking at my door [laughs]. He says, 'Do you want to join our group?' And I went, 'Yes!'

We continued for a couple of years, just playing locally, and I think we evolved the 'violence' of our stage act. We evolved our whole style and also the look of the thing. Then we started to play in London, the pub circuit, and we had the whole thing together. We were all completely unknown and we made a tremendous impact before too long. People were talking about us, writing about us in the music papers.

I read somewhere that the first album, 'Down by the Jetty' [1975], was all first takes. You'd been gigging so much you just banged it out in the studio, is that right? It's impressive.
Rather than first takes, it was all done at once. This was the mid-'70s: by then, the recording technology had achieved multitrack recording. Bit by bit you build up this big, horrible blend. I wasn't having any of this. I knew that the records I liked were all recorded once – you can hear it. So I insisted we set the band up as if we were on stage, and played. So yes, we did it like that. We might have taken one or two takes until we got the right one, but they were all done 'as is heard', yeah.

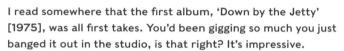

"This animosity between us grew, until one guy walks in the room, the other guy will walk out ... It's quite embarrassing to think of now."

Stupidity came out in 1976 – your first number one. You had achieved fame and notoriety. Did you enjoy being famous?
Well, you get in the situation where everywhere you go people are telling you how great you are and [laughs] everybody wants to go to bed with you, and you're getting loads and loads of money, so I hated it [laughs].

You work very hard. You had a pretty brutal touring regime.
Yeah. We certainly ended up not happy – at each other's throats. Particularly myself and Lee. I look back on it now, and I do not know why. We were good friends and we'd had such great times together. We were all Canvey Island boys and … I don't know. I suppose it got more and more frantic; in 1976 we were touring America quite extensively, and during that time this animosity between us grew up, until

one guy walks in the room, the other guy will walk out, you know? It's quite embarrassing to think of now, but that's the way it was.

When *Oil City Confidential* came out, did you feel people's awareness and understanding of you change?
I think so. I think one of Julien's motives in making the film was he felt that Dr. Feelgood had been rather ignored by history, and never, for one reason or another, got the credit, that we weren't perhaps as well known as we might have been, considering what it was that we'd started off. That was one of his motives. But I don't know. He just made such a great film.

When I was told he wanted to do this film, my first thought was 'Why?' and then 'How?' Lee is dead and there's very little footage of Dr. Feelgood, because we existed in the days before video cameras. But the way Julien set about it, he was really filming Canvey Island and capturing a moment in the '70s in the UK *and* the band. It's such a marvellous result and very gratifying.

When did you first get your diagnosis?
Just before Christmas. It's strange. One often wonders how one would feel when one hears those words, but I was absolutely calm. I knew something was wrong – I'd been having tests – but I had not been expecting that. But I felt absolutely calm. I left the hospital, and this calm turned into a kind of elation. I mean, I've always been a very miserable person, prone to depression and so on. Suddenly it was like all the things that normally I'm hung up about don't matter – past, present, future.

For instance, upstairs I've got my room; I've got all my books and my things and stuff in there, and it's really *nice* in my room. And I can remember later that day – and on subsequent days – sitting in my room

"I think of all the years I've spent wallowing in misery and hung up about the most stupid things, and now I can see that it doesn't matter."

and thinking, 'I really like my room', and realizing that normally I'd be thinking, 'My room looks really good but I'm really hung up about something or someone'; rather, I'm thinking none of that matters anymore. And this state has continued. I'm worrying that I'm going to come down crashing any moment, but as you can imagine it makes you feel really alive. You're looking at *everything*. Everything becomes very, very vivid.

I've just got back from two weeks in Japan. We went to Kyoto, up into the mountains to a Shinto temple. It was just so beautiful up there, the mountains; there was this fine snow falling with the sun shining through it, and hardly any people there.

I remember at one point I was standing on this balcony and looking out over the roofs of the temples to these mountains beyond this snow, and normally I would be looking at such a scene and trying to get it all 'remembered' for future purposes, but I thought, 'No, I don't have to do that now, because I'm not going to remember it, because I'm not going to be here to remember it.' But I am here. And I could be in that moment. And that is a fantastic feeling. The thing is, I feel completely fit in my person and I'm not suffering ill effects at all yet from this thing … so the whole idea of it is a kind of intellectual thing, you know? I've not got pain or anything like that to remind me of it. It's just this knowledge that my life is … shortly going to end. And the experience of that has not been anything like I would've imagined! I feel fine. I feel high.

You've turned down radiation therapy and chemotherapy. Was that a difficult choice to make?
No, no, I knew. I think I knew that right away. When I went in, and they gave me the diagnosis, I said, 'I'm not interested in chemotherapy. I understand it makes you feel very, very ill, and, in fact, I feel very, very well at the minute.' When I went in to see the specialist a few days later, she told me that I can expect to feel this way, to feel healthy and everything, for another four or five months maybe, before the disease kicks in.

Then she described chemotherapy to me and told me basically that I've got about nine or ten months to live. And with chemotherapy they could give me another three. But what are they going to give me – another three of sickness and misery? No, that's not difficult. I've just got this high and I don't want to interrupt it with any chemical nonsense.

And you're working on new songs as well?
I came walking out with this feeling, of course! I start writing songs! And we're going in the studio next week, and I want to bash some things down. But I'm going to take things step by step, really. Now I'm thinking I just want to be on my feet long enough to go in the studio and do some recording, and then there are some gigs planned. Now, I have said I'm not going on stage if I'm sick; I don't want people to remember me like that. So I'm just hoping that I can remain fit long enough to do these gigs properly. But I'm okay so far. I should be able to do them, I think, yeah. And then? What will I do? Wander off to some corner somewhere and curl up and die.

How does the world look to you now?
It looks pretty damn good [laughs]. I tell you man, you're walking down the street and you're just … Oh, it's intense. There are the branches standing against the sky gesturing and they're full of life – it's life, you know? I think of all the years I've spent wallowing in misery and hung up about the most stupid things and people and events and god knows what,

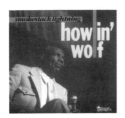

and now I can see that it doesn't matter. It just doesn't matter. When the sickness starts, perhaps I won't be quite so chirpy! I don't like being ill. Man flu is about as far as my tolerance goes, so I probably won't be so happy when I start getting sick. But right now I'm not sick; I feel fine and everything looks fine. I should've realized this years ago.

But at the same time, you've had a life in music; you've played music around the world with different groups, with some fantastic people. That's no bad way to spend a life.
I've had a fantastic life. It's just been great. All the places I've been. I was married for 40 years to the most beautiful woman in the world. Just before Christmas my son brought my grandson, Dylan Johnson, here, and he just learned to walk while he was here. I was in and out of hospital, but I've got that. Anybody that is screaming for more I think is just being greedy [laughs]. I've had more than most people.

I'm going to ask you to pick a song to finish the interview, and it can be anything you want.
I'd like to hear Howlin' Wolf singing 'Smokestack Lightning'. It was the first time I met the blues, and it's just such an extraordinarily mysterious and powerful record. It's got Hubert Sumlin's guitar on this insistent riff and the Wolf! What more can I say? I love it!

[On 22 October, 2014, Wilko declared himself cancer free – just over a year and a half after he'd been told he was going to die. Doctors found that he had a rare but potentially operable kind of tumour, so Wilko underwent an unprecedented nine-hour operation. After a long recovery, he was well enough to perform again. I spoke to him again in March 2015 at the Royal Albert Hall in London, where he'd been asked to support The Who at a Teenage Cancer Trust charity show.]

You're playing amazing shows; you've got a tour coming up. Do you wake up and every day feels like just the greatest day ever?
Well, after coming out of hospital, I had a fairly long period of getting my strength back as my body started recovering. Also, my own personality started returning, so I'm just miserable all the time [laughs]. And I found it difficult.

I mean, after a year of thinking you're at the end of your life, thinking your life is measured in weeks, to then suddenly hear, 'We fixed it, and now you're all right' – I'm taking a long time to get used to the idea that the future is more than a couple of months away. If they start talking about what we're going to be doing in August or something, I still can't quite grasp it. It's so far ahead. So I don't know how I feel about anything, really.

Have you found your musical spark has been lit again?

I've gone a year without playing a gig, and I've never, ever done anything like that ever before in my life. I've never gone more than a few weeks, maybe, without a gig. And now I'm starting to notice that you're supposed to practise every day, which I don't do. I've got to recover.

And you've got a tour coming up as well. It's quite a complex thing, because you didn't expect to be doing it.

I remember the last gigs I did before I went into hospital: they were great, because I thought I was very soon going to die. And you're just playing. And we were playing so well, and I can remember it just felt so great. You walk on stage and start playing and 'BANG!' You can feel it – going across really, really good. It's going to take me a little while to recover that position! Yeah, I'm not quite so cocksure at the moment!

Do you find it weird that now you've got more attention for your music than you ever had? Even before the original bands that made you famous?

It's been a series of events: the band just keeps getting better and better, Julien Temple's Feelgood film and lots of factors were combined, and then of course [laughs] the real winner was cancer. It fascinated everybody. I mean, my whole life took such a strange turn after being diagnosed. It was a fantastic year, it really was. Some of the experiences were very, very intense. The thing is, you can't *pretend* that you're about to die and get those feelings – you can't. I spent those months believing I was about to die. And it certainly makes you think differently about things.

The First Time Wilko Johnson Playlist

1	Roxette	Dr. Feelgood
2	Greensleeves	Antonio De Lucena
3	Come On	The Rolling Stones
4	Dimples	John Lee Hooker
5	A Shot of Rhythm and Blues	Johnny Kidd and the Pirates
6	She Does It Right	Dr. Feelgood
7	Pretty Thing	Bo Diddley
8	I'm Talking About You	Chuck Berry
9	Sneakin' Suspicion	Dr. Feelgood
10	I Want to Be Straight	Ian Dury and The Blockheads
11	Going Back Home	Wilko Johnson and Roger Daltry
12	Smokestack Lightning	Howlin' Wolf

"Our goal was always to really connect with people and make a moment, and feel like you're communicating."

WIN BUTLER

It's 2005 and I'm at the Reading Festival reporting for London radio station Xfm. It's Saturday afternoon and I'm working my way through a long list of interviews with bands on the bill. I'm tired, weighed down with equipment and hungover. A friend has been nagging me to check out a new group he's fallen in love with, even helping arrange an interview. I've never heard of them, and in my current grouchy mood, I couldn't care less. Their tour manager has suggested we do the interview by their bus – a long, muddy walk from where I was. Out of loyalty I'm trudging across a litter- and body-strewn festival field to find Arcade Fire.

I arrive eventually and the band are welcoming and chatty. I remove my microphone and minidisc recorder, switching on the power button and watching the red light wink on. The red light that means the machine is working and I can start the interview. The red light that doesn't come on. In that split second I face two choices: either I confess, make my apologies, hike back to the media room, find some new AA batteries, then trek back, or I save myself the grief and pretend to interview the band knowing that not a single word is being recorded. I am ashamed to say I chose the latter.

Arcade Fire's performance that evening was not only the best show of the festival, but one of the best performances I've ever seen. I was stunned, I was enraptured, I was baptized. They hurled themselves into an incredibly uplifting, manic, communal celebration of the power of music and played nearly all of *Funeral*, the album they discussed so enthusiastically and in such detail in the interview that never was, and not long after became one of my favourite records.

If you're a music journalist, you'll be lucky if this happens only once. If you're unlucky, it'll happen when you're interviewing a band as great as Arcade Fire. Spare batteries. That's all I'm saying.

Matt Everitt: The first thing we always ask everybody is when were they first aware of music?

My mom's a harpist, so she would always be practising. I remember being very young and hearing her play Debussy on the harp, really rolling, beautiful chords, and it was very magical sounding. There's lots of pictures of me as a little baby where she'd have a shirt that I'd be stuffed into and she's playing the piano at two in the morning; she put me under the table at nightclubs when she had gigs, so I was around a lot of music.

What about the first music that was yours?

Probably Michael Jackson, *Thriller*, or something like that, because my parents didn't listen to a lot of popular music, but that was the one thing that I think was, like, *monoculture* – kind of everywhere. The Cure was one of the first things that I really remember hearing on the radio that felt different. It was big enough that it made it to a radio station that I could actually hear, and it felt really different from the rest of the stuff that was on the radio at that time. The Cure was a big entry point for me to get into music. It was slightly more alternative than what a lot of my friends were listening to in Houston, Texas.

What do you like about The Cure?

It had all the kind of trappings of pop music – it was really catchy and melodic – but there were a lot of dark lyrical themes. And it was also kind of cool. You hear a song from *Disintegration* or *Wish*, but then if you go back and get the back catalogue, you see this incredible progression from more industrial drum-machine stuff.

A lot of the bands I was really into had either broken up or had been around for so long that you could navigate the whole back catalogue. That's something that I always relate to our own music: I think about it like I'm twenty, in terms of some kid buying [Arcade Fire's 2007 album] *Neon Bible* and then working their way forward and backwards, and trying to make sense of it all.

What about the first album that was yours, that you owned?

When I was younger, maybe eight or something, I really liked the song 'Pour Some Sugar on Me' by Def Leppard. We were in the airport and I saw a Def Leppard cassette at the airport and I was like, 'Mum, give me some money! Trust me on this. I have to buy this.' And I bought it and it was some weird album, and I got home and played it and was like, 'What is this? I do not care for this at all.' It's one of their lesser albums …

When did you start going to see bands live? What was the first gig you saw?

It would have been my mum or my grandpa. My grandfather led big bands, so I saw them play. I think the first big rock show I went to was probably U2, when I was fifteen or sixteen, at the Astrodome in Houston. Because I went to a boarding school for high school, I saw a few shows.

But really I started going to shows when I was about nineteen and I moved to Montreal and jumped headfirst into the music scene there.

There was a band called The Unicorns that gave us our first opening slot in the US. They were signed by Rough Trade; they were the first Montreal band that got signed in the UK. And there's a band called Wolf Prey – I probably saw their first 15 shows or something like that. So that for me was really cool: being contemporaries with songwriters that I thought were as good as the stuff that I like from the '80s and '90s, being in the same city with them and everything.

When the name Arcade Fire first emerged, did you have an agenda? Was there a template in your mind of the sort of group you wanted to be?

No. I knew I had to play music and I was very driven. I mean, I dropped out of school and moved to Boston with a friend that I didn't know that well, and pretty much spent a year not leaving the apartment – just writing all day, every day. Go to work, come home, write. So, for me, it was more about wanting to create. The whole mechanism of how to get

> ## "I feel that for a lot of people it's kind of backwards. They're thinking, 'Who's going to release my stuff?' And I was thinking, 'I just want to make something good.'"

a gig and how to play a show or labels? All that kind of stuff was so not on the radar. It was really just about writing and writing and writing and writing and writing.

I feel that for a lot of people it's kind of backwards. They're thinking, 'Who's going to release my stuff?' And I was thinking, 'I just want to make something good.' That was my end goal [laughs]. It was like, 'What I'm doing is not good, but I know that it can be good if we get the right combination of things.' In Montreal I was constantly trying to find new musicians to play with, and that's how I met Régine [Chassagne – bandmate and wife]. We had such a distinct writing style together, and then the whole thing grew out of that – grew out of that city and grew out of the two of us playing together.

What were your first impressions of Régine when you met her?

Um, well, I just kind of saw her across the room in the cafeteria. She looked really interesting. She was studying jazz, more from an academic standpoint, I think. But I saw her perform soon after that at an art opening, and seeing her sing with a piano player, I could tell she had a really

distinct, really special stage presence and singing style. The first time we played together, she brought all these different flutes – she could play almost anything immediately. I think that I was a real songwriter, too, at that point, so I think she was really relieved to meet someone who was actually really serious about it and not just thought it would be cool to be in a band. Because being in a band is 'cool'. Yeah.

What were those first Arcade Fire gigs like? That combination of theatrics and performance, something where the audience were involved, seemed to happen quite early on?

In Montreal, we'd play all these weird dance shows or loft parties, shows where you play in someone's home. It was always small enough that I'd play acoustic guitar and be able to sing off mic and go in the audience. I think people are used to going to a rock club and hearing music and talking and having a beer.

"Seeing images of us now playing in San Francisco, at the end of that tour, it's as punk as anything I've ever seen."

I think that our goal was always to really connect with people and make a moment, and feel like you're communicating. There's a communication happening between you and the audience. And I think that whatever place we've been in as a band, we try to use the tools that are available to make this specific show work. We just played in Haiti for Carnival, and we brought the most bare-bones equipment and ended up doing a show in this hotel, where we had two guitar amps. Everything plugged into them, the most basic ingredients, and we ended up just doing a total garage rock '60s show.

We're very in our element standing on the floor, no monitors, really just making noise. I think, in a way, that's what comes easiest to us.

What can you remember of recording that first EP [*Arcade Fire*, 2003]?

I approached Richard [Parry – producer and Arcade Fire multi-instrumentalist] to record us. We had started to get a name for ourselves, but it was really fraught internally and it felt like it wasn't really going to last much longer, so I wanted to at least document what we had done at that point, because it felt like it could fall apart at any moment. I had to really convince everyone that we should really just record this, before it goes. You never know when it's going to go. And we kind of broke up on the CD release of that first EP. But then this kind of magical thing happened once that EP was out: people started to share the music. Before that it was, 'How do you get a gig?' I was so frustrated by the whole process. I just wanted to play *now*. The idea of booking a show four weeks in advance? [Laughs] Why would you have to? It makes no sense. I want to play now. Why can't we just play tonight? But once we had the EP, people started to share it with each other, even pre-internet, and our shows slowly started getting bigger. There would be more people coming to check it out.

And then after that, half the band broke up and we were kind of left. My brother had just moved to Montreal, so it was Richard [Reed Parry], Tim [Kingsbury], my brother [William], Régine and me, and we had no drummer. And we had this EP that was from a different group. So we had these really limited resources when we were writing a lot of that *Funeral* stuff, and I think part of that energy made us focus in even harder because it was such a trying period.

When *Funeral* [2004] came out, I don't think I've ever witnessed a body of work so particularly loved by everybody across the board, everywhere. You were feted as the 'great hope of music'. How did that feel?

Well, I don't know that it was exactly like that. The reviews on the next two records, they're kind of the same. There was always one person who thought it was crappy, but overall people were like, 'This is pretty good'. There were a couple of early really positive reviews, but it wasn't like this avalanche of love. It was still very much a slow build, because we had no manager, we weren't signed.

The record didn't come out in the UK till six months after the US. We did a van tour across the US as *Funeral* came out, and you could tell it was starting to build. We went across the whole US and by the time we got to San Francisco, it was like, 'Okay, this is really starting to really happen'. But it was still very much related to the live show. Seeing images of us now playing in San Francisco, at the end of that tour, it's as punk as anything I've ever seen.

It's like Wills and Richard banging on the walls and plaster's falling off. And I was really sick and my voice just sounded like a razor blade, just like [screams] – just screaming to get any sound out. It wasn't really until the end of the *Funeral* tour, when we started playing festivals, that we had to get roadies and we had to start to navigate finding a manager and all that kind of stuff. It started to feel like we had to figure it out again, what our goal was artistically.

I was going to talk about 'Keep the Car Running' and Springsteen, because Springsteen covered it, which is a fantastic honour. When did you first fall in love with Springsteen?

I didn't really grow up listening to Springsteen. My parents didn't listen to him. I probably heard 'Born in the USA', but when I moved to Montreal the original Arcade Fire drummer was a big Springsteen fan. I remember hearing 'Born to Run' and 'Thunder Road' and all those songs on that record. And then deeply getting into *Nebraska* was my

entry point to really getting Bruce – it's just a really unflinching, very real record. For someone who had just done *Born in the USA* to come back and do a record like that is very inspiring, you know. It takes a lot of guts.

What would you play off of that record?
Oh, man. We used to cover 'State Trooper'. I love that song. It's like a little film noir in a song.

The Suburbs did so incredibly well – US number one and UK number one – and put you into the mainstream. Was it an intimidating thing, being 'the hottest band in the world'? Being an arena band is not necessarily something that may have been an ambition when you started, but then it happened.
I don't know. It didn't feel that different, to be honest. We did the Grammys and we did the Brits, and we definitely feel a bit like a fish out of the water in those kinds of scenarios, but I think, if people are honest with themselves, probably everyone does. I can't imagine anyone who wants to hang out at the Brits all the time, except for maybe some B-list celebrity who likes having their picture taken. I remember seeing Nirvana on the MTV Movie and TV Awards when I was a kid, and you think that they were on top of the world. It was like, '*Nevermind*! Biggest record in the world!', and you're like, 'Oh man, the whole world was about Nirvana'. And then I saw it again recently, and the rest of the bands are, like, C+C Music Factory, Aerosmith – Nirvana are the total weirdos on that bill.

They wanted to play 'Rape Me', and they weren't allowed to play that, so they had to play a different song. Even at that point, they didn't have the power to choose what song they played; they still had to do this tap dance. And for us, I think that we've had to compromise very little. At the Grammys we played 'Month of May', which is a total punk song.

You mentioned Haiti: what was your first trip there like? It obviously had a huge impact. The sound of Reflektor [2013], the universe around the record, is infused with that location.
When I first started dating Régine, I would go to her aunt and uncle's house for Christmas, and all her family's Haitian: they would always be speaking in Creole and we'd eat Haitian food. One of her uncles used to be an ambassador and had this very deep, commanding voice, and he would give these long monologues about Haiti. So I learned a lot about the country just from hanging out with her family.

She always wanted to go, and her mother and father both had to leave under pretty rough circumstances, during the Duvalier regime, and her mother in particular was really scared and didn't want to go back, and didn't want Régine to go back. So after Régine's mother passed away, she was just waiting for her opportunity to go. We went well before the earthquake with Paul Farmer from Partners in Health, who's close to a Gandhi, one of those great people who changes the world. We got to see

Haiti through his eyes, be in real Haiti, on a river at midnight in a dugout canoe, because some of the road has been flooded out. It was a really amazing experience. There's no electricity – everything's lit by firelight – and you just hear this incredibly deep music.

You meet a farmer who's like, 'Yeah, I'm a singer', and he sings a song for you and it's like pre-delta blues African music, lyrically deep and so incredible. It's definitely part of who I am. Our family celebrates Carnival like a lot of other families celebrate Thanksgiving or something like that. Now we have a son and that's part of his heritage, too. It's definitely somewhere that I'll be going my whole life. It gets under your skin – not a lot of places like that left in the world.

I wanted to ask about New Order, who you've referenced a lot.
'Power Out' is pretty New Order-y. They've always been an influence because when Régine was first learning to play drums, she practised to New Order. They're also one of those bands where, you know, it's more about the band and the sound and the music. 'Bizarre Love Triangle' is one of the most perfect, beautiful songs.

You get to pick the last song. It can be anything: old, new, yours, someone else's, something you heard this morning ...
That's a horrible, shitty question! Usually when I DJ, the last song I play is 'Mind Games' by John Lennon, so let's go out with that.

The First Time Win Butler Playlist 🟢 ⠗⠇⠇⠇⠗

1	No Cars Go	Arcade Fire
2	Dances for Harp and Orchestra	Debussy
3	Thriller	Michael Jackson
4	Disintegration	The Cure
5	Pour Some Sugar on Me	Def Leppard
6	I Was Born (A Unicorn)	The Unicorns
7	Neighborhood #3 (Power Out)	Arcade Fire
8	Oh! You Pretty Things	David Bowie
9	State Trooper	Bruce Springsteen
10	Ready to Start	Arcade Fire
11	Carpet Crawlers	Genesis
12	Gede Mazaka	Haitian Rara
13	Bizarre Love Triangle	New Order
14	Mind Games	John Lennon

"Both of us were very real, actually, and even a drop of reality, a drop of truth, goes a long way."

YOKO ONO

Some artists change the world to such a massive degree that it's nearly impossible to imagine how things were before them. These days, an understanding of conceptual art is inherent in the way that everyone thinks about the world: we all know that a pile of bricks, a pickled shark or a room full of handmade porcelain sunflower seeds can be art. We're not scared by that – we're fascinated. We understand that art is about ideas, not just appearances. And Yoko Ono was one of the very first people to take that theory and place it slap bang in the mainstream.

From 1966 onwards, Yoko – already a formidable and respected artist – had a profound effect on the public. The profile she enjoyed (or endured) thanks to her relationship with John Lennon meant her work was exposed and scrutinized not just by art enthusiasts, but by pop fans, plumbers and policemen, too. Just as The Beatles dropped a sugar cube of psychedelia into Britain's afternoon tea, households would read about Yoko's performance art or her 'bed-ins' with Lennon in the tabloids, while bland entertainment like *Till Death Us Do Part* or *Dixon of Dock Green* flickered on a black-and-white telly in background.

She's just as you'd expect: tiny, dressed all in black with huge sunglasses, lost in the middle of a comfy sofa at a posh London hotel. Her face is happy and open, a little pinched with age and creased in the cheeks where she smiles (which she does frequently), but her voice is exactly the same as it's always been – high and playful and punctuated by little laughs. In fact, there's more laughing during my conversation with Yoko than any other interview in this book. And that's my overriding memory of our meeting – not the little sigh she gave when I asked her to recall her first meeting with John, not that she answered my final question in the most conceptual way imaginable, but that we laughed so much.

Matt Everitt: Did you enjoy first learning music? [Ono began piano lessons at just four years old.]

Well, you know, I think many, many people experienced the same thing in those days. The parents say, 'Now, you better play well!' or something like that. I was not very good. And the reason why I was not very good, and this may be my excuse, but my father was *so* strict. When I was two and a half years old, I went to San Francisco to meet him and the first thing he said was, 'Show me your hands! Show me! Well, this part has to be long enough for the octave!' You know, a tiny little thing. So at that age my hands just kind of shrunk back [laughs].

Do you remember buying your first album?

Luckily, I never had to buy records, because they came to us. When I was a young, young girl, what I knew about music was my father playing the piano, and my mother playing Asian instruments. They were totally different from each other. I was sent to this early music school called Jiyū Gakuen, which is 'Freedom Garden' in Japanese. Many of my fellow students became serious artists, actually – serious musicians that are known in Japan. I was not one of them! But it was a pretty interesting education. The homework was – for example – to collect, in your mind, all the sounds that you heard that day and put them together.

The teachers sometimes let us listen to the clock ticking – *dunk, dunk, dunk* – then afterwards they said, 'How many were there?' You don't know how many it was. Well, you *do*. So you have to go back to it, and repeat in your mind. And you start to learn about sounds and notations and music through that. So instead of just saying, 'Okay, do, re, mi, fa – after fa is …?', it's going, 'No, it's not like that. Just let me hear what you remember.' And then you have to remember it in your mind.

"I was conceptual from the beginning, it seems like ... I was shy, and I didn't particularly want to express myself loudly."

When you first found the avant-garde in New York, what drew you there? It became such a creative environment.

Did they use the word 'avant-garde'? Yes, I suppose that it was convenient to use that word – for radio people, maybe. I was in classical music and was trying to create my own music, to get *out* of that one, so that came very naturally to me. I was conceptual from the beginning, it seems like. It's a mixture of reasons: one, I was shy, and I didn't particularly want to express myself loudly; and also, it's an environment where it was easy to live in a conceptual world.

You did some really interesting work with people like John Cage. Where did you first meet him?
In those days, I was still moving from one style to another – a growing period, you know? It's not strange, because of my father, because that's what, in a certain way, I was avoiding. And the kind of music I made came from that, I suppose.

I have to ask you about *Cut Piece* [a performance piece in which Ono sat onstage and invited her audience to cut off her clothes] – a very famous piece of conceptual art. When was the first tlme you did *Cut Piece*? And what were people's reactions?
I did that first in Kyoto [July 1964, Yamaichi Concert Hall] and it was a little bit scary. But it wasn't *that* scary, because I have this habit of immediately going inside myself. So when I was on a stage and I placed a pair of scissors in front of myself and said, 'Come out and cut wherever you want', I immediately went inside myself – let's say half inside myself.

"It's interesting that it's one of the most powerful works of mine. But for me, it was just hiding."

A guy just jumped on the stage with the pair of scissors. And everybody's going, 'Oh! What's going to happen?' But in my mind, it was like a peripheral vision that did not have the sharpness of reality. Does that make sense? But then the thing is, he settled down with this kind of posture, and we all knew that he was probably a dancer [laughs], making that posture, so he was not dangerous or anything. But that's how it started. And then I went to Tokyo [1964], and in Tokyo I did the *Cut Piece* again; the third one was in New York City [1965]; the fourth one was in London [1966]. And then, much later, I did it in Paris [2003].

It's still a really powerful image.
It's interesting that it's one of the most powerful works of mine. But for me, it was just hiding. Well, hiding my emotion, as well. I did not call my work conceptual, in the beginning. I know that it was conceptual, but I don't like labelling so much.

I'd love to ask you about your first impressions of meeting John Lennon. What did you first think, when you met him?
Do you really want to know that? There are so many times that I have spoken about it, but okay. I had this exhibition of mine in Indica Gallery [in London; 'Unfinished Paintings and Objects', November 1966], and I was preparing for it with students from Saint Martins; I think John Dunbar [Indica co-founding gallerist] brought them. It's a very wise

thing to do, because these were would-be artists and they all helped us to put it together. I was thinking, 'Okay ...' [pretends to gaze around], and then the door opened and John Dunbar came in with a friend of his.

And I thought, 'What is he doing? Didn't I tell him that I don't want anybody to get in here until I'm ready?' You know? But I thought, 'Well, I'm not going to scream about it, or anything. It's probably his close friend or something.' They went downstairs and I thought, 'What am I going to do? Oh, okay, I better go follow them', and I went downstairs. I saw them standing in front of the 'Hammer a Nail In' piece [*Painting to Hammer a Nail*, Ono's 1961 'instructional piece' in which viewers are directed to hammer a nail into a wood panel], but I didn't go near them or anything. That is the kind of person I am, you know? I don't go, 'Eek!'

So then John Dunbar noticed me and said, 'Oh, this is the artist', introducing me to John. Instead of saying, 'This is Yoko Ono', it was 'This is the artist', and then, 'Uhhh, this is ...' and he mumbled John's name, probably to protect him. But to me, it was nothing. I mean, it was just another person. So I said, 'Hello', being polite. And he was just standing in front of this blank piece of wood, which it was, because nobody had hammered a nail in it.

But very seriously, he wasn't, 'Ha ha!', you know? 'What is this block of wood?' No. He was looking at it like, 'Hmm'. And he said, 'Could I hammer a nail in?' So I said, 'Well, if you pay 5 shillings you can.' And he didn't say anything. I forget exactly how he said it, but what he meant was, 'Is it all right to hammer a nail in conceptually?' So I said, 'Yes'. But I thought, 'That's interesting that he's playing the same games as I was.'

"He mumbled John's name, probably to protect him. But to me, it was nothing ... it was just another person."

The night before, I thought, 'Well, this is an opening of a really important show for me. But how am I going to be able to sell it, or to get some money out of it, because it's just conceptual? So I said, 'Well, I can collect an admission fee?' They said, 'Ah, great idea!' So I was going to do that. And so when he said, 'Well, could I ...?' I thought, 'Okay. This is where I say it! If you pay 5 shillings, you can!' And I thought, 'Wow. This is so great!' A step forward. I'm doing something that I've never done before, making it into a showcase – a showcase people pay to see.

Did you feel something straight away?
No. As usual, I was more interested in the format that I discovered and things like that. I don't remember the sequence, but what he wanted to know was, 'Where's the *Bag Piece*?' [1964 performance piece in which two

viewers were asked to enter a large black bag and remove their clothes], because he heard that people get in the bag and everything. So I said, 'That's the one. It's not very exciting.' The black bag was just on the stand. And then he said, 'What's the event of today? Because the *Bag Piece* doesn't seem too interesting.' So I said, 'This is the event', and I showed him a card on which I wrote, 'Breathe' [laughs]. So he said, 'Like this?' [inhales dramatically], and I thought, 'Hmm, okay'.

And then he saw the *Apple* piece [1966; an apple on a pedestal engraved with the word 'APPLE'] and just grabbed the apple and had a bite! I was so upset about that, you know, as an artist – instead of respecting my work, to take a bite out of it? So, obviously, I got furious and he said, 'Oh, I'm sorry'. It's like, he wasn't saying, 'I'm sorry', but he was just, you know, upset about it and put the apple back on the stand.

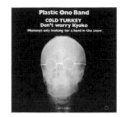

The point is, it was like a miracle that happened, because when you think about it now, everything was set right. For instance, he was in Abbey Road Studios and he just dropped in to see this show. And Abbey Road is number 3 Abbey Road; three is music – a music number. And where Indica Gallery was, was 6 Masons Square; six is the number of love. So the music came to love! Isn't that amazing? Even on that level?

The album that you made, *Unfinished Music No. 1. Two Virgins* **[1968] – it was a brave thing to do, to release that record. The cover especially, obviously [it featured a nude photo of Lennon and Ono]. But the music, it was such a jump from what anybody was expecting. Do you remember it coming out?**
Well, I know that what I did then, in terms of music, was quite different from what people were used to. But John understood it. That surprised me. Because nobody else did. My experience with music is more conceptual. The fact that I was so 'different' made it happen with my songs. They came out all right.

The first Plastic Ono Band concert was in 1969 at the Toronto Rock and Roll Revival festival. You played 'Don't Worry Kyoko'; it was a great performance! Can you remember that first gig?
I remember doing 'Don't Worry Kyoko'. It was about my daughter. I never thought there was 'pop' or 'rock' when I made it – just music. And it was a very good experience, but that's not what I was thinking. What I'm interested in about my music is very different from what other people are interested in. I think they like to see something that is comforting.

Your music's not comforting, is it? [Laughs]
I don't think so! Everything that we did was very, very close to our hearts, and we got criticism about that. You know, like, 'You guys are supposed to be artists but your work is all very personal.' And so John, he really reacted to that, and said, 'What's wrong with being personal?' He was very real. Both of us were very real, actually, and even a drop of reality, a drop of truth, goes a long way. But we had it.

'Give Peace a Chance' [1969] has become so powerful. Not just as a song, but as something that, to this day, people are still talking about. It seemed just like 'a moment', but it will be played forever. That must feel wonderful.
Isn't that great? John and I did not really accumulate anything worldly, but we had incredible, incredible richness of life that was given to us. Isn't that amazing?

It seems like you're so loved now. People really appreciate your work, whereas in the past it was easy for people to criticize you because of what they *thought* you were. How's that shift been?
Well, thank god that they criticized me instead of ignoring me! In other words, my work was criticized, not ignored. Can you imagine if everybody was saying, 'She's so good! She's so good!' I'd be dead by now!

You can see people like Elvis Costello and The B-52s starting to namecheck you as a *musician*. That must be satisfying.
Well, it's to do with being a musician and being a writer, because I started as a poet, so I'm very much into words. And that's where my mind was going, always. I think that the kind of people that you were talking about, they're great, great artists, but their emphasis might have been different. I really don't know. Some people enjoyed it, probably, I hope, and some people didn't like it!

I want to ask about 'Yes, I'm Your Angel', it's such a beautiful song. Do you remember recording that one? And writing it?
Thank you. Well, I kind of like it! But there's so many other songs that I like, too. The kind of songs that I wrote – especially *Approximately Infinite Universe* [Yoko's 1973 rock album] and after that – had a little shadow or shade, but 'I'm Your Angel' was really the tops. That's when we were so happy together, and there are very few songs like that.

One of the things that I've never told anyone, and maybe it doesn't mean very much, but John was starting to feel that he was going to be forty – the usual thing that all of us feel. So he would say, 'Jesus, I can't believe I'm going to be forty!' He was saying things like that in the middle of the night. So by writing the song I just wanted to make him feel better.

So much of your music has become better and better regarded as the years have gone on. It's like people re-evaluated it. You could release 'Walking on Thin Ice' today, and it would sound very current. Can you feel, over the past 15, 20 years, people going, 'Actually, that was some really good music'?
Well, 'Walking on Thin Ice', I know why it wasn't accepted, by the way – because right after we created it, he died. So we were more concerned about that. But I was – both of us, actually, were – hung up on when I'm singing, 'I knew a girl [who tried to walk across a lake]'. In other words,

it was not just an ordinary song. Format-wise, it's an ordinary song, but then attaching that lyric makes a big difference. And when I did that, John said, 'From now on, we should do that all the time' [laughs]. You know, it was great.

What do you think people's first impression is of you? You make playful art, but it's also very serious art at the same time.
Well, reality is always complex like that. You know, it's never one thing. People are surprised about me anyway, so I would rather that they understand it, and stop being surprised!

How would you describe your art and music, then?
Well, truth – that's big. I'm not concerned so much about how people take things from my work. I'm more concerned about the perfection of it, or how it is for me. I'm just having a normal, average life …

It's not a normal, average life!
It's true! It's true! I don't consider it as anything special. It's nothing to be impressed or not be impressed by. I think that it's my life. I feel very lucky, but I'm not concentrating on that at all. If I did, I'd go crazy.

What's the last song we should play? We'll play a piece of music at the end of this interview. What should we play?
Nothing [laughs].

The First Time Yoko Ono Playlist

1	Don't Worry Kyoko	Yoko Ono
2	Duet for Cymbal	John Cage
3	Two Virgins: Side One	John Lennon and Yoko Ono
4	The Ballad of John and Yoko	The Beatles
5	Death of Samantha	Yoko Ono
6	Oh Yoko!	John Lennon
7	You're the One	Yoko Ono
8	Give Peace a Chance	Plastic Ono Band
9	Yes, I'm Your Angel	Yoko Ono
10	Every Man Has a Woman Who Loves Him	John Lennon and Yoko Ono
11	Walking on Thin Ice	Yoko Ono

Index

Note: headings for interviewees are given in bold type.

Acknowledgments

The first thanks is to the musicians in the book and the 6 Music listeners, but also the management, record labels, promotion and marketing teams behind every interview. I owe a debt of gratitude to: Alistair Norbury at BMG; Austin Collins at AC Promotions; Barbara Charone, Moira Bellas and Fred Mellor at MBC PR; Ben Pester; Bertis Downs; Beth Morris; Bruce Garfield; Bruno Morelli, Clive Cawley and Mark Rankin at Virgin EMI; Cally Calloman and Penkiln Burn; Cameron McVey; Caroline Poulton at Out Promotion; Chris Gentry at C3 Management; Chris Slade; Claire Singers; Conal Dodds and Crosstown Concerts; Creation Management; Dan Papps; Dave Cronen; David Winterburn; Derek Birkett at One Little Indian; Didz Hammond at Quietus Management; Eleven Management; Francois Ravard; Fuzz Chaudrey and Rich Ashton at Caroline; Garry Blackburn and Katy Ellis at Anglo Management; Gillian Fleet and Domino; Grace Maxwell and Susan Currie; Graham Hodge at Cup & Nuzzle; Gregory Wells; James Sandom, Cerne Canning and Geoff Barnett at Redlight Management; Jane Arthy and Patrick Hough at Warner Music; Jared Levine; Jean Sievers; Jeannette Lee at Rough Trade; Jeremy Thomas and Coda; Joe Bennett at JBPR; John Silva and Gaby Skolnek at Silva Artist Management; Julian Stockton at JMSPR; Julie Calland and Courtyard; Kara McCabe at SJM; Kas Mercer at Mercenary Publicity; Kevin McCabe at Kevin McCabe Promotions; LD Communications: Bernard Doherty, David Cox, Doug Wright, Neil Chivers, Emma Elwood, Becky Williams, Barry O'Reilly, Alex Karol, Jamie Skinner and Alex Sutton; Live Nation; Lisa Faichney; Luv Management; Marc Gans; Margaret Murray at FMGUK; Martin Cook at Your Army; Matt Osbourne at Real World; Matthew Rankin at Nonesuch; Melvin Benn and Festival Republic; Michael and Emily Eavis, Nick Dewey, John Shearlaw and everyone at Glastonbury Festival; Michael Pickard and Rob Pascoe at Virgin; Miggins at Coolbadge; Millie Thompson; Murray Chalmers and all MCPR; Natalie Jennings at Dirty Hit; Nick Goree; Olli Dutton; Paul Crockford and Imogen Battersby at Crockford Management; Pete Black, Sam Potts, Steph Wilkinson, Manish Arora and Ferdy Unger-Hamilton at Columbia; Peter Katsis at Deckstar; Phil Youngman and Damian Christian at Atlantic Records; PIAS; Rambo Stevens; Big Ray and Metropolis; Rebecca Boulton and Andy Robinson at Prime Management; Rob Allen; Rob Cannell at Beggars; Rob Lynch at Airplayer; Ross Forrest at Radar; Sacha Taylor-Cox; Sammi Wild at ATC Management; Sara Planco at ViewpointNY; Scott Booker at Hellfire; Scott Roger at Quest Management; Steve Blackwell; Steve Guest at Guesty PR; Steve Stone; Stu Bell, Rich Dawes, Maria Barham, Kate Etteridge at Dawbell; Sue Harris at Republic Media; Tara Richardson, Steve Matthews, Cliff Burnstein and Peter Mensch at Q Prime; The Outside Organisation: Alan Edwards, Chris Goodman, Jack Delaney, Suzannah Fellows, David Lim and Nick Caley; Tina Skinner and Dave Rajan at Parlophone; Tom March, Ben Mortimer, Jodie Cammidge and Laurence Pinkus at Polydor; Tom Poole at Hesso Media; Tommy Manzi; Tony Cooke and CJ at Scream; Zena Zerai at Decca; Zoe Flower. Thank you all for trusting me.

The BBC Radio 6 Music Breakfast Show team: Shaun Keaveny, Phil Smith, Zahra Bhaluani, Joe Haddow, Matt Mills, Lisa Kenlock, Nic Philps, Claire Slevin and Mark Higgins. Plus Bob Shennan, Paul Rogers, Jeff Smith, James Stirling, Mike Hanson, Mary Anne Hobbs, Steve Lamacq, Fergus Dudley, Julie Cullen. Nathan Freeman, Sam Moy, Adam Hudson, Jax Coombes, Gary Bales, Henry Lopez-Real and all *The First Time With* ... producers. Props to Sharon Hanley and Kate Adam from BBC Press and special gratitude to Gabi Fatal and Katie Pollard at BBC Legal for their tireless work.

Love to the awe-inspiring Kate Haldane and Jeanette Linden and PBJ. Thank you to Laurence King; the most patient publishers I could hope for – Gaynor Sermon, Alice Graham, Angus Hyland, Nicolas Franck Pauly, Tim Marrs (who did an incredible job with the illustrations), Laurence himself, and my dear friend Camilla Morton, who had faith and willed this book into existence with a glorious mix of grace and determination.

Family thanks to Mum and Roger; Dad and Joy; Dave, Alfie and Ellie and Steve and Judy, and all my friends who've helped get this done: especially the collective Airds, Bensons, Brenners, Masseys and Rodds; Austin Wilde; Clive Tulloh; Ellie Parker; Mark, Ria and Marlee King; Murray Lachlan-Young; Norman (thank you for a wonderful introduction to the book), Nelly and Woody Cook; Andy Williams and Famous Tony; Sam, Tony, Joe and Daniel; Tam, Az, Amity and Lozbot; Vinette Robinson and Zoe Ball.

And finally, thanks to Joseph Gordon, who has changed my world for the better (you're a brilliant boy); to Bebe (who doesn't even know this book exists); and most of all, to Beth. This was written for you, and would have been impossible without you. You're the reason for everything. Thank you.